INDIANS
of the american southwest

Bertha P. Dutton is a distinguished anthropologist and expert on the archaeology and ethnology of Southwestern and Meso-American Indians. Among her many publications are *Sun Father's Way, The Pueblo Indian World* (with E. L. Hewett), *Happy People: The Huichol Indians,* and numerous journal articles and reviews.

Her work in the field has included research projects and excavations throughout the Southwest and expeditions to Peru, Bolivia, Ecuador, Panama, Guatemala, and Mexico, as well as attendance at conferences in South America, Europe, and the Orient.

The New Mexico Press Women presented to Dr. Dutton in 1971 the coveted Zía award for outstanding publications, and in 1974 she was appointed New Mexico representative to the National Park Service's Southwest Regional advisory committee by Secretary of the Interior Rogers C. B. Morton. She is a Research Associate of the Museum of New Mexico in Santa Fe; for a decade she served as Director of the Museum of Navaho Ceremonial Art, Inc., in that city.

INDIANS

of the american southwest

Bertha P. Dutton

PRENTICE-HALL, INC.

Englewood Cliffs, New Jersey

Library of Congress Cataloging in Publication Data

Dutton, Bertha Pauline
   Indians of the American Southwest.

   Bibliography: p.
   Includes index.
   1. Indians of North America-Southwest, New.
   I. Title.
E78. S7D79   970. 4'9   74-30311
ISBN 0-13-456897-4

INDIANS OF THE AMERICAN SOUTHWEST
by Bertha P. Dutton

Printed in the United States of America

10 9 8 7 6 5 4 3 2

Prentice-Hall International, Inc. *(London)*

Prentice-Hall of Australia Pty, Ltd. *(Sydney)*

Prentice-Hall of Canada, Ltd. *(Toronto)*

Prentice-Hall of India Private Limited *(New Delhi)*

Prentice-Hall of Japan, Inc. *(Tokyo)*

*This book
is respectfully dedicated
to
THE PEOPLE
. . . the original inhabitants
who revered this land
and its creatures
and strived to save and protect them*

MAJOR INDIAN RESERVATIONS OF THE SOUTHWEST

.........CONTENTS

1 who and where

2 the Pueblo peoples

3 the Athabascans

.........LIST OF ILLUSTRATIONS

MAPS

PHOTOGRAPHS (center section):

CHAPTER-OPENING DRAWINGS:

COVER PHOTOGRAPH:

A Navaho sandpainting (Photo by Michael Herion)

.... FOREWORD

Syntheses of topics in anthropology are assuming greater importance as the literature reaches such proportions that only specialists
in an area can be aware of the developing issues. In the
Southwestern United States especially, the continuing zeal of the
investigators has resulted in a body of data comparable to that of
any other similarly defined region of the world. In turn, the wealth
of information has served as a stimulus for greater efforts, since
sophisticated problems can be formulated and research can be
conducted in a laboratory-like atmosphere.

The attractiveness of the Southwest as a field for study has
been based on many attributes. A large number of archaeological
remains in a good state of preservation exist within regional
accessibility. The many dating techniques applicable provide excel-

lent time controls and have revealed a time depth of occupation in excess of eleven thousand years. There are links between the prehistoric populations and the modern descendants, links furnished by historical accounts beginning with the first European contacts in 1539. Today, the conservatism of many Southwestern Indians has led to a retention of a life-way similar in basic aspects to that known from the historical records.

New hypotheses about the events that transpired throughout the time that the Southwest has been occupied continue to be developed, tested, and evaluated. From the research, a general picture is emerging. While sites of greater antiquity probably exist, the earliest remains now well-dated appear to derive from peoples with a specialized hunting-oriented economy. With minor changes, the hunting-oriented pattern continued for at least three thousand years. However, a general trend toward a decrease in the effective moisture brought about changes in the economic base—the fauna—accompanied by an eastward withdrawal of the people. As that took place, there was an expansion of a pattern from the west and south that was based on an economic system oriented toward total environmental exploitation. The combination of varying cultural backgrounds represented, and the cultural flexibility to respond to the local resources in the different parts of the Southwest, resulted in the appearance of distinctive characteristic remains in the various districts.

It appears that the introduction of the idea of horticulture and of a primitive maize by at least 2500 B.C. had little immediate effect upon the tool inventory or the settlement patterns. In the following 2,200 years the basic life-way remained the same; then, changes began to occur at an increasingly rapid rate. It would require an over-simplification to attempt to isolate the numerous factors involved, given the limitations of space and purpose of this statement. However, there are some circumstances that may have played a prominent role. Perhaps an early and major impetus for change existed in the appearance, and continued flow, of ideas and traits from Mesoamerica beginning about A.D. 300. The succeeding centuries witnessed an increase in horticultural practices, population growth, the formation of large social units, continued responses to local social and natural environments, and spatial indentity of groups. The stress period brought about by changes in the environmental factors in the late A.D. 1200's and early 1300's was accompanied by dramatic demographic shifts; and, by the beginning of historic times, many regions that once held large populations were abandoned, only to be reoccupied in some cases by different peoples. Meanwhile, large increases in population occured in regions such as the Río Grande drainage of northern New Mexico. Other dislocations of people, but to a lesser magnitude, continued throughout historic times as a result of incidents such as the Pueblo Rebellion of 1680, the spread of Navajo and Apache bands into many parts of the Southwest, and the movement of Yuman groups upstream along the Gila River. Thus, the Southwestern Indians today are the products of a long and complicated sequence of events.

Early investigators in the Southwest have viewed the gathering of descriptive data about present peoples and remains from the past as a justifiable goal. Throughout the late years of the nineteenth century and the early decades of the twentieth century, their efforts have resulted in the accumulation of vast amounts of information concerning many of the major archaeological remains and the surviving ethnic groups. Of equal importance is the fact that the basis for the research tools used at present in archaeological and ethnological investigations was established during that interval. The emphasis on cultural-historical reconstructions and descriptive works about present peoples brought about the recent desire to explain the processes of cultural change and stability that have operated over a long period of time. The models exist in the present inheritors of the past Southwestern traditions.

The appreciation of the culture of the Southwestern Indians today becomes a matter of reciprocal information between the archaeological past and the ethnological present. Today, there is a continuum of the processes that have led to regional distinctiveness, have been involved in the responses to local environments, have governed the conditions of culture contact and demographic movements, and have resulted in syncretism of cultural traits. But, the documentary record is far from achieving comprehensiveness.

In the present book, Dr. Bertha P. Dutton has provided a synthesis of the Southwestern Indian cultures today, based on a critical evaluation of the data tempered by long familiarity with the people. On the one hand, Dr. Dutton has provided detailed information to make the work a valuable source for both the specialist seeking information on a problem concerning Southwestern cultures and the nonspecialist who wishes a statement that will provide an integrated view of the peoples. On the other hand, there is in the book the means for the layman to appreciate the efforts of the Southwestern Indians to adjust to alien values and still retain a life-way handed down for many generations.

Alfred E. Dittert, Jr.

.... PREFACE

The objective is to make this book generally readable for students, teachers, and travelers who desire knowledge, understanding, and authoritative information regarding the Southwestern Indians; it is for those who wish to know the basic features of Indian life, but who do not, perhaps, have the time or specialized training to read extensively of these various peoples.

"The changing Indian" is much more than an often heard phrase these days. The *changing Indian* is a fact, an almost incomprehensible fact. And changes are occurring at such a rapid pace that whatever one writes may well be out of date before the words are printed. Thus it can be said that this publication is already outdated in certain respects. However, the decade census of 1970 afforded a pivotal point, and the statements made regarding the Indian groups of the Southwest are comparable as of that time.

Throughout this work obvious changes are mentioned, and some of the more covert ones are noted. Although these may vary in kind and extent with the different Indian peoples, certain features in particular are undergoing alterations and transformations: education, living conditions locally and away from the home bases; labor opportunities, industries, economic exploitation, road works, soil treatments, dams and irrigation; health, welfare and social security; old ceremonies and new religions; and in some instances reappraisal of cultural values, appreciation of old mores, and intensification of self-esteem.

The writer has chosen diverse ways of presenting the information assembled; the material is too exhaustive for a book of this scope to be complete. Emphasis has been given to certain aspects of one culture, outstanding facets of another; some of the main features of specific organizations have been portrayed, and the complex and far-reaching traits of the Southwestern societies indicated.

No attempt is made to give equal attention to each and every cultural group. Rather, the design is to show that all of the aboriginal peoples fitted themselves to their particular environment and strove to live harmoniously with nature. To all, the land was sacred. An eminent place was given to the mountains and hills, to the water sources and streams; to the plant and animal life; to the sky above and the celestial bodies seen traversing it, and to the clouds that brought summer rains and winter snows. The individual and the group were linked unconsciously with their surroundings. And thanks were rendered for the orderly progression of season after season and for the blessings received.

The very way of life itself gave rise to keen observations, philosophical thinking; myths, poetry, song, and drama, which treat of simple things or the majestic; grief and joy, lullabies and love, with diversity of melody and of text. Each of these merits studies by itself. Some of the poetic contributions of the Indians are included, and of non-Indians who have been inspired by them. Something of the philosophy, drama, and other manifestations of Southwestern Indian life will be found in the following pages.

Not infrequently, secondary sources are cited as well as original works. These may be available to readers who wish to pursue studies regarding the Indians; and many will refer to primary works not included with the references mentioned.

It is hoped that reading this book will aid in an appreciation of the first Americans and of their intelligent responses to the surroundings; of their developments and attainments; and then of their tenacious attempts to continue living according to their philosophy and judicious practices in the face of white colonization, conquest, and alternating procedures of the Europeans whose aggressiveness, missionizing and political ambitions, and material desires were so foreign to the Indian beliefs of proper conduct and rewards.

Simply recording brief facts of history and taking note of modern conditions—some of which evidence accretions and others diminutions—have made the consistency of pattern apparent and impressive: peoples came from Asia, slowly populated the Southwest (as well as all of the New World), adopted ways of life in keeping with the conditions at hand, and developed social organizations thus dictated, recognized the limits of their domain and the rights of others, and achieved their respective cultural patterns. Then came the outsiders.

Every conceivable means has been employed to overcome the indigenous peoples and their mores, to make them conform to the white man's way of life. Through four and a half centuries, these efforts have met with relatively little success. Indians may be made to dress like Anglos, eat their foods, dwell in their types of structures, adopt their means of transportation, follow their prescribed curriculums and business methods, undergo the missionizing endeavors of various sects, practice non-Indian forms of government, and the like, but no individual or no aggregate body whatsoever can make the Indian be different from what he *is*. He may change—if he sees fit—or he may mask his feelings and appear to accept the Anglo customs; but the circumstances which produced the people that came to be called American Indians and the centuries that afforded them time to develop a racial identity and distinctive social patterns made an immutable imprint.

Regardless of outside pressures the Indians have remained Indians, and they always will. It appears inevitable that their resolute spirit will bear fruit, now that their numbers are increasing; that their pride in the accomplishments of their people has been intensified; and that they are beginning to discern their existent capabilities and power, and their rights.

.... ACKNOWLEDGMENTS

The preparation of this publication has extended over a number of years. Much of the research and writing was done during 1971. After that period no further research was pursued. However, as certain individuals undertook the reading of the manuscript several months transpired between its completion and submission to the press. Suggestions of the readers were incorporated: these include later information on occasion, and the addition of certain references and bibliographic items.

As this work took shape, I began to realize how much I owe to the mentors with whom I have been privileged to study, to many Indian friends who have guided my research and added to the knowledge and understanding of their cultures, to my anthropology associates and those in related professions, and to the institutions and foundations that have provided funds for travel and research opportunities and have printed my contributions.

I am most appreciative of the fact that several busy people have taken time to read this manuscript critically and offer advice for its betterment. Among these I give special thanks to C. Fayne Porter, teacher supervisor in language arts at the Institute of American Indian Arts in Santa Fe, who is also a well-recognized author of numerous published works. To teachers in the same school, I likewise give thanks: Michael H. Clark and Paul W. Masters. Colleagues in my profession who have been particularly helpful are Robert C. Euler, Grand Canyon National Park, Arizona; A. E. Dittert, Jr., professor of anthropology, Arizona State University, Tempe, Arizona; John Martin, associate professor of anthropology at the same institution; and Dorothy L. Keur, former professor of anthropology, Hunter College, New York. Although they have not read the manuscript, these colleagues have been very helpful: Bernard L. Fontana, professor of ethnology, University of Arizona, Tucson; David M Brugge, Curator, Navajo Lands Group, National Park Service, Chaco Center, Albuquerque; and Robert W. Young, student and teacher of Navaho culture.

Within the Bureau of Indian Affairs and the National Park Service, many persons and divisions have supplied information by means of correspondence, telephone calls, printed matter and photographs. Those to whom I render special credits are: Charles R. Whitfield, agency land operations officer, Papago Indian Agency, Sells, Arizona; Kendall Cumming, superintendent, Pima Agency, Sacaton, Arizona; William S. King, superintendent, Salt River Agency, Scottsdale, Arizona; Stanley Lyman, superintendent, Uintah and Ouray Agency, Fort Duchesne, Utah; Espeedie G. Ruiz, superintendent, Ute Mountain Ute Agency, Towaoc, Colorado; José A. Zuñi, superintendent, Hopi Indian Agency, Keams Canyon, Arizona.*

Other persons to whom I am most grateful are Al Packard, whose wide knowledge of Indian arts and crafts has been drawn upon extensively; William Brandon, writer, who has supplied several pertinent articles which otherwise might have been overlooked; Lloyd New, director of the Institute of American Indian Arts, who has furnished information and publications; and Constance (Mrs.

*Location of individuals at time of supplying information.

William A.) Darkey, Edith (Mrs. William D.) Powell, and Dr. Caroline B. Olin, who have given editorial aid.

For supplying source materials and miscellaneous data, I wish to thank the Navajo Census Office, the Northern and Southern Pueblos agencies respectively, the Jicarilla and Mescalero Apache agencies, the Hopi Tribe, the Zuñi Tribal Council, the Northern Pueblos Enterprises, and many other contributors.

To Fermor S. Church, I owe an especially great debt. Without him this publication would not have been undertaken and completed. His training in engineering (degree from Harvard University) and extensive knowledge of the greater Southwest, its peoples, and its problems—which results from years of teaching at Los Alamos, Santa Barbara, and Taos; from managing the Philmont Boy Scout Ranch; serving in high positions with electrical cooperatives for over two score years; and publishing scientific articles—complemented my learning and experience. Our discussions of matters about which I was writing and manner of presenting them added much to the significance of this undertaking. Some of the maps were prepared by him: the majority are by Phyllis Hughes of the Museum of New Mexico staff.

As author of *Indians of the American Southwest,* I have drawn on many sources and have quoted material extensively. Permission to quote direct statements was sought, and outstanding cooperation received. Sincere appreciation is expressed to the following authors and publishers:

American Anthropologist, American Anthropological Association, Washington, D. C.
American Antiquity, Society for American Archaeology, Washington, D. C.
American Folklore Society, New York
Arizona Highways, Phoenix
The Arizona Republic, Phoenix
The Caxton Printers, Caldwell, Idaho
Columbia University Press, New York (through a daughter of William Whitman III, Mrs. Philip T. Cate, Santa Fe)
Diné Baa-Hane, Fort Defiance, Ariz.
Frontier Heritage Press, San Diego, Calif.
Indian Tribal Series, Phoenix
Institute of American Indian Arts, Santa Fe
Museum of the American Indian, Heye Foundation, New York
Museum of New Mexico, Santa Fe

Museum of Northern Arizona, Flagstaff
The New York Times
The Progressive, Madison, Wis.
Southwest Parks and Monuments Association, Globe, Ariz.
Southwest Printers, Yuma, Ariz.
Time: the weekly newsmagazine, New York
The University of Arizona (Dept. of Anthropology), Tucson
The University of Arizona (vice-president for business affairs and
    treasurer), Tucson
The University of Chicago Press, Chicago
The University of New Mexico Press, Albuquerque
University of Oklahoma Press, Norman
University of Washington Press, Seattle
Robert W. Young and *The Gallup Independent*,
    Gallup, New Mexico

Specific citations are given with the references and full data appear in the bibliography.

To those who contributed their photographic works I am deeply indebted, including the renowned Laura Gilpin, of widespread fame, and Elita Wilson, who has produced outstanding records of the Southwest and its Indian peoples. These, and most of the other contributors, gave their photographs gratis for use in this publication; in other instances museums and other agencies made their contributions without charge. The name of each photographer or source appears with the pictures.

Grateful appreciation is acknowledged to those who typed the final manuscript copy of this work from the rough drafts submitted:

Mary Jean (Mrs. Edward S.) Cook, Rebecca Brown, and Sharyn (Mrs. Kimball R.) Udall.

Santa Fe, New Mexico

Bertha P. Dutton

.... LINGUISTIC NOTES

In pronouncing Indian and Spanish words, *a* is soft as in "father," *e* as in "grey," *i* as in "machine," *o* as in "whole"; no silent vowels occur. The consonant *h* is silent; *ch* is sounded as in "church"; *j* is like *h* in "hay." In *ll*, the first *l* is lightly sounded and the second takes a *y* sound; thus *Jicarilla* is Heek-ah-REEL-yah.

As noted by a recognized linguist who has worked on Southwestern languages for many years, Professor George L. Trager, "It is customary to refer to a people by the same form for singular and plural (as 'the Hopi,' 'a Hopi,' etc.)."

As with the spelling of the term *Navaho,* some writers follow the Spanish use of "j," though the word is not Spanish, while the modern trend is to use the English "h."

INDIANS
of the american southwest

1 who and where

Those who study human beings from the point of view of their physical characteristics—the physical anthropologists, or somatologists (from *somato*, meaning body)—have come to recognize that the basic characteristics of the so-called American Indians show relatively little diversity. Their closest clear-cut resemblances are with the peoples of Mongoloid stock, the peoples of Asia. In pigmentation both are between the white, or Caucasoid, and the black, or Negroid races; they have straight, coarse, dark head hair, and sparse body hair; cheekbones agree in size and projection, as do the out-jutting jaws and face breadth. Both American Indians and Mongoloids have shovel-shaped incisor teeth and, at birth, display the Mongoloid spot—a blue spot above the rump, which fades within a short time; many also have the Mongoloid, or epicanthic, fold of the inner part of the upper eyelid. The eye color is dark brown.

Aside from these strikingly similar characteristics, the Indians display a number of more or less minor differences. Some are tall, others short, some are stocky and others thin; some have long heads, while the heads of others are round; lips may be thick or thin; and noses may be high and aquiline or low and concave. Such physical divergences are amply attested by variations among geographical and cultural areas, in both prehistoric and modern eras. It has been noted that: Seemingly . . . the Indian possesses a number of relatively fixed characteristics which are clearly Mongoloid and a number which are so variable in time and space that students often look to sources in other great racial divisions for an explanation . . ." while other students "express the opinion that the Mongoloid stock of Asia is sufficiently variable in itself to account for most of the diversity among American Indians." (Gabel 1949:9-10; Agogino and Kuntz 1971:24)

Starting thousands of years ago, peoples with these characteristics began migrating from Asia by one way or another. Many came into the American continent by way of the Bering Strait and worked their way southward from time to time, in small bands—some along the Pacific coast, others through intermountain corridors, and still others along the eastern slopes of the Rocky Mountains. Although they have lived in the Western Hemisphere for centuries and are inherently part of this land of mountains, forests, mesas, canyons, semiarid stretches, and deserts, their remote Asiatic ancestry must be held in mind.

THE LAND AND THE ABORIGINAL INHABITANTS

The *Southwest* is an area with no specific limits or definite boundary, but for the purposes of culture studies, ancient and modern, it here includes all of New Mexico and Arizona, the southwest corner of Colorado, southern Utah, southwestern Nevada, and the California border of the Colorado River. The *Greater Southwest* adds the southern California Indians to the Pacific coast, western Texas, and dips down into northern Mexico on occasion. (Strong 1927:1-5)

The first known inhabitants of the Greater Southwest are commonly designated as *Paleo-Indians*, the ancient ones who dwelt here from perhaps 25,000 B. C. to around 6,000 B. C. (The earliest real date is 11,500 B. P., that is, before the present). The Paleo-Indians were highly specialized in their economy; as the environment changed and big game moved eastward, they withdrew eastward also as *Clovis*, *Folsom*, and other culture groups. The big game Paleo-Indian tradition existed in the plains area until historical times.

Those who occupied the Greater Southwest from about 6,000 B. C. until approximately two thousand years ago are recognized as being of an archaic stage of culture, the *Desert Archaic*, or *Desert Culture*. Peoples from the western basins, the California desert regions, and northwestern Mexico moved into unpopulated areas of the Southwest as the big game hunters withdrew. The Desert Culture became the basis of modern populations. On this culture horizon *maize*, or "Indian corn," was received from Mexico about 2,500-3,000 B. C. This new food made little difference in the habits or tools of the people for over two thousand years, however. It never supplied as much food as hunting and gathering; and it was only when it became a symbol that it assumed importance. (Dittert 1958) The modern Southwestern Indians well may be descendents of a variation of western Desert Culture called the *Picosa*. (Dutton 1972:2)

During their years of wandering from the Old World to the New, and as they moved into chosen locations, it was necessary for the peoples to be highly observant of elemental and environmental features. Each day man had to derive his existence from the plant and animal world about him, and so these things were of the utmost significance. Thus it was that the Indian geared his life to the scene around him. The result was a culture that integrated the natural phenomena and biota of his world with mankind. Among all factors, universal interplay was ever present; man dwelt in a world of mysticism and symbolism.

A formative type of religion prevailed over wide expanses. It may be detected in eras when the Desert Culture peoples occupied the lands from coastal southern California across New Mexico and into Texas, from southwestern Nevada, southern Utah and Colorado, and over northern Mexico. All, or nearly all, of the Indians who inhabited these regions eventually became horticulturists. Horticulture prescribes a semisedentary mode of life, and then a sedentary existence. It requires specific implements and procedures for handling them . . . and these provide the foundation for rites and ceremonies which grow out of continuing cycles of behavior and growth.

The people were held together by simple relationships based on family organization exclusively; and it is deduced that this was by recognition of the bilateral family, wherein both father and mother influenced controls. Two or more families tended to live in proximity to one another, and they habitually wintered together. Children of unrelated families married one another. The family groups had leaders, headmen who were wise and honored.

Area Defined   The *Four Corners Region* is that area radiating from the common boundary point shared by the states of Colorado, Utah, Arizona, and New Mexico, the *Four Corners*—the only place in the nation where four states adjoin one another. In the nearer reaches four groups of Indians dwell. Based on the languages spoken, including a variety of dialects, they are designated as *Ute, Jicarilla Apache, Navaho,* and *Pueblo* Indians. Somewhat farther distant from the Four Corners are other Indian peoples known as the *Mescalero Apache* of south-central New Mexico and other Apache assemblages in southeastern Arizona, commonly called the Western Apaches; Pimans (*Pima* and *Papago*) and the Cahitan *Yaqui* in south-central Arizona; Yumans, representing upland and river divisions (*Havasupai, Hualapai,* and *Yavapai; Cocopah, Maricopa, Mohave,* and *Yuma,* respectively), in the central and western parts of that state; and the Ute-related *Paiute* and *Chemehuevi* who dwell in southern and southwestern Utah and along the western border of Arizona, respectively.

DEVELOPMENT OF SOCIO-RELIGIOUS PATTERNS   The original inhabitants of this vast new land, as man today, could not *see* their deity. Consequently, an intermediary, a *seeable* personage to intervene between deity and mankind, had to be conjured, and so the headman, or "chief," who played more the part of a father and spiritual guide than actual ruler, assumed that role. With some peoples the office became that of priest.

It would seem that a universal being was generally recognized—a great, sacred omnipotence, one deity yet held as expressing male and female unification, or differing manifestations. In general, the omnipotent was believed to occupy a sphere high above that of man—just as most earthly beings view their relationship with deity. Thus, looking aloft, early peoples of the Greater Southwest—as in most of America—beheld the sun, which appeared in the east with each morning's dawn, moved in an orderly way across the heavens, and disappeared from sight in the west. The fact that one could not look directly into the sun, because of its shining brilliance, added to its celestial mystery.

Among horticultural peoples, the "chief" or a priest directed the formalities that domestication demands; he introduced calendrical observances which, by the very nature of things, gave eminence to the sun. The earth, though equally important, is here, always at hand; the Indian lives *in* it or *on* it, and *from* it. But the sun comes and goes, and alters its pathway observably from north to south, and then reverses its movement; it is something with which man must reckon. The moon divides the year into time periods and is thus a factor to be considered, almost as the earth which gives sustenance.

Such simple origins gave rise to priesthoods among the sedentary peoples, and to cults and attendant procedures, formalization, and all that follows. To make religion understandable to the people, a priest assumed the part of a sort of director-general of all deific manifestations. Just as a biologic family develops, the priesthood accommodated a growing ceremonial organization. The sun, with most peoples, came to be envisioned as the Sun Father of those dwelling on the earth, over which he spread his light and warmth. This led to a recognition of the complementary worldly sphere as the Earth Mother.

In the nature of a parable, a miraculous union of Sun Father and Earth Mother was portrayed as bringing forth offspring. This was primarily in the guise of twain, or twin boys, commonly visible as the morning and evening stars. These celestial ones function as twin war gods, an Elder Brother and a Younger Brother, whose earthly representatives are war priests, or chiefs, or war captains. On occasion the twain coalesce into one being; again they appear as a boy and a girl. As ceremonialism grew, the deific family was enlarged, and an increasing body or priesthood provided officials to represent the supernatural ones, each with specific duties and positions.

With the recitation of folk history, which is a vital part of all ceremonials, different manifestations of personages occur, resulting in multiplicity of characters. This led to the erroneous assumption by some students or researchers that the Indians had many gods, even idols, whereas these personages are actually visual aids in bringing knowledge and understanding of a supreme deity into the all-encompassing life of the people. They serve in maintaining discipline and in teaching the complex interrelationships of family and societal groups. The deific ones are portrayed bestowing their powers on earthly ones—the priests and their assistants, or whatever their designations.

According to the priestly teachings of the sedentary Indians, the first commandment of the omnipotent commonly was to build "a temple" in which he might be revered and given homage. Thus the family groups erected a ceremonial chamber, which was entered originally through a hatchway in the roof—so arranged as to permit light from the sun to shine within.

From the original bilateral family, increasing population brought lineages, or unilateral kinship groups, into being, wherein all members of a group were united through descent from a common ancestor. Among the majority of early dwellers in the Greater Southwest, this ancestor was recognized in the paternal line. With family and social growth, dichotomy commonly occurred, that is, the division of a group into two segments, which are usually designated as *moieties.* Membership in a moiety also followed the patrilineal line. With these developments, formation of small villages took place, and house-owning was a male prerogative. The people came to be controlled by hierarchal priesthoods, in which each official was subordinate to the one above him. The ceremonial chamber was built in the center of a village, contiguous to the dwelling of the priest.

In addition to the ceremonial house and the priest in charge, a third item was of utmost significance—the ark, as it were, a sacred bundle or fetish. Actually, the wrapping, or mat, of the fetish bundle is said to be its most important feature. Contents of the bundle are those things which the priest considers efficacious in the performance of his rites. They may include quartz crystals which reflect and divert the rays of the sun, turtle shell rattles and seashells felt to be potent in bringing rain, eagle feathers as representative of the messengers that carry man's word to his deity above, cone-shaped pipes the smoke of which is considered as cloud producing, rock concretions and other peculiarly shaped objects bestowed with magical attributes, and so on.

The fetish bundle is always in the care of the priest or an equivalent officer, and is regarded as the "heart of the house." Its possession is passed on to a successor in the paternal line. Such paraphernalia, the ceremonies, and the sacred chamber or a holy place are considered as being owned by societies but controlled by their respective priests, or by the head religious dignitary. According to Indian philosophy, the fetish has been with them since the time of their coming forth onto this earth—from the Place of Emergence, which is known by its proper term in each linguistic group.

Although nomadic and seminomadic peoples have been influenced by those who followed sedentary patterns of life, they tended to have more flexible systems of religion, with officers other than priests and without a structure in which their practices are centered.

DIRECTION (Papago)

I was directed by my grandfather
To the East,
    so I might have the power of the bear;
To the South,
    so I might have the courage of the eagle;
To the West,
    so I might have the wisdom of the owl;
To the North,
    so I might have the craftiness of the fox;
To the Earth,
    so I might receive her fruit;
To the Sky,
    so I might lead a life of innocence.

By Alonzo Lopez

From: *The Writers' Reader,* 1962-1966. Institute of American Indian Arts, Santa Fe, N.M.

2 the Pueblo peoples

BRIEF HISTORY   As the Spanish explorers during the sixteenth century pushed northward from Mexico, following ancient trails across desert wastes, over high mountain ranges and along flowing streams, the majority of indigenous peoples whom they encountered were those who had developed a sedentary life. When the Spaniards saw Indians living in compact, many-chambered, flat-roofed structures built around plazas, or squares, and from one to several stories in height with entering passageways, they were reminded of the villages of their homeland, hence they called each settlement a *pueblo*, and the "village dwellers" en masse were called "Pueblo Indians"—as opposed to nomadic or semi-nomadic peoples, or those on *rancherias*.

Through the centuries these Indians had developed cultures

based on hunting and gathering, to which horticulture was added in time. Stored food supplies provided for periods when products were not growing, and thus made it unnecessary for social units to move in search of food. With some 25% of their yearly food supply provided by horticulture, they were able to maintain increasingly larger groups and to attain a complex society. Theirs became an orderly way of life, with attention given to pertinent arts and crafts. Each pueblo or ranchería was established in relation to permanent springs or running water, and also to a close area having a considerable range of elevational gradients, within a short horizontal distance, which offered the maximum gathering potential. Near the villages were fertile gardens and fields where men and women shared their labors.

With the Spanish government taking formal possession of the Southwestern regions, Spanish saint names were given to the settlements. The Pueblo country was divided into districts and a Catholic priest was assigned to each. The Indians were required to take oaths of obedience and pay homage to the Catholic church and the Spanish crown.

At the pueblo of *Oke-oweenye* the Spaniards established the first capital of New Mexico in 1598, which they called *San Juan de Los Caballeros.* The next year, the Indian site of *Yunue-yungue* on the west bank of the Río Grande, directly across from the initial settlement, was chosen for the Spanish location, and this they called *San Gabriel.* It served as the capital until 1610, when the seat of government was moved to an old pueblo site which had been occupied centuries before, *La Villa Real de Santa Fe*, along the Río Sante Fe.

Becoming antagonistic toward the Spaniards who encroached upon their lands and forcibly altered their ways of life, the Pueblo peoples finally united in revolt and, in 1680, drove the invaders from New Mexico. (The name "New Mexico" as now applied appears to have been used for the northern province from 1582; the territory thus designated reached to the Pacific Ocean.) (Bloom 1940:106; *Carta Contenante . . . la Florida*) Twelve years of freedom from oppression were enjoyed until the Spaniards returned in 1692, under General Don Diego de Vargas and reconquered the northland.

Spanish rule continued until the Mexican Revolution of 1821, after which the Indians were declared citizens on equal basis with non-Indians. Life under Mexican authority, otherwise, was little changed for the Pueblos. Then the war between the United States of America and Mexico was fought, ending with the Treaty of Guadalupe Hidalgo which was signed in 1848. Mexico gave up all claim to territory east of the Río Grande (REE-oh GRAHN-day) and ceded New Mexico and upper California to the U. S. A., in return for payment of fifteen million dollars and other stipulations. Articles of the treaty provided for recognition and protection by the U. S. A. of Indian rights previously established under Spanish and Mexican rule.

Thereafter, title to Pueblo lands and those of the other Indian peoples were in question for decades. White settlers intruded upon Indian holdings in increasing numbers. In 1849 the Bureau of Indian Affairs (which had been created in the War Department in 1824) was placed under the newly established U. S. Department of the Interior, and the first Indian agent in New Mexico Territory was appointed.

According to a treaty signed on 30 December 1853—the Gadsden Purchase—the U. S. A. paid Mexico ten million dollars for all of the territory along the present southern boundary of this country, from the Río Grande to the Colorado River. Then, on 1 August 1861, all of New Mexico south of the 34th parallel was organized as the Territory of Arizona, with the boundary later to be changed as it is today. Six months before, formation of the Territory of Colorado reduced New Mexico in size, its northeastern section being included in Colorado.

Few of the pueblos could produce Spanish documents pertaining to their grants. The surveyor-general of the federal government took Indian testimonials in 1856 as to the holdings of some of the pueblos. Certain surveys were made in 1858, and a greater number the following year; these were confirmed by the Supreme Court and patents were issued to most of the pueblos in 1864, while others were not forthcoming until years later. About a half-dozen pueblos have less land today than they had according to the original patents, some have about the same, and the majority have received additional acres through various governmental actions and purchases.

New Mexico was admitted to the Union as a state in January of 1912. Twelve years later, Congress declared all Indians born in the U. S. A. to be citizens. However, the constitution of New Mexico excluded "Indians not taxed" from the franchise. Not until 1948 was legislative action taken which made Indians citizens of the state as well as of the nation, and thus entitled to vote. Arizona became a state of the Union approximately a month later than New Mexico; it had similar laws regarding the Indian residents, and took corresponding legislative action to give them the franchise at the same time as did New Mexico.

THE "PRIVILEGED PEOPLE" MYTH

Indians are not the privileged citizens that many people erroneously believe them to be. One fact widely misunderstood pertains to the relationship between Indians and the federal government. Let it be recorded here that:

> The Federal Government makes no payments to a person merely because he is an Indian. Payments made to a person of Indian blood may represent income from his property collected for him by an agent of the United States. Other payments may result from compensation for losses incurred when lands are required in connection with Federal projects. Payments may represent the Indian's pro rata share of property belonging to the tribe of which he is a member. In each instance, money available for payments belongs either to the tribe or an individual and is held in trust by the U.S. Government. Therefore, Government checks are issued in making payments to individuals and to tribes. (Papago Indian Agency 1970:4)

CULTURAL CHARACTERISTICS

The Pueblos follow a communal pattern. Society is concerned with the group as a whole. Until recent times an individual got no recognition for his personal achievements; no ancient vessel or other work of art ever bore the name of its maker.

Living in this great uncrowded region, with day following night in orderly fashion, season after season, and where cataclysmic events were exceedingly rare, the Indian had two wonderful culture-forming assets—space and time; space so that he could see things clearly, and time so that he could think and consider all matters carefully. The Indian had no system of writing; he could not jot down notes; and thus he had to remember everything and pass his knowledge on orally. Time and space and memory resulted in sound philosophy—which is reflected in all phases of the cultures which were developed in this area. No need to hurry or to make quick decisions. When some innovation occurred, it was thoroughly examined and discussed, and then rejected or accepted according to the unanimous decision of the group concerned. Changes, if made, were made slowly and for logical reasons.

The Indian, particularly the Pueblo, is restrained and affable, exceedingly polite. He wants to give you, or at least appear to give you, what you want. It seems to be a non-Indian tendency to ask leading questions, or "dumb" questions when seeking information, casual or serious. If one sees an Indian woman with a piece of pottery or a basket, or something else, and asks: "Did you make it?" the answer is likely to be yes, because she senses that is the answer desired. Should one question: "Who made that vessel? the answer might be: "my mother," or "my daughter," or "I did."

It should always be remembered that any Indian group, or even an Indian family, is now in a transitional stage. They are torn between their own ancient standards and those which are being urged or forced upon them by those of non-Indian culture.

Pueblo children have an active part in the social organization, in the family from the time of birth. A child sees and is a part of everything that goes on at home or in the plaza. From this constant participation, the manners of his people are learned early and completely. The association of a young child with those a few years older, "brings the individual at a very early age into the youth-controlled, socially accepted milieu of his own generation. (*See* Hawley and Senter 1946:142-143) Pueblo Indians think that a baby should be kept happy, for "when it grows up it will have many troubles." If a baby cries, it is given attention—picked up and entertained, not punished. If a baby cries for food, it is fed. When children are scolded, it is done quietly with low, controlled voice. Whipping is a form of punishment used when other measures have failed, but it is done in the privacy of the family only (excepting some ceremonial occasions).

Indian children are given and assume responsibilities at an early age; gradually they learn and participate in all phases of life which they will follow as adults. The boys are miniatures of their fathers, the girls of their mothers. Not until they take on more and more of the non-Indian cultures are the Indians confronted with problems of so-called juvenile delinquency.

Sexual standards among the Indians are different from ours, and may well be more realistic than those which we have long endeavored to maintain. Living in close association with other members of a family, children grow up knowing as much about sex matters as any other aspect of their culture. Premarital sexual experiments are common. They are not secret, but usually take place in the common sleeping room of parents and brothers and sisters. Pueblo adolescents usually were given sexual instructions by certain elders, so that girls and young boys suffered none of the stresses and strains and clandestine affairs to which non-Indian youth are subjected.

Traditionally, if a child is born out of wedlock, no stigma is attached to that child. The girl's parents usually raise it, and it takes a normal place in society. Certain it is that Indian youth have not suffered the physiological disturbances and oftentimes psychotic results that befall the youngsters of our society which has often failed to recognize adolescence as a distinct period when one is neither child nor adult.

The Pueblo Indians practice monogamy, whether they be married according to Indian customs or the ever-increasing civil and church ceremonies. Postmarital sexual infidelity is disapproved but is not uncommon. An erring wife, if caught, is usually punished by her husband, though a pueblo official may be sought for this purpose. Extramarital sexual relations are not uncommon either. Divorce, as well as marriage, is characteristically a family affair with the Indians. Among the Río Grande Pueblos divorce appears relatively rare; among the Zuñi it is more common.

Until modern patterns of life resulted in unbalancing the Indian economy and cultural mores and particularly in recent years of drought, wartime hardships, expanding economic, health and welfare programs, no Indian group failed to provide for its own orphans, old people, the ill and handicapped; and the group enforced punishments for infractions of its laws.

Most of the Pueblos, though they do not like death any more than we do, accept it for what it is, the end of man's material existence. It is the spirit which counts, and the spirit continues. A body is ceremonially prepared after death, dressed in traditional attire, and supplied with food, drink, and items of industry for use in the next world. Burial occurs as soon after death as possible, usually before nightfall of the same day of cessation of life. In its grave or cranny in the rocks, the body is watched for four nights, to keep away prowling dogs, coyotes, or other molesters. By then the spirit, it is believed, has reached the spirit world . . . and what happens to the earthly remains is of naught. Body orientation in burial is important among some of the Indians, while others appear to disregard the position of the corpse.

The Pueblos, like all other Indians, have taboos, avoidance practices, and other customs that they hold significant. Their reluctance to being photographed is not just a whim; it is a social matter with deep roots, and is related to sympathetic, or imitative, magic. If one has your likeness, he may exercise controls over you—usually to your detriment.

Gossip, criticism, and ridicule are major means of social control among the Indians. These factors tend to keep an individual from deviating from the norm of his culture. Indians are keenly sensitive to being singled out for public disapproval, laughter, or ostracism. They refrain from wrongdoing on the basis of such censure. Even where Christian training has spread to the Indians, the concept of postmortem reward or punishment has made little impression. Rather, they expect imminent and observable justice. For instance, if one does wrong, illness may befall his village or family group, a disastrous flood may destroy his property and crops, or severe drought may lay waste his season's efforts. It is much safer to observe the rules.

Indians feel that silence is part of the concentration that compels results. Speech, therefore, is restricted or taboo in certain ritual circumstances. The Pueblos have a profound conviction about the reasonableness of secretiveness. As long as one remains silent "his power is still in him." (Parsons 1939-I:433)

Even unto the present, some Indians regard long hair as "the badge of an Indian." It is considered by a man a necessary concomitant of his ceremonial life. As one Indian man put it: "When they cut [my hair], my heart hurt." Some were reluctant to have their hair cut, fearing they might be mistaken for Spanish-Americans, to whom they consider themselves superior. One of the most severe blows to many an Indian's status came when the armed services insisted on cutting the hair of adult Indian men. According to their mores, the kerchief is acceptable for Indian men to wear; hats are considered improper. Blanket wearing, like long hair, is another symbol of status. Moccasins are proper, whereas shoes are not. But with the demands of today we see all these less and less regarded. Conflicts result as acculturation progresses.

GENERAL APPEARANCE Understandably, the Pueblo Indians are not a homogeneous group of people. They reflect differing physical strains and admixtures. In general, they hold an intermediate position, not being of greatest stature or the smallest. They differ in head form and other respects, and fall close to the Indian mean. In the New Mexico pueblos,

NORTHERN RIO GRANDE PUEBLOS, NEW MEXICO

where cereals long comprised the principal food-stuffs, a tendency to stockiness is observable, especially among the women whose lives center in the household. The Hopi (HOH-pee), who are the pueblo dwellers of Arizona, commonly are of small stature, due in part doubtless to their rigorous environment and basically strenuous life.

Usually the Pueblo peoples wear attire appropriate for homekeeping and farmer-stockmen activities. On festive occasions they have special clothing, either traditional or modern.

LOCATION AND POPULATION
Today, not only in their pueblos along the Río Grande and in Zuñi, southwest of Gallup, New Mexico, Pueblo Indians may be seen in and around the metropolitan centers of Albuquerque, Santa Fe, Taos and Gallup. One also may see Pueblo men, women, and children displaying their handicrafts in such public places as bus stations, airports, restaurants, hotels or motels, or museums; or they may have *ramadas*—temporary shelters—set up along the highways. In Arizona, the Hopi are much in evidence in the towns of Holbrook, Winslow, and Flagstaff.

As a matter of convenience, the pueblo dwellers of the Río Grande drainage are commonly spoken of as the Eastern Pueblos, while those of Zuñi and the Hopi villages are called the Western Pueblos. On occasion, Acoma and Laguna are included with the western peoples.

One sometimes sees Indians trudging down the roadway, perhaps signaling for a ride with a lifted hand or protruded lips. Or they may be riding. If on horseback, they take the softer footing along the fence that bounds the highroad, and one sees an unforgettable picture of profiles of dark skins and bright kerchiefs. A few years ago, a common sight was a family traveling to town in a farm wagon—perhaps a shiny one, its red and green paint reflecting good care, or an old one evidencing long use, its dished wheels making eccentric curves in the sand. Today, nearly all travel by automobile, some rusty and clunking, others bright and smart with a new paint job, or a late model station wagon or truck; the all-purpose pickup is favored by most.

Traces of the Pueblo past—scattered fragments of pottery, rock chips and worked stones, mounds of earth and rock, and crumbling walls that mark former villages—may be found on every hand. Great and small deserted dwellings and ceremonial structures falling into ruin, silent and impressive, also abound. One never escapes the consciousness of the centuries that these people have lived a vivid and constructive life upon this land.

The Pueblo Indians do not constitute a tribe as that word is understood by anthropologists and related researchers. Usually with them the term means something of this nature: "A tribe is a social group of a simple kind, the members of which speak a common dialect, have a single government, and act together for common purposes such as warfare." (Or *see* Hoebel 1958:661) A characteristic feature of a tribe is that it is a closed society (a group of individuals who have adjusted their interests sufficiently to cooperate in satisfying their various needs). (Eggan 1950:4) Its laws and morals apply to its members and not to outsiders. Each Pueblo group functions as an entity, each an independent lot of farming, house-building people, alike in some features and dissimilar in others.

New Mexico's Pueblo Indians in 1970 totaled approximately 29,335, and the number is slowly but consistently growing. The Hopi number a few more than 6,000. The chart on pages 271-73 gives the population of each of the pueblos and reservations, and these are located on the maps on pages viii, ix and 16.

LANGUAGES   The Pueblos, and all other Indians, may best be considered with view to the languages they speak.* For instance, the people of Taos (rhymes with house), Picurís (pee-kuhr-EES), Sandía (Sahn-DEE-ah), and Isleta (ees-LAY-tah) speak dialects of the *Tiwa* (TEE-wah) language.

On the reservations of San Juan (sahn HUAhn), Santa Clara (SAHN-ta KLAH-rah), San Ildefonso (sahn eel-day-FOHN-so), Pojoaque (poh-HWA-kay), Nambé (nahm-BAY), and Tesuque (tay-SOO-kay), the *Tewa* (TAY-wah) language is spoken. Tewa is also the language used at Hano in the Hopi country of northeastern Arizona, where some Pueblo Indians from the Río Grande valley migrated about 1700. Jémez (HAY-mez) is the only pueblo in which the *Towa* (TOH-wah) language is now used. Tiwa, Tewa, and Towa are related tongues that derive from a common linguistic family, the TANOAN, the parent stock being known as *AZTECO-TANOAN*.

The language of Zuñi, the westernmost pueblo in New Mexico, belongs to the ZUNIAN family, which appears to derive

*Linguists for the most part follow the J.W. Powell classification of Indian languages. Here, the editor adheres to this system of grouping Southwestern languages. (*See* Powell 1891:3-142 and Swadish 1967)

from the *PENUTIAN* stock. If true, ZUNIAN and TANOAN may be very distantly related.

Keres (KAY-rays) is spoken with dialectic differences in the other pueblos of New Mexico—in Cóchiti (KOH-chee-tee), Santo Domingo(SAHN-toh doh-MEEN-go), and San Fellipe (sahn fay-LEE -pay) along the banks of the Río Grande; in Santa Ana (sahn-TAHN-ah) and Zía (Tsee-ah) on the Río Jémez; and in the Laguna (lah-GOO-nah) and Acoma (AH-koh-mah) villages, roughly fifty miles west of Albuquerque. In general, linguists feel that Keres is quite distinct from any of the more inclusive language families of North America. Evidence indicates that the Keresans have been in the Southwest for a long, long time—as they say, "since time immemorial."

Excluding those who live in the pueblo of Hano, the Hopi Indians speak a single language, with several dialects, grouped under the UTO-AZTECAN family tree, of which nine branches have been identified as stemming from a Proto-Uto-Aztecan parent language spoken about five thousand years ago. (Miller and Booth 1972).

SOCIAL ORGANIZATION

Viewing the map on page 16, it is seen that loose geographic unity exists among the various linguistic groups. The northern Tiwa villages seem far removed from those of their kindred in Sandía and Isleta; considerable distance separated the eastern Keres from those of the western pueblos, Laguna and Acoma, and the dwellers in Hopiland are still further distant. What then makes these Indians seem to be one people and gives them the appearance of being a cultural unit? The answer undoubtedly is found in their attitude toward life as a whole, their religion in fact.

With the Southwestern Indians in general, and with the Pueblos in particular, religion transcends and permeates all else. It is the very core of their existence, day by day. All aspects of Pueblo life—the arts, crafts, industries, social structure, and religion— are inextricably interwoven, thoroughly integrated. From the simple tenet that *man must so live as to be in harmony with nature* ("nature's basic rhythm"), the Pueblo Indians developed a rich dramatic art—poetry, legendry, song and dance; by these means religion is given outward expression.

Sacred rites are performed in their fields prior to the planting, and appropriate ceremonies are conducted throughout the seasons—prayers for germination, growth, and maturation of the crops, and then thanks are given for prayers "answered and unanswered," as one old Indian has told it. Their hunts are ceremonially ordered and conducted, as are their salt gathering missions and other practices. Many of the designs on their pottery and other works of art are derived from motifs connected with their ceremonial life. Through religion all else is given significance; the lean or bountiful years are attributed to faulty or proper observance of religious retreats and rituals. No understanding of Pueblo life apart from its religious beliefs and procedures is possible.

Basically, each of the Pueblo communities is a closely united and highly systematized organization. Similar social patterns may be observed among the pueblos, yet great differences exist in regard to emphases upon certain organizations and practices. Some are meeting current stresses which the modern world puts on them by relaxing certain of their customs; others hold fast to their age-old strictures. Let it be kept in mind that the Pueblos are broadly alike, yet distinct. The people mingle, but hold apart. They do not favor marriage outside one's own village; while it may not be forbidden absolutely, it is often made difficult. The ceremonial dances are similar, but variations may be observed; these are important. Physical differences exist. Taos, for example, was the buffer pueblo on the north, receiving the brunt of raids by hunting tribes from the Great Plains, and its people exhibit a mixture of blood. Foreign elements show in traditions, societal practices, ceremonies, and in stature, wearing apparel, hairdress, and adornments.

Authority between the ecclesiastical leaders and those who serve in secular offices is sharply defined in each Pueblo group.

In the New Mexican pueblos, in accordance with a decree of the King of Spain in 1620, the secular officers' titles follow Spanish designations. In general these are a governor, two lieutenant governors, *alguacil* (sheriff), and *fiscales* (men who serve as church assistants—deriving from the office of prosecutor). These take office during the first week of January—usually on the first—and serve for one year, except at Isleta, Nambé, San Ildefonso, and Zuñi where the term of office is currently two years. Metal-topped canes inscribed with the Spanish cross became the badges of authority for the secular officers.

THE CANES OF OFFICE When Mexico won independence from Spain, sovereignty was successfully established and new staffs, silver thimbled, were presented to the pueblos, and the governors were authorized and commissioned to function in line with their long custom, having two canes each in symbolic support of the office. Ten years after the Gadsden purchase, President Abraham Lincoln ordered black ebony canes, silver crowned and inscribed with his signature, "A. Lincoln," for each of the then nineteen pueblos, extending the continuing authority and commission of the governors. Thus, in 1863, a third cane symbolizing the office under the new sovereignty came into possession of the pueblos in New Mexico.(Barton 1953; Faris n.d.)

The Spanish canes and the Lincoln canes bearing the name of a pueblo, the year, and the name of President Lincoln, are in evidence at any ceremony or gathering of the Pueblo Indians in any season of the year. Some of the pueblos have handed their Mexican canes over to the lieutenant governors; it appears that one or two of the villages have lost their Mexican canes and acknowledge having only two—the Spanish and Lincoln canes, as they are usually designated.

In 1883, Picurís lost the silver crown and ferule from its Lincoln cane. The stick was taken to an Indian Agent for replacement. Unfortunately, a heavier crown with paneled floral decoration was mounted, and an error was made in the date, showing the year as 1862. Pojoaque people lost the silver crown from their cane, having only the ebony stick left. But today, it is said that Pojoaque has a silver-headed, engraved cane. (Hayes 1971) Some of the canes are battered, but for the most part they are kept in fine condition. The respect for the pueblo canes is no less than is the congressman's respect for the mace in the U.S. house of Representatives.

In 1960, silver medals showing the profiles of Lincoln and President Dwight D. Eisenhower side by side, surrounded by the wording, "Republican Centennial, 1863-1960," were struck, fashioned into pendants, and strung on ribbons of red, white, and blue. Each pueblo governor was presented with one of these. They, with beribboned canes, serve as impressive symbols of office.

.... THE TANOANS

The Tanoan domain formerly extended widely from south to north and west to east. Tanoan social organization is characterized by strong dual organization, or dichotomy. In the northern Río Grande region, where the Tanoans now dwell, the two divisions—complementary ceremonial groups—are referred to generally as those of the north and south peoples, respectively, or as the summer people and the winter people. These divisions have been identified as moieties. (*See* Ortiz 1969:57-59, 73, 84, 108)

TIWA INDIANS Of the Tanoan subfamilies, the Tiwa apparently were the initial Pueblo Indians to have entered the northern Río Grande. In prehistoric times Tiwa pueblos dotted the Río Grande valley from northern Mexico to the region of modern Albuquerque.

Usually overlooked in works on the Indians of the Southwest is a Tiwa group that dwells near University Park at Las Cruces, New Mexico. Commonly known as *Tortugas* (tor-TU-gahs), the official name of this village is Guadalupe Indian Village. It is controlled by an Indian corporation, *Los Indígenes de Nuestra Señora de Guadalupe*. An elaborate celebration commemorates the patron saint's day on 12 December, with activities the day preceding and that following the major event. The colorful ceremonies, influenced by long association with the Catholic church, include ritualistic singing, candlelight procession, pilgrimage to the summit of Tortugas Mountain, and dancing in front of the village church—all conducted under strict rules passed down by generations of Tiwa Indians, even though they now are Hispanized considerably. The number of those who may be counted as Indians today is unknown.

Although the Indians of the Southwest have the franchise after a hiatus of many years, and Indian people are taking their place in the legislative bodies, it is worth noting that, during the 1927 session of the New Mexico legislature, one of the Tiwa men of the Tortugas group served as representative from Doña Ana county. He was a diligent committee worker, and was frequently called to preside over the House of Representatives, a position which he filled with skill and dignity.

Throughout historical times, the other Tiwa have occupied

two locations. A northern group, of which the pueblos of Taos and Picurís remain, is separated by some 75 miles from their southern kinsmen who dwell to the north and south of Albuquerque, in Sandía and Isleta. Indians of the latter pueblos can readily converse with one another, as can those of Taos and Picurís; and the people of Sandía and Isleta can understand the dialects of Taos and Picurís, but the reverse is not true–Sandía and Isleta are understood by the northern Tiwa with difficulty. This suggests that the division occurred long ago and that the more isolated northern people have maintained the original character of their speech to a greater degree than have the others.

In the dual system of the Tanoans each division has, or had in the past, its own priest, or *cacique*. (The term *cacique* [kah-SEE-kay], is a Haitian word that was used extensively by early chroniclers to designate the priest-chiefs; it was incorporated into the Spanish language with this significance, and was added to the Indian vocabulary.) The cacique of the north, or of the summer people, has control during the summer, and that of the south, or winter people, during the winter. The cacique is the head of all pueblo organization; he holds office for life and has a staff as a badge of authority. The cacique, the kiva chiefs, and their appointees or selectees to the secular offices, constitute a hierarchial form of government.

At Taos and Picurís, six round ceremonial chambers are utilized. These are subterranean or semisubterranean rooms, built apart from the dwellings. Such a chamber is generally referred to as a *kiva* (KEE-vah), this being the Hopi name of a sacred ceremonial, assembly, and lounging chamber, characteristic of ancient and modern Pueblo settlements. "Kiva" embraces circular and rectangular structures of a specialized nature, whether they be built below ground or above, detached or among the houses. At Taos, each kiva is surrounded by a palisade of tall poles. Visitors are advised to keep a respectful distance from these. Paternal kiva membership is the pattern, but at Taos the choice of kiva is now optional, though the tendency persists for a father to "give" his child to his kiva or kiva cluster. The males are also the house owners.

In addition to its six kivas situated in the north and south segments of the pueblo—with a "chief" in charge of each—Taos has a seventh chamber of similar form which lies outside the village wall; it is sometimes described as "disused." Actually, it is used for retreats and prayers. Its original association was with a scalp society, or warrior cult, under the direction of the war chiefs. Picurís also has its structure designated as a scalp house, which undoubtedly has similar associations. Curing and healing were functions of the warrior society.

Formerly, if not at present, each Tiwa pueblo, as Taos today, had a race track as part of the village plan. Such tracks extend in an east-west direction, representing the courses of the sun and moon. Footraces are part of ceremonial ritual, being run to give power to travel to those celestial bodies. They represent contests between the north division of the pueblo and the south division. In the form of relay races, runners represent the north and south kiva groups, respectively; starting in the east, as the rising sun, they run to the west, touch another runner who races eastward, and so on until the winner is proclaimed.

Among the southern Tiwa the pattern regarding ceremonial structures is not so apparent. Inasmuch as deep subterranean chambers are known to have been in the region as long as a thousand years ago, it seems possible that the original kiva system may have been like that of Taos and Picurís. But Isleta and Sandía were in the main path of the Spanish *conquistadores*, and for over four and a quarter centuries they have been subjected to cultural disarrangements. The pueblos have been deserted, reoccupied after intervals of time, perhaps relocated, and admixtures of peoples have inhabited them.

The modern situation includes two rectangular ceremonial chambers built within the house blocks which are arranged about a central plaza. Isleta, largest of the pueblos in this group, has two rectangular kivas built among the dwellings and, in addition, a large circular chamber built almost wholly above ground and detached from other structures. It is a prominent feature of the architecture and is known as an "outside house." This is said to be used for maskless ceremonial dances, for painting the clowns, and for race ritual; it was primarily the place where scalps of enemies were kept.

At Isleta the divisions of the dual organization are known by the terms "Black Eye" and "Red Eye," respectively; everyone in the pueblo belongs to one or the other. Officers of the Red Eye (*Shúre*), or summer division, and the Black Eye (*Shifun*), or winter division, are prominent in the irrigation rituals and in certain maskless katsina dances; they direct the clowning, hunting and ball-playing, and other group activities.

In general, *katsinas*, or supernatural beings, are *not* impersonated by masked dancers among the Tiwa, although the small kiva groups make offerings to those personages.

Everyone belongs also to one of seven "corn groups" that hold winter and summer ceremonies for the sun; these signify seasonal transfer of official duties. An Isletan belongs to his mother's corn group. The corn chief, who may be referred to as "Corn Father" or "Corn Mother," serves as an intermediary with the curers, or expediter of deceased ones. The corn fathers and their helpers operate as a priesthood. The moon is regarded as "our mother moon," and stars are considered to be sons of the divine parents.

Isleta shows resemblances to both the Keres and Tewa systems. It has a cult of the dead, believing that weather and crop spirits dwell in the mountains. Their supernatural beings, like the katsinas of other pueblos, are impersonated in dances, but no masks are worn.

It is said that the office of cacique no longer exists at Isleta. Ritual matters are supervised by the war captain.

In 1947, this pueblo was the second in New Mexico to adopt a constitution to govern itself. In 1970 the document was replaced by a new constitution. All enrolled members of at least twenty-one years of age have the franchise. The top vote getter becomes the governor, the second is declared president, and the third highest, vice-president. A council is appointed, four members being named by the governor, and three each by the president and vice-president. The president is executive officer of the council, and the governor is chief executive of the pueblo. None of the elected officials receive a salary.

The pueblo of Sandía has two rectangular ceremonial chambers, although one is in disrepair. Here the division into summer and winter people is said not to exist; only one cacique holds office. He serves for life as the head of his people. The present cacique of mid-age, succeeded an old man who had been in office since the 1940s. When choice of a cacique comes about, the privilege of naming him is traditionally rotated among the clans. The cacique appoints all secular officers annually. Directly under the cacique is an executive officer, the war chief, who also serves for life; he controls the nonsecular activities, supervising the keeping of rituals and the holding of dances. The governor works through the war chief in reporting on affairs of the pueblo—all business dealings. Five or six fiscales assist the governor in carrying out the dictates of the council, which is composed of former governors and war chiefs.

Sandía has been affected by influences of many peoples; perhaps as a result of this, the pueblo is said to have several matrilineal clans, "the number varying as some die out." (Hume 1970a) Corn groups like those of Isleta are evidenced.

With the Tanoan peoples, clan organization is generally nonexistent, or is weakly represented—indicating its adoption from neighboring Indian groups. A clan is recognized as a social group comprising a number of households, the heads of which claim descent from a common ancestor.

TEWA INDIANS   Each of the Tewa villages in the upper Río Grande drainage is made up of small, loosely connected clusters of dwellings; their arrangement is irregular, with rooms generally offset, but they adhere to north-south and east-west axial lines. With growth, and possibly from long association with the Spanish-Americans—who customarily built their communities around plazas, and frequently enclosed sections within walls—the pueblo clusters came to assume plaza form, at least to a degree. In some instances, squares surrounded by structures are in evidence, in other cases the so-called plazas are only a matter of loose application of the word. Certain it is that little or nothing comparable to the compact buildings and courts of the prehistoric peoples of the Four Corners region, or of the Hopi pueblos of today, exists in the Río Grande Tewa villages.

The Tewa people live in five pueblos, all to the north of Santa Fe; in addition, some one hundred odd individuals of Pojoaque affiliation hold title to the Pojoaque reservation, and reside there or nearby. In each of these pueblos, dichotomy is of prime importance. Formerly, and to some extent today, a cacique presides over each division; Nambé, for example, has not had a cacique for several years. As with the Tiwa Indians, the summer cacique is in charge of the north people, while the winter cacique is in charge of the south people. Their office is for life.

The seasons are not evenly divided. Summer is considered to begin in February or March and to extend to November; winter lasts from November to February or March. Thus it appears that with the Tewa and Tiwa, and probably with all Tanoans originally, it is not the solstices that are of foremost importance in establishing the ceremonial calendar, but the seasonal transfer. The headman (cacique) of the north group gives the people to the headman of the south group in November, and the latter gives the people to the former in the spring. The winter solstice ceremonial is observed in January, while the summer solstice is celebrated in June. In matters of importance the cacique of the summer people has precedence over his counterpart.

Membership in the dual organizations is patrilineal, but the affiliation may be changed. A woman may join the division, or moiety, of her husband on marriage, or may remain as she is; the husband may transfer from one group to the other if he desires. It is the custom for each moiety to have a specialized, rectangular chamber built in the respective house blocks. The summer people are associated with the squash chamber, and the winter people with the turquois chamber.

In varying degrees the old ceremonial groups and moiety organizations of the Tewa pueblos are now broken down and their former distinct functions are mingled and confused. Traditionally, initiation into a moiety took place in a "big kiva." (*See* Hawley 1950:289) Today, San Ildefonso and Tesuque each have two moiety houses; the former also has a large circular chamber. In Santa Clara and Nambé the houses of the moiety chiefs are used in lieu of separate moiety rooms.

At Santa Clara the government is run under a constitution adopted in December, 1935, making this pueblo the first in New Mexico to adopt a constitution. This action was instrumental in healing a factional dispute that began in the late 1800s, when the then conservative ones of Santa Clara "were opposed to the acceptance of federal programs designed to upgrade the living conditions of the pueblo."

"The constitution effectively divided the secular from the religious, allowing the conservatives to concentrate on retention of the old religion and the young people to concentrate on the secular government." (Hume 1970b) The governing officials number six: governor, lieutenant governor, secretary, treasurer, sheriff, and interpreter. These are elected annually. The governor receives a nominal salary, and all officers receive expense allowances when on pueblo business.

It is said that the constitution divides the pueblo into four groups, two subgroups in each of the moieties, the summer and winter. Each of these groups can nominate candidates for any of the elective positions, and the candidates then run in a general election. Those eighteen years old have the franchise in regular elections, but on constitutional amendments the age limit is twenty-one.

Santa Clara's council is comprised of the elected officials plus two representatives from each of the pueblo's subdivisions. They have their own law and order setup, with a tribal judge whose decisions may be appealed to the pueblo council.

As is traditional with the Tewa, Santa Clara has a cacique at the head of its ecclesiastical organization. The position is for life.

Among the Tewa the extended family is emphasized, on both the father's and mother's sides. These large family groups often assemble in the home of some leader-member to discuss important matters. Clans, if they ever existed, have no significance today— although the term has frequently been used in speaking of various groups or societies. The simple family consists of a man and his wife and their unmarried offspring, or a widow or widower with children.

Heads of families, except old men and women, are responsible to the pueblo officials for such services as may be demanded of

---

A LULLABY OF NAMBÉ

Go to sleep,
Go to sleep,
Lest something come,
To take away
My little one.
So you must sleep,
My little one

From: *Songs of the Tewa*, by H. J. Spinden
© 1933 by H. J. Spinden (Spinden 1933)

them. They may be called to clean the irrigation ditches, sweep the plaza before dances and feast day observances, and to perform ceremonial duties.

Patrilineal descent is the rule. House ownership is male, for the most part; and a tendency to build houses within a man's moiety seems evident. Originally, this created the basic architectural pattern.

At San Ildefonso, although a small pueblo numbering a little over 350, the outward evidence of past ceremonial organization is still manifest. The pueblo has two rectangular chambers, that of the winter people built in the northern most house block, and that of the summer people detached and in the southwestern part of the village. The large circular structure, built mostly above ground with an opening toward the southeast, appears prominently in the southern part of the pueblo. Entrance is by means of a stairway— formerly a ladder—leading to the top of the structure, where a hatchway gives access to the interior. The old ladder symbolized ascent from the underworld to a higher plane, or to an eminence. This chamber is said to be the oldest building in the pueblo; and it "belongs" to all of the people. It is used as a dance place. As at Isleta, this circular building is designated as the "outside house."

In certain of the pueblos, the war chiefs are also called "outside chiefs," and it appears that the outside house at San Ildefonso related to affairs of the warrior cult. The warrior society is no longer extant in the pueblo, although the paraphernalia is said to have been preserved.

Until a few years ago, the remains of a small, one-room building were observable on top of a low hill near the sacred spring of the west, of San Ildefonso. This was the chamber to which the old priest retired for his retreat.

The late William Whitman reported that the religious hierarchy at San Ildefonso is based on paternalism, and he stated that: "The Cacique is not a priest in the sense that he is an impersonation of godhead. He. is 'father and mother' of the people, mortal as his children, whom in his wisdom he leads and directs. . . .To insure divine blessing it is believed that propitiation must be made not only by the priests (headmen) but by the group as a whole, and that through the efforts of the group, led and supplemented by those of the priests, the forces of nature are compelled to act in accordance with the needs of the people." (Whitman 1947:118*)

---

*Reproduced by permission of Marjorie Whitman Cate.

San Juan has two rectangular kivas built in the house blocks. The reader is referred to the extensive work of Alfonso Ortíz, himself an Indian, who dwelt in that pueblo with his family and has had unusual opportunity to study San Juan in detail. (Ortíz 1969) Santa Clara has two similar chambers, but detached from the dwelling structures. Tesuque has rectangular kivas built in the house blocks, and probably utilized two at a time; the pattern has become confused due to recent demolitions and rebuilding. At Nambé one finds only a large, circular structure in evidence. Archaeological excavations there exposed a small underground kiva, the floor of which was six feet below the present surface. It was twelve feet in diameter; it had vertical walls, the adobe plaster of which curved slightly at the floor level. The chamber was dated around A.D. 1400. The excavator observed that: "Small underground kivas used in prehistoric times as ceremonial chambers of religious societies, were replaced in most of the Río Grande pueblos by aboveground houses built for that purpose, or even by adaptation of one room in the house of the leader of the society." (Ellis 1964:38*)

The Tewa of Hopiland are mentioned later.

SONG OF THE SKY LOOM (Tewa)

Oh our Mother the Earth, oh our Father the Sky,
Your children are we, and with tired backs
We bring you the gifts that you love.
Then weave for us a garment of brightness;
May the warp be the white light of morning,
May the weft be the red light of evening,
May the fringes be the falling rain,
May the border be the standing rainbow.
Thus weave for us a garment of brightness
That we may walk fittingly where birds sing,
That we may walk fittingly where grass is green,
Oh our Mother the Earth, oh our Father the Sky!

From: *Songs of the Tewa* by H. J. Spinden
© 1933 by H. J. Spinden

---

*Reproduced by permission of the Society for American Archaeology, from *American Antiquity* 30:38 (1964).

TOWA INDIANS   The pueblo of Jémez is the remaining member of a third Tanoan subfamily, the Towa. It is located on Jémez Creek, or the Río Jémez, west of Santa Fe in the mountains of the Jémez range. Seventeen survivors from the pueblo Pecos moved to Jémez in 1838, and descendants of Pecos parents and the Jémez people are presently enumerated together. Being located quite apart from the Tiwa and Tewa peoples, but close to non-Tanoan villagers, Jémez displays many characteristics which are attributable to the Keresans.

There are two large rectangular kivas, but the dual organization has broken down, although summer and winter people are recognized; no moiety houses exist. Society houses occur in the regular house blocks. The Jémez developed clans, with descent reckoned through the maternal line. One has to marry outside the clan. Clans play but a minor part in the economic and ceremonial life of Jémez. Weakness of the clan system probably reflects a borrowed trait, or a marginal occurrence. House owning rests with the males for the most part.

One cacique serves for life; he possesses a "Mother" fetish. The cacique is assisted by two men who are probably relatable to the war chiefs of old. Foremost duty of the cacique is to watch the sun, that is, to determine the arrival of summer and winter and set dates for ceremonies accordingly. Races of the kick-stick type are held on a north-south track.

.... THE KERESANS

The origin of the Keresan people is unknown. One linguist subdivides them into four groups: Acoma and Laguna, Zía and Santa Ana, San Felipe and Santo Domingo, and Cochiti. He says that Acoma and Laguna, usually considered as the western Keres, "have had a history of linguistic development independent to a certain degree of the other dialects," (Davis 1959:78) that is, of the eastern Keres. Acoma and Laguna also have distinct histories extending into prehistoric times. (Davis 1959:83*) Some evidence of a closeness between the language of Zía and the western Keres has been detected. (Spencer 1940; Hewett and Dutton 1945:19) And viewing the maps it is seen that the eastern and western villages share a continuity of terrain. Keres people have demonstrated a preference for locating their pueblos atop eminences, usually lofty sandstone mesas above the valley lands. Trails led directly between the two regions; and pueblo ruins now existing may have been occupied by Keres people.

Archaeological investigations indicate that those who now occupy the Keres districts have been there for a very long time. Like the Tanoans, their former territory well may have been more widespread.

One belief, although remote, is that the Keresan language may be of HOKAN-SIOUAN affiliation, suggesting that the Keres represent an intrusion of peoples who pushed into the Southwest around 4,500 years ago—thus being descendants from Archaic peoples (Sapir 1929; Dittert 1959; Eddy 1965:24) who came from a southerly direction and merged with northerly ones. Such a position and history of the Keres would be in harmony with the finding of Strong, (Strong 1927:57) who believed that certain peoples, including a Yuman-speaking enclave, pushed themselves into what had previously been a continuous Azteco-Tanoan domain.

Regardless of their origin and regional developments, the Keres display cultural features that differ in varying aspects from those of the Tanoans. Acoma was established at or near its present location as early as A.D. 900, and its occupation has been continuous since 1075. (Dittert 1959) Its structures are built in parallel rows of

---

*Dr. A. E. Dittert, Jr., recognizes these two peoples as distinct in central western New Mexico for at least 4,500 years.

terraced house blocks, tending in an east-west direction; all face toward the south. Among the dwellings, seven rectangular ceremonial chambers are situated on the ground floor. The head kiva differs from the other six in having a floor vault over which a plank is placed, acting as a resonator when used as a foot drum.

Contrary to Tanoan organization, with the Keres peoples clans are, or were, of foremost importance. Each Acoma Indian is born into his mother's clan. These clans are exogamous; that is, one must marry outside his clan, and so the chief function of the clan is to regulate marriage. Descent is reckoned in the maternal line, and houses are property of the women. The economic unit is the household. Although the part that clans play in ceremonies and general pueblo procedures may now be minor, in olden times the clan heads owned fetishes, settled disputes between members, went into a series of summer retreats for rain, assisted the medicine societies—particularly during the winter solstice observance—and conducted ceremonies relating to supernatural ones associated with the clans.

Only one cacique holds office at Acoma, and he represents and cares for the whole pueblo, reflecting lack of dichotomy, or dual organization. The cacique is the highest religious officer and the political head of the pueblo; his most important ceremonial function is to watch the sun and determine the solstices; he sets the date for practically all ceremonies. Here, as with the Azteco-Tanoans, the sun is recognized as representative of a supreme deity.

Laguna was without ceremonial chambers for many years. Formerly, two rectangular ones were built aboveground, one on the east side of the village and the other at the west end. The east kiva was the repository for all of the paraphernalia belonging to the warrior society, which performed the scalp dance. The west kiva housed all ritualistic property of the katsina cult. Children joined the kiva of the father, and wives that of the husband.

A few years ago, a new chamber was constructed at Laguna, in the southwest part of the pueblo, and this is being called a kiva. It is said to be "all modern."

At Laguna, one cacique was chosen for life; he spent his time in prayer and sacrificed for the welfare of his people. The cacique was assisted by war chiefs, representing twin war gods; they were concerned with warfare, hunting, and guarding the people and the rituals. They were aided by chiefs' helpers.

Laguna followed a matrilineal-matrilocal pattern of organization, with exogamous clans bearing totemic names; they had ceremonial, judiciary, and economic functions. For many years, two groups—one conservative and the other progressive—have been observable at Laguna.

A degree of unanimity is found in the organization of the eastern Keres Pueblos, but their social pattern differs considerably from that of the western peoples, and from the Tanoans with whom they are in proximity. As a rule, the Keres did not live east of the Río Grande. Generally speaking, their settlements were on the west side of that stream, and their domain extended no farther than the eastern mountains which border the Río Grande valley, that is, the Sandía range and the Ortíz-San Pedro mountain group.

Today, five pueblos are extant among the eastern Keres: Cochiti, Santo Domingo, San Felipe, Santa Ana with outlying farming communities, and Zía. Whether large or small, each pueblo has two round ceremonial structures built above ground and apart from the dwellings. One of these is associated with summer (squash) people and the other with winter (turquois) people. Each kiva group is associated with particular clans, and with certain medicine societies—thus involving a triple organization.

The spiritual leader, the cacique, in the larger pueblos is appointed by the war chief for life; he has to be a member of a particular society (Flint), and he is associated with a "clown" group. In no instance is the clan organization strong. It follows matrilineal descent for the most part, clan exogamy, and matrilocal residence. In the pueblo of Zía, however, clans display patrilineal descent; matrilocal residence is followed for a while, then the groom builds a new home for occupancy.

Because of the prominent two-kiva system, relating to seasonal divisions made manifest by the occurrence of the winter and summer solstices, and in view of the ceremonies relating to each season, a general dichotomy in the social organization prevails. This has been identified as a moiety system by some investigators. Keresan society is better considered as clan-based, although the clans now function but weakly. Then, realizing the seasonal divisions and accepting the probability of influences from the strong Tanoan dichotomy system, it is possible to visualize an original Keresan pattern quite diverse from that of their neighbors. The Keres evidence a complicated social structure, embracing clans, kiva groups, and medicine societies. Under the control of its single cacique, each Keres pueblo in the east has two circular ceremonial chambers built apart from the dwellings, while in the west these are rectangular, built among the house blocks, and may number two or more. All are aboveground structures.

THE ZUNIAN PEOPLE

Archaeological and linguistic evidence indicate that Zuñi-speaking people have been in their present location for some eight hundred years, or more. And it appears likely that Indians traveled between Mexico and the regions to the north for centuries; no boundary existed until the time of the Gadsden Purchase. In the 1530s, verbal accounts concerning Indians of the unexplored lands of the Greater Southwest reached the ears of the Spanish conquerors in Mexico. By 1535 they had heard of many-storied houses built of stone and adobe, in which the Indians dwelt. Don Antonio de Mendoza, the Spanish viceroy, soon became interested in the opportunity of adding new territory and expected riches to the empire of Charles V, and of Christianizing the Indians. Accordingly, a Franciscan friar, Marcos de Niza, was sent forth at the head of an exploring party, in the spring of 1539.

Among a group of Piman Indians—the Sobaipura (so-BAI-pu-rah) who occupied the Río San Pedro and the Gila valleys until about the end of the eighteenth century—Fray Marcos met the first Zuñi Indian of whom specific mention is known. The old Indian told the friar of the pueblos of his homeland and of neighboring peoples. He was the original informant concerning Hawikuh, or *Ahacua,* which he described as the largest of the Zuñi pueblos.

Fray Marcos sent a member of his party, a black man named Estevan (es-TAY-vahn) de Dorantes, ahead with a few companions to scout the way to Zuñi and to pacify the Indians. Estevan is credited with having had a gift for dealing with strangers, but his reception among the Zuñi was anything but friendly. The Indians refused his entrance to Hawikuh; they stripped him of his possessions, sent him forth, then fell upon and killed him. Some of the party escaped and took word back to the friar, who retreated to Mexico. Another explorer, Francisco Vasquez de Coronado, entered Zuñiland the following year (1540).

Aside from the Estevan incident, the Zuñi, like the Pueblo Indians of the Río Grande, were friendly toward the Spaniards when they first entered the region. Other explorers and missionaries came and went; some of the latter were admired and respected by the Zuñi, others stirred resentment which caused their dispatch. The Zuñi took part in the Pueblo Rebellion of 1680, although they were less involved than were the Río Grande Pueblos, who were closer to the scene of the uprising. When Vargas effected his reconquest in 1692, he found the Zuñi withdrawn to the eminence called *Towayalane*, or Corn Mountain. Shortly thereafter, they began the building of their present pueblo, including the old site of Halona on the Zuñi River.

Currently, most of the Zuñi people live in that pueblo; a few have permanent dwellings in nearby settlements. The lands of Zuñi were not recognized by executive order of the U.S. government until 1877. The boundaries then established were amended by Presidential order in 1883 and again in 1885. The reservation now covers some 440,000 acres to the southwest of Gallup, New Mexico. Zuñi is one of the most populous of the Pueblo groups, numbering around 5,640 Indians. Nonresident Indians increase the population by several hundred, making about 6,000 in all.

Traces of a dichotomous organization have been detected at Zuñi, with recognition of north people and south people, or summer and winter people. The summer cacique is considered to be speaker to the sun, and the winter cacique, rain priest of the north. Clans are of considerable significance, although as such they have no social or political functions. They number about thirteen, are totemically named, each being composed of one or more unnamed lineages; they are exogamous. Both the mother's and father's lineages are important; their social and ceremonial duties are differentiated sharply. Formerly, the clans were grouped into phratries, that is, major groups including a number of clans, which were associated with the six directions—the cardinal points, the zenith and nadir. The economic unit is the household, normally composed of an extended family based on matrilocal residence—occupying a series of adjoining rooms which are owned by the women, since descent is matrilineal.

It has been noted that an individual is "fitted into an intricate and closely knit social organization." Also, "The elementary family, so important elsewhere, is merged into the household group, and the specific roles of relatives are affected by their position in the social structure. A Zuñi is born into a certain household, which determines his clan affiliation and kinship status, and, in part, his future ceremonial roles." (Eggan 1950:191*) Ritual activities are primarily in the hands of the father's household, while economic activities are primarily in the hands of the mother's household and lineage.

Zuñi has an elaborate ceremonial organization centering in six kiva groups (one for each direction), associated with medicine societies and an extensive esoteric cult (*kóko*) and priesthoods—all of which cut across clan and household groupings. The kivas, like those of the western Keres and the Tanoans, are rectangular and aboveground; some are built in the house units, others are detached. Sacred fetishes are in the care of the women and their brothers. On ritual occasions the men return to their natal household to carry out important ceremonial duties. Medicine societies are not tied in with the kiva system.

The Zuñi people, perhaps more than most of the Río Grande Pueblo groups, have maintained their social organization insofar as has been possible in the face of inevitable change. In recent years, isolation of the pueblo has ceased. Improved roads and pavement, modern vehicles, public utilities, development of resources, and government projects of varied types, have brought the Zuñi into cultural ferment, slowly but surely. Education has been available on the reservation since 1882, first through the primary grades only, then through high school since 1956. Over 80 percent of the Zuñi who have been graduated from high school have continued in commercial and vocational schools and/or in colleges.

Alert officials at Zuñi became aware of a federal law of 1834 which had never been used, but which allowed Indians to administer their own reservations with the approval of the Secretary of the Interior. The Zuñi Tribal Council held a ratification election on a proposed constitution to replace custom laws which had been followed for centuries. All registered tribal members over twenty-one were allowed to vote, and they favored the change to home rule. Currently, eighteen-year old Zuñi people are allowed to vote.

Formal agreement by which the Zuñi took over direction of the federal agency on the reservation was signed on 23 May 1970. This agreement was the culmination of a comprehensive development plan that had been worked on for a period of years. The plan contains forty-three programs, with the major goals of increasing individual income, enhancing educational opportunities, and improving living conditions. The agreement is described as being flexible; it can be canceled by either of the signing parties on 180 days written notice if it does not work out. By taking this impressive action, the Zuñi became the first tribe in the nation to take control of its own affairs. The council was presented the first Interior Department Indian Leadership Award for its initiative.

THE HOPI GROUPS

The Hopi, the pueblo dwellers of Arizona, have occupied their domain for over a thousand years. The designation *Hopi* is abbreviated from *Hopituh Shi-nu-mu*, which means "the peaceful people." For the most part, their villages are perched atop three high, barren mesas located northwestward from Keams Canyon, where an Englishman, Thomas V. Keam, started a trading post in 1878. The federal government established offices there in 1887, Keam's holdings being purchased and made part of the headquarters. From there, the mesas were called "First Mesa," "Second Mesa," and "Third Mesa," going from east to west. This was just opposite to the order in which the Hopi themselves regarded their highland sites.

In ancient times the location of the Hopi settlements on the three southern prongs of Black Mesa served as a natural protection from enemies. The dissected highland, some sixty miles in diameter, is drained by streams that carry sand and silt southward to the lower plain. There the prevailing southwest winds separate the soil materials and blow the sands back to form large dunes. These absorb the water and lessen the runoff when rains fall. Permanent springs thus result.

The villages on these mesas, like those of the Río Grande pueblos, have an intricately interwoven social structure. They have never had a tribal government of any kind. Each village has its own organization and each individual has his own particular place in the operation of his community. The clan system is basic; it is matrilineal and matrilocal, resulting in blocks of houses built adjacent to the home of the matriarch. The clan is stronger among the Hopi than elsewhere among the Pueblos; and a strong clan system correlates with a weak political system. (Eggan 1950:117-118) It has been stated that to a casual visitor in a Hopi village, "its government is so lacking in form as to seem almost nonexistent." (James 1956:107*) Nothing of a dichotomous organization is to be seen. The household is the economic unit; labor is judiciously divided between the men and women. Each major clan has a fetish which is kept in the clan house and is presided over by the woman considered to be the clan mother.

*Reproduced courtesy of the Caxton Printers, Ltd.

Women own the houses, food, seed for the next year's planting, the springs and cisterns, and the small irrigated gardens that they work. The men do the herding, hunting, and farming away from the village. They gather and haul the fuel, and theirs are the duties of spinning, weaving, and moccasin making—all of which are becoming less and less evident today. Married men live in the household of the wife, but they continue association with their mother's and sisters' homes—their "real homes"—and participate in ceremonial activities of the family clans.

The Spaniards visited Hopiland, or old Tusayan, under Don Pedro de Tovar, a lieutenant of Coronado, and occupied a village believed to have been the now ruined *Kawaiokuh* (kah-WAI-oh-kuh), from which the Indians had fled at the approach of the small party of armed invaders. The first contact between the Spaniards and Hopi followed—a friendly encounter apparently, for the Indians brought gifts and Tovar assembled his men in a camp near the pueblo. There, the Spaniards learned of a great river flowing in a deep canyon—the Colorado River of present days—and Don García de Cárdenas was ordered to search for the mighty stream, which has always played a major part in Hopi mythology. For forty years the Hopi were not again visited by the Spaniards.

In 1583, Antonio de Espejo and a few soldiers passed through the Hopi towns. They spent several days in *Awatobi* (ah-WAH-toh-bee), now in ruin a few miles east of Walpi (WAHL-pee), and in other villages. The Indians were cordial and gave the Spaniards many presents before Espejo continued on, seeking gold (but finding silver). Juan de Oñate visited Tusayan in 1598 and in 1604. From 1629 until 1680, Franciscan missionaries tried to convert the Hopi to Christianity. Missions were established at Oraibi (oh-RAI-bee) Shungopovi (shung-OH-poh-vee), and Awatobi. (Montgomery, Smith and Brew 1949; Smith, W. 1952 and 1971) The period was one of great unrest among all of the Pueblo peoples; their priests resented the Spaniards' interference with the native religious ways; they chafed under the enforced labor demanded of them; and they deplored the ravishing of their women. Distrust and unfriendliness toward the intruders grew and intensified.

Like the Río Grande Pueblos, those of Tusayan were ripe for rebellion, and they joined in the uprising of 1680. They killed four friars and demolished the churches and outlying *visitas*. Vargas, in 1692, was in Tusayan and gained some submission from the Indians; Oraibi did not give obeisance, for Vargas did not visit that village. The Spanish reconquest meant little to the Hopi. Their isolation and the aridity of the region did not attract Spanish colonists. From those days, nearly three centuries ago, Spanish influence has faded into history.

Settlements have been moved. Shungopovi people went atop the second, or "Middle Mesa," and built a new pueblo in 1680; and those of Walpi moved to the tip of First Mesa after 1700. Following the Pueblo Rebellion, Tano Indians (Tewa from near Abiquiu in New Mexico), who wanted to escape the vengeance of the Spaniards who they feared would return to their pueblos, were invited to establish a village at Hano (HAH-noh)—as THAN-noh was pronounced in the western region—and serve as guards at the top of the trail. Hano and Sitchumovi (seet—CHEW-moh-vee), which was built in the 1700's as an overflow from Walpi, make the First Mesa structures appear almost continuous.

A new pueblo, Shipaulovi (shee-PAUL-oh-vee), was founded in its present location on Second Mesa, and Mishongnovi (mee-SHONG-noh-vee) was moved to the end of the mesa from a lower site near the Corn Rock shrine (originally two imposing sandstone pillars, now one has fallen).

A farming settlement was set up along Moencopi Wash in the western part of Hopiland by Chief Tuba, in 1870, and Upper and Lower Moencopi (MOH-en-koh-pee) came into being. A short distance from there, a government agency established by Mormon missionaries and named for Chief Tuba, or *Toovi*, from Oraibi, has become Tuba City. The Mormons hoped to produce woolen textiles on a large scale and founded a woolen mill there in 1879—a venture which was short-lived. The Mormons believe the American Indians to be descendants of the "lost tribes of Israel," so they feel obliged to treat them in a friendly manner. Their efforts to convert the Hopi have been but mildly successful.

Old Oraibi has occupied the same locale since about 1100; it vies with Acoma as being the oldest continuously inhabited village in the nation. It was one of the largest of the Hopi towns until 1906, when dissension brought about the founding of Hotevila (now more commonly spelled Hote-villa, but pronounced hoh-tah-VILL-ah), then Bacabi (BAH-kah-bee) in 1907, and New Oraibi (1910) on Third Mesa. (Cf. Coze 1971:4)

During the first quarter of the nineteenth century, Americans were visiting the Hopi country in steadily increasing numbers—explorers and trappers, soldiers and surveyors, traders and missionaries, government agents, and others. In 1853, the villages were ravaged by smallpox, an introduction of the white man. Lieutenant A. W. Whipple of the Topographical Engineers reported that at one pueblo he found "only the chief and one other man remained of all the able-bodied men of the town." The living dragged the bodies to the edge of the mesa and threw them over the cliffs. This cut the Hopi population drastically, as did another epidemic around 1892.

Hopiland was part of the U.S.A. for about twenty years before an agent was assigned to take over supervision of these Indians, in 1869. A year later a Protestant group established a mission school at Keams Canyon; like other attempts to convert the Hopi the results were negative. Their age-old religion provided security for the Hopi and their way of life—the "Hopi Way"—satisfied their needs.

A Mennonite preacher, H. R. Voth, without approval of the Oraibi people (but with the consent of government officials) built a stone church on the mesa near the pueblo in 1901. It stood as an "offensive eyesore" until it was struck by lightning and gutted by fire in 1942. (James 1956:30) The ruin may be seen as one passes along the roadway a short distance from the pueblo.

When conditions became more settled, some individuals began moving to ranches on the lowlands, generally south of the mesas; others went to places such as Keams Canyon, where many work for various governmental divisions in numerous capacities, or to Polacca built below First Mesa, to Moencopi or Tuba City. Perhaps 1,200 work in more distant communities—Holbrook, Winslow, Flagstaff, and Grand Canyon or elsewhere. But most of these wage earners will be back in their hereditary homes on the mesas for the seasonal ceremonies. In these modern times, many ceremonials are scheduled for weekends, so the increasing number of off-reservation workers can return and take part.

Among the Hopi Indians today are many qualified carpenters, painters, masons, mechanics, and other laborers who can secure work in non-Indian communities with no difficulty. The Hopi are shrewd businessmen. Many have proven to be adept machine operators and skilled forest firefighters. Those men who stay at home care for their sandy fields which they dry-farm, or on which they practice flood irrigation, wresting their livelihood from a harsh, though beautiful, environment. Considerable income is derived from the carving of figurines, watercolor painting, basketry, jewelry, and to a decreasing degree from weaving traditional textiles. The average annual income per family is estimated to be $2,050. (Gilliland 1972) The women tend their fertile garden plots;

some fashion beautiful pottery, others weave belts or make baskets. They are famous for *piki*, a tissue-paper-thin breadstuff made of cornmeal and baked on a red-hot rock slab. Several layers are rolled together while still warm. The rolls become crisp when cool; they are tasty and highly nutritious.

All educational facilities for the Hopi have been upgraded in recent years. These include a dormitory housing 320 boarding school students, and six additional elementary classrooms at Keams Canyon, which were constructed in 1956, as was a complete new school at Polacca. A consolidated school at Second Mesa, and facilities at Hotevilla have been occupied over ten years. Formerly, children were educated through the tenth grade; however, the ninth and tenth grades have been abolished and Hopi students go to off-reservation boarding schools and elsewhere for their high school training. Plans have been finalized for a four-year fully accredited Bureau of Indian Affairs high school on the reservation. The Hopi Indians are very much interested in education. Accordingly, attendance is good and dropouts are few. Some 145 Hopi students are enrolled in schools above the high school level. Many Hopi leave the villages after completing school and make their way in society along with non-Indian groups.

Development of paved Highway 264, with hard-topped tributary roads leading to the north and south through Hopiland, has had severe effects upon the Hopi, both in the number of visitors who intrude upon their quiet way of life, and in the number of their younger generation who are drawn away from their hereditary world and culture. On 15 January 1971 a Hopi Culture Center built along traditional pueblo lines by a modern architect was opened by the Hopi Tribe. It contains thirty-three deluxe hotel units, and has a restaurant and conference room. A museum and crafts shops are included in the complex, on Second Mesa.

As one walks by the house blocks or enters the small plazas of the Hopi pueblos, rectangular structures detached from the dwellings add striking features to the architecture. Tall, slender poles, two in number, stand high above the flat-roofed chambers—the kivas.

At Hano, established by Tewa from the Río Grande, clanship affiliations of the kivas are obscure. Every member of the village belongs to one of the two kivas, but when the winter solstice ceremony is observed, part of a clan may go into one kiva and part into the other. Since the Tewa migrated with a patrilineal moiety system to join the matrilineal clanship organization of their hosts, the non-Tewa-speaking Hopi, this may well account for the variances found. When the Tewa were invited to live on First Mesa, they gave heed as an entire community—not by any clan—to their town chief's council. He was chief of the summer moiety.

In the other pueblos of Hopiland the social organization displays its basic Hopi pattern. Walpi, the main village of First Mesa, has five kivas—four separated from the houses, but one attached to a house block. Sitchumovi has two kivas, back to back in a plaza.

On Second Mesa, where three pueblos were built at their present sites in the 1680-1700 period, all of the kivas are detached; Shungopavi has five, Shipaulovi three, and Mishongnovi four. Of the Third Mesa group, old Oraibi has had a long history of rectangular kivas built apart from the houses; but since the total population is now less than 150, the ceremonial organization has suffered decline. Hotevilla, Bacabi, and the outlying farming community of Moencopi have detached kivas in active use.

A respected friend of the Hopi, who spent much time with them and gained knowledge and understanding of their ways, recorded that the nearest thing they had resembling a legislative body was the meeting of the chiefs—"Chiefs' Talk"—held each year at the end of the important *Soyala* ceremony, or winter solstice; other meetings might occur whenever a situation demanded consideration. The chiefs of the ceremonial societies constituted this assembly, with the village chief as headman. According to Hopi organization, the village chief selected his successor from among the sons of his brothers and sisters—the one believed to be best qualified—and trained him for the position. (*See* James 1956:105)

The time-consuming deliberations of the Hopi elders continually frustrated government officials, who wanted quick responses to their proposals and propositions. Eventually, they devised a "tribal council" comprised of a progressive faction and imposed it on the more conservative ones, thus achieving a body with which dealings could be carried on, whether the "old ones" approved or not. When a constitution and by-laws were submitted for ratification by the Hopi, on 24 October 1936, they were adopted by a vote of 651 for and 104 against. In this election only some 30 percent of those entitled to vote cast their ballots. (*Hopi Reservation* leaflet n.d.:5)

This tribal council is made up of members who must be twenty-five years of age, speak their own language, and have lived on the Hopi reservation for two years. Representation is based on village population. After certification by the respective village leaders, the representatives are certified by the outgoing council annually on December first. The council elects a chairman and vice-chairman from among its members; it appoints a secretary and treasurer who may or may not be council members, two interpreters and a sergeant-at-arms who are not members.

From early times, land limits and boundaries have grown to be a problem for the Hopi. After many centuries, the Hopi lands gradually came to be completely surrounded by the Navaho, whose presence became recognizable after A.D. 1500. Some 2,428,000 acres were federally acknowledged in 1882 as the Hopi reservation, but were long in dispute between the two groups of Indians. Attempting to improve the situation, the government ruled in 1937 that the Hopi should have exclusive use of only 631,174 acres and should share the remaining acreage with the Navaho. In 1962, a decision of the Arizona District Court confirmed this ruling and it was upheld by the US Supreme Court a few years later. The remaining acreage (nearly 1,800,000) was held between the two groups "in joint, equal and undivided shares." So the conflict continued.

In April, 1970, the Hopi filed a brief in federal court seeking to drive the Navaho off this shared area and to allow the Hopi living within their reservation, but outside the excluded land, to share grazing rights and leases on trading posts with the Navaho. The Indian Claims Commission meeting in Washington at the end of June, 1970, ruled that the Hopi should have been paid, by the 1937 land rates, for the 1.8 million acres taken from them and that they should have been paid, by 1882 land rates, for an estimated 5 million acres in aboriginal claims. Further hearings and more years of waiting are in store—specific acreages are to be determined and values fixed, or other arrangements made.

SECRET CULTS AND SOCIETIES A very important feature of social organization among the Pueblo peoples is curing; this is under the control of medicine societies operating within an esoteric cult generally known as katsina. The early Spaniards recorded this as *catzina*, (Hackett 1937, III:131ff.; *see* Dockstader 1954:148) which would be their rendering of the Keres "K'AH-tseen-ah" or of the Hopi "cot-SEE-nah." In written literature, the word is given diverse spellings such as katzina, katchina, kachina, cachina, katcina, kacina, and audible pronunciations approximating the native language concerned.

Remember that none of the New World peoples had a written language of their own*; so the spellings of Indian words followed systems of the recorders—some simply personal, others in accord with recognized phonetic or orthographic systems. It is likely that this gave rise to certain of the debased usages of today, for readers frequently do not give attention to the fine print or explanatory notes. For instance, Dr. Bunzel in her reports on Zuñi uses *katcina*; she gives a "table of sounds" in which "c" has the value of "sh" and would be heard as "kátshina," with accent on the first syllable. (Bunzel 1932a:471)

Beliefs concerning the katsinas are similar, pueblo to pueblo. These supernatural beings are represented in various ways, all of which are associated in the Indian mind. First, they are *spiritual guises* of an anthropomorphic nature. Again they are masked, painted, and properly *costumed individuals* who appear in the village plazas and kivas as impersonators of the spiritual ones enacting esoteric rites and ceremonies. In another guise, they are *wooden figurines*—small representations of the life-size beings—by means of which Indian children become familiar with the katsinas as part of their religious training and culture history.

When the katsina cult functions fully, every man, woman, and child of a pueblo is supposed to be initiated into it, and every man takes an active, lifelong part in its ceremonies. Men only impersonate the male and female katsinas. Primarily, the katsinas are recognized as benevolent beings who dwell in the mountains, springs, and lakes, and who are the bringers of blessings, particularly rain, crops, and wellbeing. Some katsinas, however, are ogres or demons with disciplinary functions.

Throughout the millennia of man's struggle for existence in the semiarid Southwest, the dominating factor has been rain. Inasmuch as the Pueblo Indians are farmers, their ceremonies are primarily for rain. The building or decorating of a kiva is said to be a prayer for rain or crops. And the feeling is that the correct performance of numerous ritualistic acts brings the desired results. Thus the katsinas, the spirit rainmakers, truly symbolize the climatic drive or weather control of Southwestern man past and present.

Upon death, it is believed, a Pueblo person becomes a katsina; he may appear henceforth as a cloud—that is, as a masked personator. A boy belongs to the kiva of his father, into which he is

---

*Unless some of the Meso-american glyph systems prove to relate to true written tongues.

initiated; girls also may be initiated, but they do not wear masks or belong to the kiva groups. Although the cacique is not a curer, or "medicine man," he has authority over the curers and the kiva chiefs. The duties of the cacique keep him somewhat aloof from the people; on the other hand, the war chief is the most important officer, visibly, but his authority is virtually under the authority of the cacique. Thus, the katsina organization is under the direct control of a cacique and his assistants.

According to legend, in bygone days the katsinas used to come to the people when they were sad and lonely and dance for them. They brought gifts to the people and taught them their arts and industries and how to hunt. After a time the people began to grow their own foodstuffs. When rain was needed the katsinas would come and dance in the fields; then the rains always came.

Pueblo versions vary slightly, but all agree that the people came to take the katsinas for granted. Respect and veneration for their benevolence were lost by some; others had violent fights with the supernatural ones. The katsinas left, refusing to return. However, they taught a few of the faithful young men some of their ceremonies and showed them how to make masks and costumes; as long as the earthly ones followed their instructions properly, as long as "their hearts were right," they were permitted to act as if they were katsinas, and the "real katsinas" would come and possess the persons of the masked dancers. Rain would follow. On this assurance the masked katsina dances are performed to this day.

Serving as a means of uniting man and spirit beings, the katsina masks are very sacred. In some instances they are privately owned, in others they are communal property; they may be kept in certain households along with other ceremonial paraphernalia, or kept in the kivas.

The katsina cult, then, exists for the purpose of impersonating the supernatural rainmakers, so that weather controls may be exercised with resultant moisture for the crops and pastures. The organization is composed of various groups, each managed by a medicine society. Initiations take place in the house of a medicine society. A great deal of accoutrement is necessary. When masked dances are presented the masks may be all alike, or specific combinations, or they may be of mixed character.

Many of the Spanish officials and zealous missionaries did all they could to destroy the aboriginal religious rites. In the Río Grande valley where the Spanish influence became so strong the masked ceremonies were forced underground, or away from foreign eyes, for the most part. Frequent changes among the governmental officials and agents of the Catholic church, with alternating policies and practices, resulted in the Indian's compounded confusion. Within a hundred years after the *entrada* of Coronado and with less than a half-century of colonization, the culture of the Indians had been irretrievably altered. After preceding administrations had rigidly suppressed the Indian religious observances, Governor Bernardo López de Mendizábal, who was exceedingly oppressive in most ways, not only gave permission for the performing of katsina dances, but commanded the Indians to enact them. Accordingly, from about 1660 on, these previously forbidden ceremonies were held in the Tewa and Tiwa pueblos, as well as among the Keres, and even in the plaza of Santa Fe!

Among the western pueblos, where Spanish influence was less disruptive, masked dances continued to be performed much as they were in pre-Spanish times. Later "reformers" in the Southwest found the Indian rites offensive, "horrifying and unclean." But those who understood—some of those white people who were intimate with the Indians and were allowed in the kivas—refuted such charges.

It must be remembered that values differ from one culture to another, and they alter from time to time. Actions that appear innocent to us may be considered extremely vulgar by those of another social group; and things appearing obscene to us may be inoffensive to others.

It is now a rare instance when a white person is allowed to witness a katsina dance at one of the Río Grande pueblos; even Indians of other Pueblo groups are frequently kept from viewing such events. At Zuñi outsiders are permitted to view many of the masked dances. For instance, in the spectacular *Shalako*—a fertility and house-blessing ceremony—masked personators dance before large audiences of white people, as well as Indians, local and otherwise. And in the Hopiland villages restrictions are even less evident. There, some two hundred and fifty or more katsinas are known; the number is highly flexible for a variety of reasons. (*See* Dockstader 1954:23ff.)

Studies that have been permitted in pueblos of the Río Grande region have revealed that Keres ceremonialism is highly complex. In common with most Southwestern Indians, the Keres hold that they emerged from the dark underworld. They have a long myth which recites the facts of their life in the netherland. There they appointed priests, or organized societies, to take their places, and each deity, or group of spirits, taught their human successors how to perform the rituals that were essential to human welfare. Then came the emergence—the coming out of the people at *Shipop* (SHIP-op). It is said that after they emerged they made an extensive trip "around the world"—their world, bounded by certain mountain ranges with specific directional peaks, sacred springs, and related features.

Through the years the Pueblo Indians have been faced with a variety of situations which have altered their traditional beliefs regarding illnesses and curing. Slowly, they became influenced by the white doctors' knowledge of medicine and medical and surgical practices. In some pueblos, or in towns nearby, clinics were established, providing nursing assistance and professional consultations. In fewer instances, hospital facilities were provided. On availing themselves of these newer services, some Indians received sympathetic treatment and kindly attention to their needs; others fared less well, and many were the occasions of long or fruitless waits to secure aid. The Indians reacted accordingly.

In 1950, during the first session of the 83rd Congress, Public Law 568 was passed, transferring health services from the BIA and placing them under the U.S. Department of Health, Education and Welfare. This act was opposed by the Pueblo Indians at that time. They feared that the change would result in less understanding of their problems and requirements. As they came to comprehend the Public Health Service plans better, they became more hopeful. Soon, great improvements in health facilities for the Indians were initiated; and the trend has continued.

Countless surveys relating to Indian health conditions have been made, and many volumes have been written on the subject. Readers interested in learning more on this subject are referred to PHS publications and related sources.

Today, an increasing number of Pueblo Indians seek and receive modern medical and surgical treatment, just as do the majority of the population.

With the Keres, medicine societies as well as clans are important.

Great attention is given to the combatting of disease. The small, secret medicine societies are composed of male members who have the knowledge of the initiated and possess mighty supernatural powers by virtue of that knowledge. Their ideology, paraphernalia, ritual, and ceremonies are grouped together under the term "medicine cult." (White 1935:120) The medicine societies deal only with sickness due to supernatural derivation. Benevolent and malevolent supernaturals being recognized, the latter call forth the services of the curers most frequently.

At Santo Domingo, largest of the eastern Keres pueblos, four major medicine societies are known: the Flint, *Cíkame*, Giant, and *Bóyakya*. These societies work together for the good of the pueblo, uniting their efforts in serious cases. Their power lies not in themselves but is believed to have been secured from supernatural animals. To gain power from these, and make use of it, the curers employ their extensive collections of fetishes and figurines, medicines and numerous efficacious items. Cures may be conducted at any time of the year. The curers wear prescribed attire. Although females may belong to medicine societies they do not know all the secrets. Several channels of attaining membership are recognized, voluntary or by compulsion. In addition to their curative functions, some of the religious societies also have important governmental controls.

The Keres have no moiety houses. Each medicine society has a chamber in which its initiations take place, solstice ceremonies are performed, and retreats held; each society has its headman who exercises some authority over his fellow members. These society chambers, or houses, built in the midst of the pueblo dwellings, are linked with the circular "big kivas" of the Keres system which are used for dances and ceremonies pertaining to the village as a whole. They function intimately in the katsina order, each kiva group being associated with particular clans and with two complementary divisions of anthropomorphic personages. These manlike spirits are recognized as sacred clowns called *Koshari* and *Kurena* (and by comparable terms in other Pueblo languages). The koshari societies do not practice curing; they are concerned with fertility and growth.

The koshari are members of the Flint society which is associated with the turquois kiva—thus the winter people; while the kurena are members of the Cíkame society and function with the squash kiva—the summer people. The kiva heads organize the katsina dances, act as custodians of the masks, and supervise preparations for dances; they also select dancers for special parts such as those who enact the buffalo dance.

Santo Domingo has four other curing societies of minor importance: Ant, Snake, *Kapina*, and *Beraka*. Each has power to cure some ailment. Some of these societies occur in the other Keres pueblos, and similar organizations are found among other peoples.

The legendary belief is that Koshari came from his home in the east, near the sunrise; and Kurena had a home close to Koshari, at a spring somewhat to the south. Long ago, these beings also are said to have lived with the people; but, when they went back to stay in the east, arrangements were made that ordinary men might represent them if properly initiated, costumed, and otherwise prepared. When these personators function it is as if the "real" koshari and kurena were present. Thus they serve as mediators between the people of the earth and their ancient spirits. Those of the koshari organization whom we see are held to be the living embodiments of the spirits of the ancient ones.

Differences in attire and accoutrement, body painting, and hairdress help to distinguish the kurena from the koshari. The trunks, limbs, and faces of the koshari are painted white with black horizontal stripes (or sometimes the bodies are painted grey, sometimes with spots instead of stripes). Black circles surround the eyes and mouth. The hair is daubed with white clay and is done up with cornhusks into "horns" on either side of the head. An old dark rag serves as a breechclout, looped over a thong around the waist and from which cow hooves may be suspended. At times rags are tied about the wrists, knees, and neck. The feet are usually bare. Narrow strips of dried cornhusks are symbolic of the koshari.

Bodies of the kurena are painted in vertical divisions—the right side orange, the left side white. Vertical stripes of orange and black are painted on the face. The hair is worked into a single bunch on top of the head. Ragged loincloth and arm and knee decorations are like those of the koshari. A blue and red necklace made of cornstalk with beads may be worn. Feathers of the desert sparrow serve as symbols of the kurena. But as Pueblo customs break down, traditional features show certain changes.

Members of the medicine societies accompany the masked dancers in rites from which the public is excluded. They also participate in some of the open ceremonies, such as corn dances, where they dance in and out among the formal dancers. Men and boys who dress like the koshari and kurena and act like them, but who are not members of the societies, may dance, too, on such occasions. Frequently, both the koshari and kurena function as clowns to the merriment of Indians and visitors alike. Indian cultural mores provide for a balance of pleasurable or amusing activities and grave or sedate pursuits. The serious duties of these society members, however, are far more important. Each of these societies goes into individual retreats before a dance is held. In

September the kurena society has a dance of its own, and in February the koshari has its dance; obviously these pertain to seasonal transfers.

On occasion, among the Keres peoples, certain other impersonators are seen who are identifiable by knobby protuberances on their masks and accentuated circles around the eyes and mouth—the commonly called "mudheads." These relate to times when the Indians had not yet emerged from the dark underworld. Each Pueblo group recognizing these characters explains their origin as their migration myths are recited. The mudheads serve as messengers of the people and their deities. The western Pueblos place greater emphasis on them. *Gomaiowish* of Acoma, for instance, equates with Kóyemshi of Zuñi. More will be said of these personages under the discussion of the secret orders at Zuñi.

In the past, each pueblo had a warrior society, membership in which resulted from killing of an enemy and taking his scalp in a prescribed ritual manner. Even though a society may now be defunct, masked warriors' dances or scalp dances may be performed. Patron deities of the war cult are the twin war gods (*Masewi* and *Oyoyewi* of the Keres). The koshari and kurena collaborate with the warriors' society in the scalp dance. Although created as clowns to amuse the people, they have other functions that are serious and far-reaching.

Another important organization is the hunters' society, in which membership is voluntary. It is composed of medicine men who manipulate supernatural power in order to control game, thus assuring plentiful animal food for mankind. Their power is believed to have been derived from the beasts of prey. The society has, or had, its own ceremonial house and considerable equipment. It has a prominent part in the communal rabbit hunts, and plays a role in the buffalo dance.

Among the Tewa peoples, as noted above, the large surface structure of circular form—serving an entire pueblo—has association with the warrior cult. Ceremonial emphases originally were on war, not on rainmaking as is found among other Pueblos. Medicine societies were not part of the social organization, although curing was effected by officers of the warrior cult. The concept of katsinas apparently was lacking in the primary pattern. Later, esoteric organizations with powerful priesthoods, the katsina cult, clowning orders known as *kossa* and *kwirana*, and various ceremonial procedures—largely borrowed from the Keres—were added to Tewa practices.

Among the Tiwa, Isleta gave asylum to a conservative group of Laguna (Mesita) people around 1879, inviting them to establish a colony at the western limit of the pueblo; this is called Oraibi—the same name as that of one of the Hopi pueblos. Two groups of medicine men, who are both curers and weather controllers, function at Isleta—the Town Fathers and the Laguna Fathers. A hunt chief is recognized, and a war chief who is more or less the executive for the town chief and his assisting bow chief.

Properly speaking, no katsina organization into which all of the youth are initiated exists at Isleta, but they have katsina chiefs, the headman being chief of the yellow corn group. Their supernaturals, like the katsinas of other pueblos, are impersonated in dances, but no masks are worn. What katsina organization prevails was introduced from Laguna. The medicine men derive their powers from animal spirits. Clowns, *kápyo*, are associated with the katsinas and appear with their bodies painted in stripes, with spots, and contrasting colors: six represent each kiva and a young boy wearing small deer horns dances at the head of the line of dancers.

It has been stated above (page 23) that Taos and Picurís have chambers used by the warrior cult and scalp societies, and that curing was a function of the warrior society. The clowns are called *Chifunane* (Black Eyes), or commonly pronounced *Chifonetti*; their bodies are painted similarly to the koshari of the Keres groups.

At the Towa pueblo of Jémez, some twenty groups of a ceremonial nature exist, and they include two clown orders, each relating to a kiva; one, the *tabŏsh*, is associated with the squash kiva which has charge of the summer activities, and the other, *tsúnta tabŏsh*, is associated with the turquois kiva which has charge of winter ceremonies. Most of the pueblo men belong to one or the other of these groups; they are self-selective. Women also are members. The tsúnta tabŏsh is concerned with the sprouting of plants, and the tabŏsh with their maturing. The latter group represents the turquois people and the other, the ice people; they are said not to recognize themselves as summer and winter people. The chief of the tabŏsh retreats to the turquois kiva in November, and the tsúnta tabŏsh chief to the squash kiva in the spring. The tabŏsh have two fetishes, or "mothers," and the other order has one. The tabŏsh participate in dances in September and on 12 November, while the tsúnta tabŏsh come out only on 2 August—the feast day of the Pecos people who migrated to Jémez in 1838.

Jémez has no katsina organization, as such, but it has adopted the concept of katsinas from neighboring peoples and has related them to their secret ceremonies, manifest through masked dancers who personate the supernaturals. Jémez katsinas, recognized in pairs of male and female, are envisioned as cloud people, identified with their deceased ones; they bring rain for the growing crops.

A father to the katsinas is appointed by the cacique and is called "chief." He is entrusted with a corn ear fetish, or "mother," and he is in charge of ceremonial whipping. Wherever katsina organizations obtain, the principal initiatory rite is that of whipping by a katsina whipper. Girls as well as boys are whipped—a rite of exorcism to drive off evil spirits.

Ceremonial races of the kick-stick type are held at Jémez on a track oriented north-south.

Two medicine orders function in the pueblo, a fire society and an arrowhead society. (Parsons 1925:49) They treat illness caused by supernaturals of bird, animal, and human form—the so-called "witches." They also engage in weather control. Each group has its chief and each member possesses a fetish, or "mother." The fire society may have women members. The chief of the arrowhead society has charge of the war god figurines. No warrior society now exists. The chief of an under-chief society is in charge of the scalps; this society holds a scalp dance, a function of the warrior's society elsewhere.

As has been noted, the Zuñi have an elaborate ceremonial organization. This includes a large number of esoteric societies, each of which is devoted to the veneration of special supernaturals or groups of supernaturals. Each society has a priesthood, a special meeting place, a body of secret ritual, permanent possession of fetish-derived power, and a calendrical cycle of ceremonies. According to Zuñi philosophy, the sun is the source of life and is duly honored at solstice observances. The most revered and most holy man in Zuñi is the sun priest who has charge of solstice ceremonies and is keeper of the calendar. He is held responsible for the welfare of the community; thus his duties are those of the so-called cacique in Tanoan and Keresan societies. The Zuñi calendar also includes lunar observations.

Utmost attention is given to a cult of rainmakers which is comprised of twelve priesthoods. Membership in these is usually hereditary in the matrilineal family residing in the house in which the fetish of the group is kept. These fetishes are said to be the most sacred objects in Zuñi. Rather than presenting public ceremonies, the rain priesthoods observe retreats in the household of the fetishes; their rites are primarily concerned with weather control—securing rain for the growing corn.

A significant feature of Zuñi ceremonial organization is its emphasis on ancestors, resulting in an ancestor cult. Every Zuñi participates in their veneration, and "they are involved in every ceremony. They guide, protect, and nourish human life," being identified with clouds and rain. It is said that while priests and medicine men pray to special groups of ancestors, the ordinary Zuñi prays to ancestors in general. (Eggan 1950:203)

The katsina, or kóko, cult is pueblowide, including every adult male, but normally not the women. Upon death, a deceased one goes to join the katsinas, but "only those intimately associated with the cult can be sure of joining them after death." Chief concern of the katsina priests is with fertility, rather than with rain.

Zuñi has a strong cult of the beast gods under management of twelve curing societies, in which both men and women may hold membership. This cult centers around the animals of prey "who live in the east, control long life, and are the givers of medicine and magical power." Each society practices general medicine and specializes in certain diseases or afflictions.

The cult of the war gods is in the hands of the bow priesthood, whose members are those who have killed an enemy. It is in charge of an elder and younger bow priest, who represent the twin war gods, sons of the Sun Father. This priesthood serves as the executive arm of the religious hierarchy. In recent years, the warrior society has deteriorated. Membership has come to be limited; some have said the society no longer existed, and others that it did.

In the recent past, certain members, or surviving relatives who possessed the fetishes and other ceremonial gear, have sold these surreptitiously. Collectors paid well to obtain such rare paraphernalia of a passing culture trait. The opportunity to secure like benefits inspired clever artisans (Indian and non-Indian) to produce similar fetishes—fashioned of antler and embellished with feathers, beads, and other symbolic features—and ceremonial pottery, especially old jars covered over with tiny flakes of turquois, and to which fetishes and feathers may be tied with leather thongs. The antiqued specimens show traces of pollen or sacred meal, and readily pass as authentic. About a decade ago some of these spurious items began appearing in the hands of dealers who commonly kept them under cover. It was a while before the quantity available aroused suspicions as to their authenticity.

At the end of January 1970, press notices made it known that Owaleon, the "last of the old Zuñi war chiefs," had died. His age was estimated to be 106 years. A son is quoted: "Now all the memories of his Indian prayer are disappeared forever . . . none of the new war chiefs visited him after he was sick." And the son remarked, "He wanted to be buried at the new cemetery because he believed in God, not in the old way." (Anonymous 1970f) This betokens cultural changes which have occurred among the Southwestern Indian peoples during the past century and particularly the last fifty years. A warrior society continues to be recognized at Zuñi, but the "new war chiefs" have a vastly different role than did the old ones.

The Zuñi run ceremonial races that are contests between the elder and younger war gods; these are of the kick-stick type, comparable to the Keres races. Clan races also may be held, or ceremonial races by kiva groups.

It appears that the social organization of Zuñi is the most complex to be found in the Southwest.

According to their mythology, the twin sons of the Sun Father guided the Zuñi from the undermost world to this world. Here they organized four esoteric fraternities. The people traveled about for many years. Then the rain priest sent forth two of his children, a youth and a maiden, to search out a good place and build their village. The two ascended a mountain where the maiden stayed to rest while her brother looked over the country. When he returned his sister was asleep; she appeared so beautiful that he desired her. His act of passion enraged the girl, and this unnatural union resulted in the birth of ten children, that very night. It is said that thenceforth "they talked a changed language, but there was no change in appearance." The first born was normal in all respects, but the others lacked the seeds of generation, and thus were infertile. As evidence of this abnormality, their seeds are contained within knobs growing on their heads; from the puckered mouth flows unintelligible talk. "Silly were they, yet wise as the gods and high priests."

Realizing that it was not well for him and his sister to be alone, the youth hurried to make things ready for the coming of their people. He created two rivers and a lake with a village in its depths. When the people reached the river—said to be the Little Colorado of today—many were afraid; strange happenings occurred. Following their leaders came the women with little children on their backs. As they became crazed and terrified, many of the children dropped into the water and instantly became aquatic creatures—tortoises, water snakes, frogs, tadpoles, other vertebrates, amphibians, and reptiles. Those transformed ones went from the river to the lake village, the home of the koko, or rain people who have died; there they "were restored to normal condition" and immediately attained maturity.

The rain priest's son who had sired the "nine lastborn children" and his offspring became mudheads, or kóyemshi—old dance men; the mother became the mother of the gods—old dance woman, *kómokatsi*. After creation of the gods, Father Koyemshi decided they must not appear outside of their dance house unmasked. The head of one of the esoteric fraternities, the *Néwekwe*, copied the mask of Father Koyemshi, and others of that fraternity copied the remaining nine masks. The masks are made of cotton cloth of dun color, with a piece of black cloth at the base; under the latter, packets of seeds of the native crops are concealed. A black kilt and brown moccasins are worn; fawnskin pouches hang from the right shoulder. Each koyemshi differs slightly from the others in appearance and conduct. They became the attendants of the koko—sages and interpreters of their ancient dance dramas.

Whereas the Hopi are known far and wide for their katsina dances and their snake dances, Zuñi is famous for its Shalako ceremonial held annually in late November or early December. This is a re-enactment of the creation and migration of the Zuñi people to their "middle place," or *Héptina*, from their sacred lake village. The Shalako—giant-sized messengers of the rain gods—come to bless the houses constructed in their honor (a maximum of eight may be built—one for each of the six Shalako, one for the mudheads, or koyemshi, and one for the Council of the Gods) and to offer prayers that the Zuni may enjoy fertility, long life, prosperity and happiness. Every member of the pueblo is committed to honoring the Shalako by aiding his clan and kiva relatives; this is done by contributing labor and material goods.

The religious enactments are under control of caciques of the six kivas which represent the cardinal directions, the zenith and nadir. Each kiva has a spectacular group of dancers—the koko, or so-called katsinas—in magnificent attire. The Shalako ceremonial closes the Zuñi year. Their New Year comes near the time of the winter solstice, usually the first part of January. Then the cycle of religious activities begins, and the initial preparations for the Shalako are made; the personators of the dance characters are selected, and households accept responsibility for building new houses or remodeling old ones wherein the Shalako will be entertained. The year-long duties of the personators are assumed; these consist of religious activities, usually held in private, through which the long chants are learned and their presentation practiced.

Date of the Shalako is determined in the fall, and announcement is made that the return of the gods will occur in forty-nine days.

DEATH IN THE WOODS (Keres)

Corn swaying in the rhythm of the wind —
    Graceful ballerinas,
    Emerging at the edge of the forest.
All dip and dance;
    Wind tunnels through long silken hair.
    Golden teeth-seeds.
Trees chatter nervously
    Awakening sky in fright,
    Pointing at Woodman.
A mighty thud! Blow leaves deep scar;
    He strikes again . . .
Corn mourns golden tears,
    Rows, praying for fallen brother.
Jay mocks the greedy beast
    Who has doomed majestic brother,
    His life home.
Wind tosses leaves aside as
    Woodman tramps on his way,
    Ax dripping oak's blood.
The forest, damp and silent,
    Mourning for lost Oak.
    And now remains but a
    Chirp of a lonely cricket and
    Silhouette of Woodman,
    Diminishing,
        beyond the
           saddened hill
             as the far
                sun sinks.

By Harold Bird, Laguna-Santo Domingo
From: *The Writers' Reader,* Fall, 1966, The Institute of American Indian Arts, Santa Fe, N. M.

On Shalako day, about midafternoon, activities which visitors may witness are begun. The little fire god and his ceremonial father come from the south and cross the Zuñi river; they are followed by a retinue of splendidly adorned personages. After their retirement, intervals occur during which the ceremonies are covert, but the great drama continues throughout the night, with all participants appearing in the pueblo and certain ones dancing in the Shalako houses. As sunrise comes, activities cease and a few hours are spent in resting. Then rites are resumed. Around midday, the Shalako and their assistants come forth for a culminating spectacular which is performed on the south side of the river—the six giant figures, like great birds, engaging in a ceremonial relay race.

One who has observed many Shalako ceremonies has prepared a small publication which should be read by everyone attending this unique and centuries-old enactment. (Gonzales 1969)

The Hopi have been influenced by contacts with the Río Grande Pueblos for centuries and they have borrowed extensively from the Zuñi. They have a strong katsina organization in operation. New katsinas are introduced from time to time, some coming from other pueblos and some from non-Pueblo peoples such as the Havasupai, Apache, and Navaho. The Spaniards brought the horse, cow, sheep, and domesticated fowl to the Southwest, and these came to be represented by katsinas; more recently other representations—even Mickey Mouse—have been portrayed.

We are told that if a first performance by the personator of a new katsina is followed by good weather, rain, and fertile crops, he is adopted and becomes an integral part of regular performances. If such an introduction appears to cause bad weather, drought, and loss of crops, rarely does he come again. The older katsinas are generally held to have superior power, more prestige, and greater dancing skill, but *Hŭmis* (often wrongly called *Niman*)—regarded as originating at Jémez—is held in extreme reverence and is a most popular katsina.

It is said that few katsinas "function as clan ancestors: the names by which some of the ancient kachinas are known are the same as clan names, and living clan members claim that the kachina of the same name as their clan is also their clan 'ancient,' or ancestor (*wöye*). Usually the *wöye* masks are kept in the custody of their respective clan mothers, who see to their safe-keeping, and ritually feed them regularly.

The totemic aspect is present, but very few of the kachinas that are traditionally regarded as the most ancient have any marked totemic character—

most of the apparently totemic kachinas seem of more recent origin, and some are of recognizably alien provenience, either alien-Indian or White. (Dockstader 1954:14)

Only a few of the katsina ceremonies are given on set dates. After the opening of the katsina season in November, with enactment of the emergence from the underworld, any individual katsina or groups of katsinas may be selected for presentation. If the village chief gives permission for a ceremony, word goes out as to date, place, and katsinas to be impersonated. Series of night dances in the kivas are performed freely between the time of Soyala in December and the beginning of *Powamû* in February. The latter is the major ritual of the katsina cult in Hopiland; it is a nine-day ceremony. One of the chief features is the promotion of fertility and germination in the approaching season. Growth of beans is forced in kiva rites by Powamû members, and dramatic performances portray Hopi mythology.

Young people are initiated and learn the many aspects of the katsina mysteries. Then come curing rites, "for Powamû is regarded as having strong medicine for the cure of rheumatism." (Stephen 1936:156) While curing is ostensibly secret among the New Mexico Pueblos, it is under little specific prohibition among the Hopi. Rainmaking receives greater emphasis than does curing. Powamû, or bean dances, are presented and the horned water serpent ceremony, or *Pálulukoñ*, is performed with night dances in the kivas. These two ceremonies are closely connected, the main elements of both being similar. It is early April by the time all of the activities involved are terminated. The weather then permits daylong katsina dances in the village plazas.

After costume preparing and rehearsals, which take place in the kivas, the public ceremony is ready for presentation. On the day announced, "the performers, painted and costumed, proceed to one of several shrines outside the village, where they ritually don their masks. In the regular dance pattern, there may be from thirty to forty performers all costumed alike. These are usually accompanied by six masked *kachinmanas* (kachina maidens), or female kachinas, who are thought of as the sweethearts, or sometimes sisters, of the kachinas. These *manas* are usually men dressed as women. As the sun rises, they start for the village where they are met by the *kachina-amu*, usually an old man not in costume, who has the function of encouraging the dancers, guiding them, and offering to them the prayers of the villagers." (Dockstader 1954:18)

A significant feature of the masked dances at the Hopi villages, as well as at Zuñi (and seemingly in the Río Grande pueblos), is the processional order of the participants. In certain instances the same individual takes a given part each time a ceremony is performed; he is followed by a particular personator, and so on down the line. In the Hopi observances the old, uncostumed man, or "father," usually leads the dancers in single file into the plaza (*kísonvi*) along a path he has prepared by sprinkling sacred cornmeal on the ground. The meal symbolizes feeding of the dancers; during the dancing the father sprinkles meal on the participants' shoulders and thus feeds them strength. The dancers are led to the south side of the plaza where they line up facing the east. The leader of the dance group is in the center of the line. He shakes his rattle and starts the singing. The other dancers join in, one by one taking up the song and rhythm. Each comes in on cue down to either end, where the poorer singers and novices are placed.

When the songs have been sung once, the father leads the dancers to the east side of the plaza where they face toward the north; the songs are repeated. Next, the line is led to the north, where the participants, facing west, sing the songs again. Then the dancers leave the plaza and go to a secluded part of the mesa, where they remove their masks, smoke, eat, and rest; they also have a short rehearsal of the next set of songs. They return to the village and present another round of singing and dancing. Such a ceremony continues from dawn until sundown. During the midday break, women of the proper clan bring food to the participants. The family of the dance sponsor has the major responsibility for providing this food.

This usual procedure differs from another type of dance performance, which is more akin to the Río Grande pattern. In it, all the dancers are costumed alike; the dancers do not sing, but are accompanied by a chorus of a dozen or more singers—usually older men.

Gifts from the katsina personators or other villagers are commonly brought into the plaza. Then, at the end of the third songset, the dancers distribute them. A bow and arrow for boys and a carved figurine for girls are traditional; now, gifts may include foodstuffs, store goods, and a variety of items.

Other participants in these dances include a number of mudheads, (Coze 1952:18-29) similar to those of Zuñi; in Hopiland they are called *Táchukti*. Individuals may elect to give an impromptu show, or several organized clown groups may take part. They hold privileged positions in the katsina observances and, in their vari-faceted manifestations of jester-great hunter-medicine man, they are immune from taboos.

Still another katsina performance involves individual dancers who may enter a village singly, in pairs, or in small bands. These are the "character actors," some of whom have distinctive actions or calls which give rise to their names; others are known for their unique costuming. They may come almost any time during the katsina season, even while regular katsinas are performing, or in mixed katsina dances.

As the summer solstice approaches, the dance season draws to a close, and the final act of the katsina drama commences. Whereas at Soyala the badger clan ushers in the katsina ceremonies, the katsina clan has charge of the ceremonial departure of the katsinas, when they "go home" to their legendary dwellings. This, the Niman ceremony, usually occurs in July. At this time, impressive dances are given in the villages.

The people of Hano (Tewa) have adopted the katsina cult and considerable of the ritualistic activities from the Hopi, but they have not borrowed the major Hopi ceremonies. They do not have men's societies. Katsina dances, games, races, and other observances—including competitive events like those of the Río Grande Tewa—are frequently held by kiva groups. It seems probable that kiva membership is associated with katsina initiations or with the winter solstice ceremonies. A Tewa clown organization exists; and great emphasis is placed on curing. All religious matters are in the hands of a hierarchy headed by the village chief. A war chief is responsible for guarding the pueblo against enemies and witches, and for settling internal quarrels.

OPEN CEREMONIALS   To newcomers in the Southwest, the promise of Indian dances is often a strong lure. The term "dance" as used here has little of the meaning of dances of modern western society, or of esthetic and interpretive dances. The Pueblo Indian (as does his racial kindred) feels he is an important part of nature, that all parts of the universe are interrelated, and that he and the universe must be kept in balance. If this equilibrium is upset by selfish or hostile attitudes, disaster will result. Each considers it his duty to perform ceremonies to help the seasons follow one another in proper succession, to promote fertility of plants and animals, to encourage rain, and to insure hunting success. All this is voiced in his prayers and dramatized in his dances—rhythm of movement and of color summoned to express in utmost beauty the vibrant faith of a people in the deific order of his world and in the way his ancient ones devised for keeping man in harmony with the universe.

Numerous Indian dances are given which visitors are permitted to witness. Some are purely social dances, performed for the pleasure of dancing and having an enjoyable time. To these, non-Indian people and other Indians are welcome. Many of the dances occur on fixed dates, each year (see pages 265-69). Some of these are the culminating performances of rites which have been going on secretly for days in a pueblo—purification rites, retreats, prayers, and sacred enactments.

It is well to keep in mind that centuries of communal life have taught personal restraint. Consequently, the fact that visitors are admitted to certain dances does not mean, necessarily, that their presence is desired. (On occasion, non-Indian neighbors of the Pueblos, commonly operators of trading stores, erect "WELCOME" signs and direct traffic by their places of business, en route to a pueblo that is holding dances.) The Indians may not resent the presence of outsiders, but, remembering that the ceremonies being enacted have been going on for centuries—long before the white man came into this land—we can hardly feel that our being there is a truly welcome addition. We should feel honor bound not to abuse our privilege.

Some pueblos allow the use of cameras—*if these are carried under permit from the governor*, and usually *after payment of a fee*. Other pueblos are deeply opposed to picture taking, and permits for cameras are never granted. Anyone taking a camera or tape recorder into a pueblo should go at once to the governor or his representative and make sure of the existing conditions. Sketching and note taking are also forbidden unless special permission is granted.

Visitors sometimes commit offenses unintentionally, such as getting in the way of dancers, walking across the dance plaza, or standing or sitting in places that cut off the view of the pueblo residents, even to crowding them from their own premises. Others are shamefully rude, making unkind comments about the Indians or the ceremonies they are performing (as if the Indians do not understand English perfectly well), talking loudly, complaining because "nothing is happening," walking into homes where they are not invited, and utterly disregarding the fact that they are attending a ceremony which may be as sacred as any held elsewhere, in church or temple or synagogue. The Golden Rule should be observed in an Indian pueblo as well as—or perhaps even more than—any other place.

Participation in ceremonials is a communal duty and privilege of all the Pueblo people. Individuals are trained to take part in the dances from early childhood. Some of the most colorful and attractive dances are performed by children exclusively, as for example, Christmastime and Eastertime ceremonies at the pueblo of Santo Domingo.

Every item of the dance attire has a special significance—the things worn, body decoration, and accoutrement carried. Spruce or fir twigs held in the hands, or which adorn the body, symbolize longevity and everlasting life. Gourd and tortoise shell rattles imitate the swish of summer rain on the growing crops. Feathers and tufts of down or cotton are cloud and sky symbols. Before he can take part in a dance, each performer has to wash his hair as a rite of purification. Both men and women dance with their hair hanging loosely, the beautiful black tresses often falling below the waist. Crests of varicolored feathers worn on the men's heads are symbolic of the glowing zenith. The women's headdresses— fashioned from thin boards, or tablets (*tablitas*)—are decorated with carved-out or painted figures indicating the sky arch, cloud terraces, sun and moon, and other motifs of a sacred nature. Colors here, as with many aspects of Pueblo and other Indian cultures, have significance such as turquois of the sky, yellow of pollen, green of vegetation, red of life, and black of death, with recognized connotations.

The men wear moccasins ornamented with black and white skunk fur, to repel evil spirits from the feet of the dancers. In the summer ceremonials, the women's feet are traditionally bare, and they are scarcely lifted from the earth—thus representing the closeness of womankind to Mother Earth, and betokening fertility.

Men's kilts and sashes are decorated with sacred symbols in colored embroidery or brocade. Weaving has been a traditional art of the men. The white braided girdles with long flowing tassels represent falling rain, and are often referred to as "rain sashes." The brocaded sashes show a conventionalization of the katsina mask, Broad Face. This design is not embroidered but woven in the weft. These sashes are made by the Hopi men (or, nowadays, by students in the Indian schools or participating in projects which have been initiated in recent times) by whom they are sold or traded to other Indian groups, where they are widely used in dances. Many textile designs have lost their original significance or have been altered in their details, but this particular decoration is always essentially the same in design and colors. The zigzags indicate teeth, and the central diamonds represent eyes. On each side of the eyes are figures called "angular marks." In the black bands, the vertical white lines are called "face marks."

From a man's waist, in the center of the back, a fox skin hangs. This is worn by many dancers, especially, by most of the dancing katsinas. It is considered to be a relic of the earliest days of man, for the katsinas "were transformed while mankind was still tailed and horned." (Bunzel 1932b:870) Often a string of shells is worn over the left shoulder crossing to the right hip; and several necklaces of shells, silver, or coral and turquois beads may adorn a dancer. Above the elbows may be painted rawhide armbands, and at the knees, turtle shell rattles (now commonly replaced with clusters of harness bells) and hanks of colored yarn.

The women usually wear a one-piece dress called a *manta*, secured at the right shoulder leaving the left shoulder bare, or exposing a cotton undergarment of bright color. Silver and turquois pins or buttons serve as decorations on the sides of the mantas. The waist is encircled by a woven belt of red and green or black. Around the neck are numerous necklaces, and on hands and arms many rings and bracelets.

These are the principal costume features of the summertime dances; the same items may be used in varying assemblages in yearround ceremonies. Through them all forms of life are represented: animals, birds, and shells of the sea; vegetation of all kinds; all the elements and features of the universe.

Each pueblo has a fixed date for a ceremonial, or fiesta, in the Río Grande groups, honoring its patron saint as introduced by the Spaniards. In prehispanic times, the Pueblos had certain set or relatively definite dates for ritual observances. The Spanish priests found it advantageous to select the name of an appropriate saint for such ceremonies, hoping gradually to accomplish a transfer from veneration of a sacred personage of the Indians to reverence for a Catholic patron. In part, they were successful. In one way or another, saints' names were applied to specific villages, with accompanying feast day observances.

Through the years, a blending of Indian and Christian ceremony came to be observable. Perhaps Mass is held early in the morning in the Catholic church of a pueblo, with Indians in the choir and congregation taking part in the service—with apparently the same reverence and fervor that they bring to their own, aboriginal ceremonials. After Mass, an image of the patron saint may be carried into the plaza and placed under an arbor of boughs (ramada), in front of which the Indians later dance. The Indian cosmography includes many supernatural beings, so the people seem able to acknowledge the Christian God while holding to their own faith. Throughout the dancing Indians may be seen going into the ramada, or improvised shrine, and dropping on their knees before the image of the saint.

Corn Dances   Probably the so-called corn dances, or tablita dances, are seen most frequently. For centuries corn has been the main staple of the Pueblo Indians. It has become more than nutritional, taking on a symbolic character. The corn fetish is most sacred. Corn is exchanged as a sign of friendship. The public performances that we witness occur at the culmination of purification rites which take place in the kiva; these last from one to five days. The corn dances relate to the germination, growth, maturation, and harvesting of the crop and, therefore, are held throughout the summer months. All summer ceremonials are concerned with rain. The corn ceremonies may be very spectacular and onlookers are often deeply moved, even though comprehending only a fraction of their significance.

A typical corn dance, like that at Santo Domingo, may begin with historical pageantry. First, one sees the koshari emerging from the turquois kiva. These ghostly figures encircle both divisions of the pueblo, thus symbolically throwing the protection of the ancestral spirits around all the people. They will perhaps meet the kurena who have come out of the squash kiva, and an excited conference takes place. Runners are sent out in the cardinal directions. They disappear into the kivas or rooms of nearby houses. The spirited parley continues.

After a time the runner from the east returns, and the excited throng crowds round him to receive his message. Animated speeches are made, accompanied by dramatic gestures. The runner from the west comes back, and the same performance is repeated. These are the runners who having been sent to the frontiers, have brought back word about the enemies—Apache, Comanche, Navaho, Ute— prone to make raids upon the Pueblo crops. Then from the north and south, runners arrive with liquids of which all partake—a rite of purification before warriors set forth to meet the enemy. One then sees a dramatization which may be interpreted as preparation for battle. After its conclusion, the participants file back into the kivas, and the historical portion of the ceremony ends.

Where the two-kiva system prevails, a great standard, a long ceremonial wand, will be observed on the roof of each kiva. By watching these, it is possible to know when dancing in the plaza is about to begin. When a wand is brought down, elaborately costumed figures, equal numbers of men and women, alternating, come forth from the kiva. The summer people usually emerge first. They form into two rows and enter the plaza, following a rain priest who carries the great wand. They are accompanied by a drummer beating a large double-headed drum and a male chorus that provide the song and rhythm for the dance.

The wand is highly symbolic. At the top of a pole some fifteen feet in length is a bunch of brilliantly, colored feathers, traditionally those of the macaw. Just below this cluster are bunches of parrot and woodpecker feathers tied on with strands of colored beads and ocean shells. Near the top, a fox skin, bespeaking the long ago, is suspended. An embroidered banner—decorated with clouds, rain, and related symbols—is fastened lengthwise along the pole; it is trimmed at intervals with eagle feathers which float out from the one edge of the banner, and a cluster of small medicine pouches. This wand represents all life in nature. The rain priest stands alongside the dancers and waves the throbbing sacred emblem over them throughout the ceremony. During the course of the day, all of the participants are supposed to pass under the wand as an act of purification.

In a complete presentation of a corn dance, the group from each kiva dances four times, and at the end of the day, the two groups join in a final grand spectacle.

Animal Dances   During winter months, the most important ceremonies include hunting or animal dances, variously called buffalo, deer, antelope, or game animals dance. These are dramatizations of the supposed relationship between the Indians and the larger game animals which, during the centuries, furnished their principal wintertime food. Dancers dress to represent bison (buffalo), deer, antelope, elk, and sometimes mountain sheep. They wear headdresses and horns or antlers which make the likeness to the various animals even more realistic. They carry slender sticks in the hands and by leaning forward on these as they dance, increase the likeness.

In a buffalo dance, the leader is dressed as a hunter and several other hunters may participate. The animal dancers are usually in two lines, with a woman, or two, between them. In December, the woman wears a sun symbol on her back and she is called the buffalo mother (or buffalo woman); but in January, she wears a feathered headdress, and is then called the wild turkey. The buffalo mother is the symbolic mother of the larger animal life of the region. At dawn, she goes out to look for game, and leads the animals to the village. The coming in of these animals from hills surrounding a pueblo and the pantomime which follows is one of the most spectacular dramas that one is ever likely to see. Small evergreen trees may be planted in the plaza, suggestive of the forest. Participants in the ceremony enter their kiva after all are gathered in the plaza. They come out and dance four times during the forenoon, and four times in the afternoon. The dancers are accompanied by a drummer and male chorus whose leader wears a Plains Indian costume; for it was to the great plains that the Pueblos had to go for the largest of all the game animals, the bison. The final event of the day is the enactment of a hunt. In the end, the game is "killed," and the limp bodies are carried from the plaza. The other animal dances are performed along these lines.

Eagle Dance   The eagle dance as we see it today is a fragment of a ceremony which was formerly common to all the pueblos. It is performed in the early spring and is likely to be repeated throughout the year. The eagle has direct communication with the sky powers and is highly venerated. It is not uncommon, even now, to see a specimen of the Golden or American Eagle kept in captivity in a pueblo, where it is treated with every mark of respect. The eagle dance is a dramatization of the relationship believed to exist between man and the eagle and deific powers. Two young men are costumed as eagles, one a male and the other female; in the course of the dance, they imitate almost every movement of these great birds. One sees them in the act of soaring hovering over the fields, circling, perching on high places, resting on the ground, and going through mating gestures. Although the costume may vary from pueblo to pueblo, the basic features are the same.

Each dancer's body is painted realistically; he wears a kilt, usually decorated with an undulating serpent design. On the head, is a close fitting headdress covered with feathers; the eyes are indicated, and at the front, is a long, curved beak—in all, a very good representation of an eagle's head; over the shoulders and attached to the arms, are great feathered wings; and a feathered tail is attached to the belt in the back. Being such a spectacular display of artistry, this dance is a favorite with the public and is frequently performed at public exhibitions.

Basket Dance   One of the most beautiful and significant of all the seasonal dances of the Pueblos is the basket dance, which takes its name from the use of the food baskets in the ceremony. The baskets in the dance symbolize their normal contents—not only the food which preserves the life of the people, but the seeds that are planted in the ground and which must be fructified in due time; the fruits or grain that the earth yields in response to the efforts of the people; the meal which is produced when the harvest of corn is ground; and finally, the loaves of bread ready for sustenance of the Pueblo groups. The invocations for fertility which occur in a basket dance embrace not only the food plant life, but the human race, which must multiply and transmit the gift of life from generation to generation. A complete series of the scenes presented in this ceremonial would constitute an epitome of woman's life, her consecration to childbearing and the sustaining of the life of the pueblo. All participants are costumed spectacularly—men and women—and the basketry display is outstanding.

Miscellaneous   In most of the pueblos, Christmas, New Year, and Easter are
Dances   definite dance dates. Generally, the Indians dance on these holidays, and on the three following days. A few other dances occur on fixed dates, as will be seen from the calendar on page 265-69, but the dates of most ceremonials are optional and variable with the Indians. Among the dances commonly performed are the snowbird, bow and arrow, feather, butterfly, turtle, horse, crow, basket, hoop, sun, cloud, Comanche, Kiowa, Navaho, dog, pine or evergreen, and war and peace dances. Comanche and Kiowa dances were adopted from the Plains Indians. The idea of frightfulness in connection with the Comanche has been intensified by the enormous feathered headdress—which was never a part of Pueblo costume—as well as by the action of the performance. In the typical war dance, formerly performed in preparation for battle, the body is painted black. Nothing is more significant than this painting of the body: when the Indian painted himself from head to foot, it meant war. This was the supreme symbol of anger and deadly intent. Many of the so-called war dances are in reality peace dances, enacted in religious spirit to celebrate the close of hostilities.

ON CORN (Tiwa)

The green corn stands
in the field
close to Mother Earth
earth worms sacrificing
themselves to hungry birds

Look at their golden
tassels like hair
hanging, touching
earth, close
to moist soil
and getting ripe

I danced for the gods
She danced for me
I prayed for rain
She prayed for me

Singing to the sun
She sang of me

I dreamed not of her
But of animals
She dreamed of me . . . .

By Joseph Concha, Taos

From: *The Writers' Reader*, Fall, 1970. Institute of
American Indian Arts, Santa Fe, N. M.

Snake Dance   Other than the katsina dances, the best known of the Hopi dances
are the snake dances. These are among the most involved of
enactments. They take place in late August, in one or more of the
villages. Many days of preparation are required before the public
dance is presented on the final day: at Hotevilla or Shipaulovi and
Shungopavi in even-numbered years, and at Walpi and Mishongnovi
in odd-numbered years.

As part of the preparation, men and boys of the snake and
antelope fraternities enter their kivas. They emerge, painted and
costumed, and spread out on the desert flatlands; equipped with
snake whips, they gather snakes over a period of four days from
each of the directions. Day after day, rites are performed in and
outside of the kivas and other sacred places. Then comes the day of
the great spectacle that has long attracted the local citizenry and
visitors from all points of the compass.*

As the sun lowers in the afternoon, a single file of antelope
priests enters the plaza, singing a solemn chant. After circling the
plaza, they line up along one side to await the arrival of the snake
priests. The atmosphere is tense and exciting by the time the latter
enter the plaza, opposing the antelope priests. In the plaza center is
a small bower made of cottonwood branches, the *kisi*, in which the
snakes are kept. In front of it is a wooden drum—a heavy plank
atop an excavation in the ground. This symbolizes the *sípapu*, or
entrance to the underworld. The snake priests stomp on the drum
"to notify the gods of the underworld that the ceremony is
beginning."

As the two groups of spectacularly attired and painted priests
face each other across the plaza, "the gourd dance rattles vibrate to
emulate the sound of some giant rattlesnake, and a deep, sonorous
chorus that now begins reminds one of some tremendous tempest
approaching from the distance. As the song increases in volume, the
lines of the priests sway back and forth and, at a climax in the song,
break up. Thereupon, the snake men reform in groups of three, and
these groups dance with a strange leaping motion entirely different
from any of the steps so far used. From an observer, we learn that:

As these dancers pass the *kisi*, the first man of each trio reaches in among the
boughs of cottonwood. The priest hidden within hands him a snake which he

*At the end of summer 1971, the village chief at Mishongnovi, Second Mesa, made
a firm announcement that the Snake Dance there would be closed to the public. Acting
without proper authority, the tribal council and the BIA at Keams Canyon attempted to
override this statement of policy by issuing their own announcement that public
attendance would be permitted. The village chief, upholding his decision, was able to keep
the Snake Dance closed to outsiders.

immediately places in his mouth, grasping it with his teeth and lips a few inches back of the reptile's head. The second man puts his arm over the shoulder of the one carrying the snake, and the third man walks behind. If the snake becomes unmanageable, the second priest distracts it by stroking it with his snake whip, or wand.

Each snake priest dances the circle with his snake four times, then he drops it to the ground and the third man of the trio, the gatherer, picks it up. If the supply permits, the first man will reach into the *kisi* for a second, a third, and even a fourth snake. The length of the performance is determined by the number of snakes that have been caught—as many as seventy or eighty—and the number of men participating. . . .

As the dance continues, a priest who preceded the dancers to the plaza continues to sprinkle corn meal on both dancers and snakes. At one point, several women, garbed in old-style Hopi costume, enter the plaza. They bear in front of them baskets containing finely ground corn meal, pinches of which they, too, sprinkle on both snakes and dancers. When all the snakes have been danced with and are being held by either the gatherers or the antelope men, the priest with the corn meal uses what is left of it to draw a circular design upon the ground. All the snakes are then tossed onto the design and the women scatter the rest of their fine meal upon the writhing mass. The Hopi spectators near the spot add their spittle to the sprinkling of corn meal—and woe betide any white visitor who happens to be too close!

There ensue a few minutes of confusion. Snakes dart in all directions, and the gatherers have a difficult time keeping them heaped upon the corn meal design. Occasionally an unusually swift one gets well away into the crowd, and the screams and laughter that follow serve well to direct the gatherer to it. Then the Snake men dash in, seize handfuls of the writhing reptiles, and rush out of the village and down the steep trails. . . .

Back in the village, the Antelope men circle the plaza a few times, stamp on the plank to tell the underworld that the ceremony is at an end, and then march back to the kiva. . . . After the Snake Dance, the entire village relaxes and for four days there are feasting and jollity. Games and races are frequent. . . . Most of the white visitors leave the village as soon as the Snake men have left to liberate the snakes. (James 1956*; *See also* Forrest 1961)

Dramatic buffalo and mountain sheep dances—both very old observances—and a more modern butterfly dance are given in the Hopi villages; these are social in nature to a degree. All three are believed to have derived from the Río Grande Pueblos. Only the buffalo dance is given at a set time (*see* page 266). Many dances are scheduled but a few days prior to their occurrence.

We are told that most of the main Hopi ceremonials are performed twice a year, once as a minor (preparatory) form and then as a major presentation. "Winter in the upper world is summer in the underworld and reciprocal ceremonies are believed to take

*Reproduced courtesy of the Caxton Printers, Ltd.

place—a major ceremony in the underworld is parallelled by a minor ceremony in the upper world and vice versa." (James 1956:183*) Ceremonies may last from one to seventeen days, with much of the time spent in preparations.

REGRET (Keres)

I have made a name for myself.
Of this, I am ashamed.
I have failed to sprinkle cornmeal
To the Great One above.
Knowing the day is ending,
I pray to you,
You who have given
The beauty of Mother Earth.
I dare not ask anything more
. . . but forgiveness.
It was evil of me to fail you;
I regret that I have no excuse.
Sincerely, from my heart, I promise,
I will never fail you again.
Whatever the punishment may be
I will take,
But still . . . I am ashamed.

By Rosey García, Santo Domingo

From: *The Writers' Reader*, Fall, 1966. The Institute of American Indian Arts, Santa Fe, N. M.

---

*Reproduced courtesy of the Caxton Printers, Ltd.

3 the Athabascans

Long, long after the original, and successive, peoples began to inhabit the western hemisphere and scattered over the two continents, other migrants started to trek from Asia into the New World. Looking to their advent here, perhaps around three thousand years ago, (Young 1968:3) it is found that family groups or small bands of people began coming from northernmost Asia via the Bering Strait. The major body, designated by linguists as the *Nadene*, includes subfamilies called Tlingit, Eyak, Haida, and Athabascan—which is by far the largest.

At one time, Nadene peoples occupied much of Alaska and wide expanses of northwestern Canada; eventually, they reached into northern Mexico. Some of them were skilled fishermen, others were great hunters, and all were food gatherers who followed their preferred game and favored foodstuffs along various routes. Today, small enclaves still remain along the Pacific coast as far south as California; of these latter, the Tolawa and Hupa are representatives. What caused certain groups to come into the Southwest, and why they selected the routes they traveled, have been matters of conjecture in large part. However they came, they considered themselves to be "The People," the *Dine'é*.

A form of chronological evidence known as the lexicostatistic dating method, or glottochronology, places the divergences of these Dine'é from the northern Athabascan groups some seven hundred to a thousand years ago. Computations fix the southern movements at a time about one thousand years past, and continuing for approximately four hundred years (which fits well with traditions). This method, then, indicates that the arrival of Athabascans in the Southwest took place in the mid-fourteenth century, (*See* Hoijer 1956; Young, 1968:4) or slightly later.

Certain indications suggest that some of the Dine'é traveled through the intermontane region west of the Rocky Mountains (Willey 1966:232; Huscher 1942, 1943; Harrington 1940:523, 525, 527-529), but no evidence of this has been established. And archaeological findings of the last few years and historical references to a limited degree reveal that significant movements of Athabascans followed down the eastern slopes of the Rocky Mountains during the 1400's. Some of these migrants reached the southern limit of present day Colorado around 1500. Part of them edged eastward into southwestern Kansas, the panhandle of Oklahoma, and central-west Texas to become known as Kiowa-Apache. Certain of the bands continued southward, some centering in southwestern Texas as the Lipan Apache, others turned westward to occupy chosen locations in southwestern New Mexico and eastern Arizona. And those who were to become known as the Jicarilla Apache and the Navaho found their way westward through mountain passes which brought them into north-central New Mexico, into the upper reaches of the San Juan River.

The New Homeland   The region into which the Jicarilla Apache and the Navaho found their way had been occupied by small numbers of village-dwelling peoples from about A.D. 400-700; after 700 until 1050, the population had increased. These facts are recognizable by distinct phases of Pueblo occupation. (*See* Eddy 1966) The district, then, like most of the Southwest, suffered long periods of drought during the late thirteenth century. It was not the first time this had happened. The significant fact which caused abandonment of pueblos and movements of people into more favorable areas was the shift from a summer dominent precipitation pattern to a winter pattern. Having occupied higher elevations where rainfall was sufficient for cultivation of crops, the change in precipitation with its shorter growing season caught the people living above what was an area of a sufficient growing season. They had either to revert to a Desert Culture economy—which meant the break up of large social units—or move. They moved. (*See* Schoenwetter and Dittert 1968; Eddy 1974) The Athabascans, because of their basic hunting and gathering economy, were able to exist in small groups. It is possible that the earliest of them coming into the Colorado-New Mexico border locations from the east were wandering raiders who, discovering the abandoned pueblos and adjoining lands of the upper San Juan, deemed it expedient to move into the then promising region. Several investigators of Navaho history have determined that the earliest area of Navaho occupation in the Southwest is the traditional *Dinetah*, meaning "among-the-people" in the Navaho language; this is identifiable as an area centering in the Gobernador and Largo tributaries of the San Juan river, about seventy-five miles northwest of Santa Fe.

CULTURAL CHARACTERISTICS

Through the preceding narration, it has become evident that the culture of the Pueblo Indians may receive additions which are grafted onto the basic social structure, and that losses may occur during time and from outside pressures or other contingencies; but change with regard to traditional mores, or lifeways, has been resisted resolutely. In the latter respect—change—adherence to a dual ceremonial organization dictated inflexibility; the Pueblos have held on with age-old tenacity. Major concern has been for an entire village or community, the *group as a whole*, with little thought for the individual, although changes in minor traits could take place.

In contrast, the Athapascan-speaking peoples have a culture system of completely opposite nature. With those of our special concern, the Navaho and his closely related cousins, the Apaches, who constitute a single ethnic group, sharing a common culture core, (Steward 1955:37) it is the *individual* who is of primary importance.

HABITAT AND SOCIAL ORGANIZATION

Fundamentally, each Athabascan band had its headman who selected a location for his people in an unoccupied district that provided good hunting and gathering opportunities. In the Southwest, they chose protected canyons and high plateaus, or mesas, with extensive grasslands and the timbered mountain fastnesses where game was plentiful. Constant streams were not so vital to these transient ones as they were to the sedentary peoples who dwelt in pueblos or other permanent communities. The Apaches and Navaho moved about at first, camping or living temporarily near good springs for the most part, or by small streams, ponds, or lakes. Residential shifting was seasonal in accordance with the climatic fluctuations that controlled food supply and forage.

From various lines of evidence, it is apparent that these newcomers followed a patrilineal system of descent, with patrilocal residence, and it is believed that they had "a shamanistic-individual religion preoccupied with curing," without priestly officers such as obtain among the Pueblo Indians (*See* Hester 1962:87) and without permanent religious structures.

As they passed along the eastern side of the Rocky Mountains, marginal to the great plains, the immigrants came into contact with Plains Indians (the Kiowa and others) who had culture traits unknown to the Athabascans. Being quick to see the advantages some of these features offered, they were promptly added to the meager trait list of the immigrants, who brought only the knowledge they could carry in their heads and things they could carry on their backs and perhaps the backs of dogs.

Among the possible additions to their original culture may have been conical dwellings of forked-stick construction or crude rock shelters and cylindrical pottery with roundly pointed bottoms—a Woodland type. The immigrants could have become familiar with agriculture from the Plains peoples. (*See* Willey 1966: 232) These items and knowledge, apparently, the Dine'é brought into the Southwest, with a new type of weapon, the sinew-backed bow which was a far more formidable instrument than the simple wooden bow long used by the Pueblos.

ORIGINS OF BAND NAMES

Accounts of the Spaniards, who entered the Southwest not long after the arrival of the Athabascans, make little reference to people who may have been of that subfamily. Chroniclers of the expedition of Coronado (1540-1542) made slight mention of

Indians who can be so identified; but the Espejo expedition of 1582 encountered a band near San Mateo (Mount Taylor), New Mexico, which was probably ancestral to the Cañoncito Navaho of present times. (Brugge 1969)

It is believed that the term "Apache" was derived from the Zuñi word, *ápachu*, meaning "enemy." The Spaniards appear to have met members of the southern bands first. To differentiate one group from another, they noted particular characteristics or locations. Those who gathered an agave species, *mescal*, for food were called "Apache de Mescalero," the Mescalero Apache. The ones that occupied the Chiricahua mountain strongholds became the Chiricahua Apache; and those farther north were designated as "Querechos," and later as the Gila, San Carlos, White Mountain, Tonto, Cibecue, and so on, utilizing regional terms. Because some of those who took up locations in the north made fine basketry containers which served purposes of small gourds, or *jicarillas*, with which the Spaniards were familiar, they were called "Apache de Jicarilla." And others who were found cultivating crops became "Apache de Návaju." This term is believed to have derived from the Tewa word *Návahu'u*, or "the arroyo with the cultivated fields."

FIRST SNOWFALL (Navaho)

The snow has come at last;
Coming down in soft flakes,
Caressing my face with tenderness
As if it were telling me,
"You are the first I've touched."
And, as I walk along,
The snowflakes seem to sing
A song that has never been heard,
A song that has never been sung—
Unheard!
Unsung!
Except in my heart.

By Tommy Smith

Winner of the Second Prize, Scottsdale National Indian Arts Exhibition, 1964.
From: *The Writers' Reader*, 1962-1966. Institute of American Indian Arts, Santa Fe, N. M.

.... THE NAVAHO INDIANS

According to their legends, the Navaho came to this earth through a progression of underworlds. The number of worlds may vary. In some versions these are recognized as numbering twelve, which are grouped by fours into three layers, or "rooms," known as the Black World, the Red World, and the Blue world, respectively. (*See* Young 1968: .2; Yazzie 1971) Again, four underworlds are recognized, the world in which we dwell, the sky immediately above, and one still higher—Land-beyond-the-sky. (*See* Reichard 1963: 14ff.)

It is believed that not only did The People originate in underworlds, but so did the land itself and all forms of water, the animals, all vegetation and other features. All were brought to the surface by supernatural beings. The place of emergence, *Xajiinai*, is considered to be a hole in La Plata Mountains of southwestern Colorado. The Navaho origin myth is long and detailed. (*See* Matthews 1897: 63–159; Schevill 1947: 29-48; Moon 1970)

Once in this region—tradition sets the time six hundred to eight hundred years ago—The People wandered about. As they say, "many groups joined the original people, to become the progenitors of the earliest clans." By accretion the groups grew, some coming "from the ancient pueblos; some from people who spoke a language similar to Navaho . . . ; and, at a later date, Mexicans and Utes." (Young 1968:2)

BRIEF HISTORY

The Beginnings of Change

Archaeologically, two phases of culture appear to be distinguishable in the Dinétah domain. The earlier one—as yet not clearly defined, due to a paucity of datable remains—brought the immigrants into contact with eastern Pueblo peoples. One of the results was that the Navaho, the interjacent ones, recognizing the Pueblo culture to be more advanced than their own, began to adopt practices which were advantageous to them. Modifying their hunting-gathering mode of life, they acquired horticultural knowledge and began raising corn, or maize. In time, farming brought about a semisedentary residence pattern.

Prior to the coming of the Spaniards, Pueblo peoples occupied river valleys from Old Mexico to northern New Mexico. Don Juan de Oñate brought the first Spanish colonists to settle in northern New Mexico in 1598, after which time comments were made about

Apache or Apachean peoples. Certain historical documents speak of them as raiders who, following attacks, were traced back by the Spaniards to their homes, where they were found to be growing corn—which suggests that these were Navaho.

Fray Zárata Salmerón first referred to the Navaho as a specific Apachean group, in 1626. By the third decade of the seventeenth century, the Navaho had became a large and powerful people, spreading from the Chama to the Little Colorado River, in eastern Arizona. Various bands had their recognized headmen; and it would seem that war and peace chiefs were distinguished. The Benavides report of 1630 refers to Apache and Navaho chiefs, as well as those of the Pueblos, without giving their names—as was common in the Spanish accounts.

The People were dwelling in earth-covered houses and were growing crops: corn, beans, squash, and other Southwestern products. They also gathered wild foods and hunted widely. And they engaged in extensive trade with other Indians and the Spanish settlers. They were holding large gatherings where dances were performed.

As the Spaniards increased in numbers, they edged into the desirable Pueblo holdings and demanded more and more of the Indians. Frequently, they attacked the pueblos, capturing or killing the people, or burning their structures. Prisoners were impressed into servitude or were sold as far south as Mexico. Undoubtedly, the Pueblos, resentful of the growing Spanish pressures and domination, encouraged attacks on them by the Apache-Navaho. At any rate, strife mounted and reprisals increased. Fray Alonso de Benavides, in 1630, published an account of conditions of the period. (*See* Young 1968:12-16; Forrestal 1954:44-52) He established contact with the Navaho and endeavored to achieve peace between the divers peoples and to introduce Christianity to the Indians—both without much success.

It was recorded that in 1653 a Spanish punitive expedition surprised some Navaho holding a native ceremonial. Although no pictographs or petroglyphs on the cliff walls or in caverns have been identified for the earlier archaeological period, it is possible that impermanent art portrayals (dry paintings?) may have been made in connection with ceremonials. The Spanish phraseology also suggests that, by the mid-seventeenth century, the Spaniards had asserted themselves to such a degree as to cause the Navaho, as well as the Pueblo Indians, to go underground, as it were, with their ceremonial practices.

After the Pueblo Revolt of 1680 and the reconquest of 1692, many of the pueblos were abandoned, and the Indians there from were pushed northward toward the San Juan, which brought them into significant contact with the Navaho. In some areas, the two peoples mingled. As a consequence, "In the space of a few years the Navaho adopted the Puebloan styles of architecture, manufacturing techniques, and religious paraphernalia, plus many elements of non-material culture such as clans, matrilineal descent, matrilocal residence, the origin myth, and ritual." (Hester 1962:91) But with these changes, the preferred residence of the Navaho continued to be the *hogan*, a house type traceable to the Asian World.

Immediately after 1696, sites of the upper San Juan consisted of open clusters of hogans and masonry *pueblitos*, or small pueblos, of three or four rooms, indicating that Pueblo refugees were living as isolated family units. Like settlements did not appear in the Gobernador and Largo canyons until some twenty years later, showing that the Navaho and the Pueblo refugees were moving southward.

Huge masonry compounds and pueblitos were built in the Gobernador, in defensive locations on high rock pinnacles. Some of the buildings were in the form of towers equipped with loopholes. Certain sites contained as many as forty rooms. It has been noted that the "only peculiarly Navaho architectural features were the hogans and sweat lodges inside the masonry compounds." (Schaafsma 1966:4)

Archaeologists have called the period dating from 1696 to 1775, the *Gobernador phase*. By the terminal date, Ute, Comanche and Spanish enemies had brought such pressure to bear on the Navaho that they had completely abandoned the eastern Dinetah—the area east of Blanco Canyon. For the Gobernador, data are much more numerous than for the pre-1696 phase. The economic pattern included hunting and gathering of wild plants, with some herding and dry farming. Water was controlled by storage behind sand dikes in a few instances. By 1706, herds of sheep, goats, horses, and cattle were kept—all Spanish introductions. Corrals and horsegear have been found in archaeological excavations. And pecked and painted depictions of people are portrayed on the cliffs—some as black-robed friars on horseback, some wearing fringed attire of Plains Indians, and others with manta-like garments of the Pueblos; with these are *yé'ii* figures (Holy People), eagles, corn plants, bison, and a variety of symbols.

During the earliest part of the eighteenth century, the Pueblo culture dominated the San Juan basin; the Navaho had adopted it in full force. However, in the last half of the century, Pueblo traits were modified or simplified; and by the end of the period, with abandonment of the upper San Juan-Gobernador-Largo districts, the refugees had been absorbed by the Navaho. (*See* Schaafsma 1966:9)

Pueblo and Navaho ceremonial paraphernalia have been excavated from the same caches, giving credence to the belief that much modern Navaho ceremonialism is derived from early Pueblo contacts. Pueblo influences—including sandpaintings, metate and firepit styles, and weaving at least in part—altered the basic Navaho culture, and within a few centuries, distinguished it from that of the Apaches who were less in contact with the Pueblo peoples.

Not the least of the changes was in the spoken language. At the time of the entrada of Coronado, the Athabascan groups spoke closely related, if not essentially similar tongues. Linguists have calculated that the Navaho and Chiricahua Apache were close relatives and historically very friendly, and that their languages became distinctive one from the other during a period of only 149 years. (Hoijer 1963; but *see* Schroeder 1963:17) The Navaho, by the same calculation, are separated by 279 years from the San Carlos and Jicarilla Apaches, and by 335 years from the Lipan Apache. (*See* Young 1968:4)

Shifts of Location   The folklore of the Navaho, as well as their symbolic portrayals on available rock surfaces, and archaeological remains traces their movements from the original locations in the upper San Juan region, down through the Gobernador, Largo and Blanco, into Chaco Canyon and to the Big Band Mesa districts some thirty or forty years later; there, Navaho ceremonial art appears to be relatively scarce. Farther to the west, where Canyon de Chelly in northeastern Arizona was settled by Navaho people before the earlier sites in New Mexico were abandoned, some of the initial art forms seem to have proliferated, while others are absent. Tree-ring dates for archaeological remains have been found to show later occupation going from east to west.

In one instance, however, investigations at an archaeological site at the base of Mariana Mesa, some ten miles north of Quemado in west-central New Mexico, are said to have yielded "the earliest tree-ring date yet obtained from a Navajo forked-pole hogan—

1387." Fifteen additional tree-ring dates supporting the antiquity of this site were also obtained. (Navajo Tribal Museum 1968*) Perhaps this late fourteenth century dwelling was inhabited by migrant Athabascan people who entered the Southwest by an intermontane route, rather than by the common trails leading into north-central New Mexico.

In general, each Navaho community had certain individuals known as men of wealth, with influence, ceremonial knowledge, and good judgment. These usually were referred to as *naat'áani*, or headmen (men—peace leaders—who always knew the Blessingway, which is intended to gain the good will of Navaho supernaturals and to bring good fortune; it is not primarily curative). (*See* Van Valkenburgh 1945:71-72; Shepardson 1963:78)

The White Intruders   Numerous accounts have been written of the Navaho and Apache during the years following their entrance into the Southwest and the decades that saw them fighting against many odds, including other Indian peoples and, especially, the white men who came in ever-increasing numbers—the Spaniards and then the Anglo-Americans. References to pertinent publications are given in the bibliography of this book.

Juan Bautista de Anza, who served as governor of New Mexico from 1778-1789, initiated a plan whereby Navaho headmen were called "captains" or "generals" in the Spanish army. At that time, a prominent Navaho known as Antonio el Pinto was recognized as a general. He received gifts regularly from the Spaniards and was influential in maintaining peaceful conditions until the time of his death in 1793. This type of bribery was carried on after Mexican rule prevailed.

Early years of the nineteenth century were filled with strife, with short periods of peace. The first treaty that defined a boundary between the Spaniards and the Navaho was agreed upon in 1819. The population center was then in Canyon de Chelly, from which westward movements were made into the canyon and valley lands of Chinle, Black Mesa, Navajo Mountain, Klagetoh, and Steamboat Canyon.

Mexican control covered the period from 1821 to 1846. From the time of the arrival of General S. W. Kearny with the U. S. Army, in the latter year, the Americans made intermittent attempts to achieve peace with the Navaho, who were warring and

*This interpretation is questioned by other archaeologists.

raiding. Through the mid-nineteenth century, a few Navaho chiefs were identified by name. Antonio Sandoval was mentioned as leader of the Cebolleta Navaho band. He was a "medicine man." The renowned chief, man of great wisdom and foresight, Narbona, comes to attention, and Zarcillos Largos. When a treaty was signed by Colonel A. W. Doniphan and the Navaho on 22 November 1846, these three were signers (with "X" marks), as were: Caballada Mucha, Alexandro, Kiatanito, José Largo, Segundo, Pedro José Manuelito, Tapia, Archulette, and Juanico and Savoiette Garcĭa. (Young 1968:33-34) Much has been written of these chiefs and other historical figures.

Treaties were proposed, some made (always with communication difficulties) and shortly broken. By 1849, American emigrants were crossing the Southwest in their rush for gold in California. It was common practice for them to abuse and take advantage of the Indians—Navaho, Pueblos, and others alike. Increasing encroachment of the Anglo-Americans on lands which the Navaho considered to be their own, added to misunderstandings and mounting violence. It is recorded that by 1858 the Navaho lived "scattered over a wide area, from the Jémez Mountains to the Hopi Country and from the San Juan River to the region south of the Little Colorado." (Young 1968:38; *see* Harrington 1945:514, fig. 32)

Forts and garrisons established by the U.S. to control Navaho uprisings were left unmanned, in general, following the outbreak of the Civil War of 1861. The Navaho and Apaches were quick to take advantage of the situation and soon were the scourge of the countryside. A few army troops did engage in war against them rather ineffectually. Then it was that Colonel Christopher (Kit) Carson, of Taos, was called to lead a campaign that was destined to bring the turmoil to an end. On 20 July 1863, he and his troops, joined by a band of Ute Indians, reached Fort Defiance, Arizona, to fulfill the ruthless policy formulated by General James Carleton who, in the first place, proposed to resettle the Navaho and Apaches. On a reservation created at Fort Sumner, New Mexico, they were to become farmers like the Pueblos. All captives who surrendered voluntarily would be taken there and all male Navaho who resisted were to be shot. Their livestock and food supplies were to be destroyed; and they were.

Days of Captivity   As under Spanish oppression, the Navaho scattered into isolated canyons, attempting to avoid Carleton's attacks. From November, 1863, nevertheless, captives were rounded up and forced to go to

Fort Sumner, or *Bosque Redondo* ... on the Long Walk. By
December, 1864, the Navaho there numbered 8,354; and 405
Mescalero Apache were confined there also. The next year, it was
reported that 6,447 Navaho were concentrated at Fort Sumner, and
it was estimated that 1,200 had escaped captivity and remained in
Navaholand. (*See* Young 1968:41) Chiefs Manuelito and Barboncito eluded Kit Carson's roundup and refused to surrender to the
army. They and other chiefs held out in their isolated locations.

The Carleton experiment was a horrible failure. Crops that the
Navaho and Apaches were forced to plant produced a disheartening
yield; confinement, and crowded and unnatural conditions resulted
in discontent and disease and great numbers of deaths. The
enormity of Carleton's despotic regime was finally recognized and
he was relieved of his command in the fall of 1866. The following
January, custody of the Navaho was returned to the BIA.

On 1 June 1868, a treaty was concluded and on 12 August of
that year, it was signed, establishing a 3.5 million acre reservation
for the Navaho within their old domain. Signers of the document
were W. T. Sherman and S. F. Tappan of the Indian Peace Commission, and twelve Navaho chiefs: Barboncito, Armijo, Delgado,
Manuelito, Largo, Herrero, Chiquito, Muerto de Hombre (Biwos),
Hombro, Narbona, Narbono Segundo, and Ganado Mucho. All
signed with "X" marks. (*See* Link 1968)

Though this was but a small portion of their former holdings,
the Navaho were jubilant. Many tribulations, however, had to be
met and endured before the return to their homeland was actually
accomplished. Old Fort Fauntleroy, renamed Fort Wingate, was
reactivated in 1868 and served as an agency for the returning
Navaho for a time. Then the agency was moved to Fort Defiance.

Political Reorganization: The Tribal Council

As late as 1922, no political body that could be considered as tribal
existed among the Navaho. Chapters were initiated in 1927 on a
community level, where two types of leaders were recognized:
formal and informal. The informal leaders, in some communities
at least, are influential men who to a certain extent continue the
traditional naat'áani system. (*See* Young 1961:371ff.; Hill 1940)
Showing something of the counterbalance, or dichotomy, of
Navaho social organization is the fact that war leaders were
recognized also—men who always knew the Warway.

Formal leaders came to hold elective offices in the chapters
and/or agencies of broader authority. Chapter officers are a
president, vice-president, and secretary.

The Navaho population was increasing significantly and the people's relations with the rest of the nation were growing more and more complex. Need for an entity that could serve the interests of all the Navaho people became critical. A Business Council, on which three influential Navaho served, was established. Its first meeting was held on 7 July 1923. One of the three was Henry Chee Dodge, who had served as Navaho interpreter for some years. Intelligent, educated, and with great leadership abilities, he "became the ladder along which the Navajo people tortuously made their way out of the early post-treaty period into the modern age." (Young 1968:50)   Chee Dodge was leader of the Navaho for over seventy years. Organization of the Business Council was only a step toward a workable arrangement. Gradual developments continued. Fifteen years later, a tribal council was formed; and this led to organization of the Navajo Tribal Council in 1938. By 1950, this was well established and "the tribe was fast becoming a political entity." (Young 1968:63)

After a Century   Now a century has passed and successive generations of Navaho have come into being since the days at Fort Sumner. Only a few of the old ones lived to witness the Centennial observances which were prominently featured during 1968. Varieties of activities were held, including a re-enactment of the Long Walk to Bosque Redondo; and a series of publications was issued. In these, one finds a wealth of information concerning the Navaho of the past and of today (*see* bibliography).

As one views modern maps, he may locate the Navaho domain generally as the region bounded on the northeast by the Continental Divide, on the southeast by the Río Puerco, on the south by the San José and Puerco rivers,* on the west by the Little Colorado and Colorado rivers, and on the north by the San Juan River. The entire area, broadly speaking, is an almost level plateau, averaging some 5,500 feet in elevation. In places, however, mountains rise to a height of more than 10,000 feet, and deep, sheer-walled canyons cut into the plateau. This results in spectacular landscape, with isolated mesas and buttes, desert wastes, arroyos that are usually dry channels—but which, in seconds, may become raging torrents

---

*In accord with a decision rendered by the United States Board of Geographical Names between 1 July 1936 and 30 June 1937, it should be understood that the Puerco River "rises in township 16N, range 13W, McKinley County, New Mexico, and flows west and southwest to join the Little Colorado in Navajo County, Arizona. Henceforth [the Board stated] this stream will be known as the *Puerco River* and not the Río Puerco or Río Puerco of the west." (Southwestern Monuments 1937) that gouge out the earth and cause erosional destruction. The topography is matched by great contrasts in climate. Winters are cold and summers are hot; and, always, insufficient moisture renders the country marginal insofar as agricultural pursuits are concerned. Only the arroyos and limited areas on which water can be utilized by gravity flow are suitable for farming ... unless modern irrigation techniques are employed. And these are slow in coming to Navaholand. Steps have been taken by the BIA to train the Navaho in modern farming methods, and the tribe has appropriated hundreds of thousands of dollars for the training program.

THE MAIN NAVAHO RESERVATION   Land holdings of the Navaho have been increased periodically and substantially since the days of their return from Fort Sumner. But never have the increases kept abreast of the growing need of the people. The main reservation now embraces 14,450,369 acres, or about 25,000 square miles, reaching out from the Four Corners to include northeastern Arizona, northwestern New Mexico, and southwestern Utah, in that order of acreage. Much of the land is desert and semidesert, sandy or rocky and of little productive value. In some districts, 240 acres are necessary for pasturage for one sheep for a year. Approximately 68,000 acres are farmlands. The acreage under irrigation varies, including federally planned projects and others not formally designated. Perhaps 10,000 acres are now under irrigation. And the population is ever growing. Brandon (1969:14) says they are growing "twice as fast as the national average. The people want to stay together as members of living communities." The Navaho registered as of 1 January 1970 were 126,267. (Navaho Census Office, Window Rock, Arizona) Not all Navaho are registered, so the total number is several thousand more than this figure.

With the completion of a dam on the San Juan River and the diversion canals in prospect, 110,000 acres of irrigable land should be added. When water becomes available, however, it will not give the Navaho what they desire for the most part—land and water for individual working and production. Rather, large commercial enterprises are destined to control the water; and most of the Navaho will be laborers for "the other fellow." Some 36,000 acres are dry-farmed.

Until the present time, the Navaho never settled in communities that could be called villages or towns. They lived in desirable locations scattered over the entire reservation. Following the matrilineal pattern, a Navaho grandmother is the center of the family. The children belong to her and are members of her clan. Because it is taboo for a Navaho man to look at his mother-in-law, or to talk with her, a woman and her husband do not live with the wife's mother. Instead, they erect a home nearby, so that the woman and her children can frequent the maternal abode. Thus, one may find several generations dwelling together or in proximity: grandmother, mother, daughter, and grandchildren. It is usual for the dwelling, the crops, and the livestock to be cared for by the mother and her children, so these are owned by the woman.

Inasmuch as property ownership among the Navaho is individual, a woman disposes of the rugs she weaves, and of her crops and stock; she spends her money however she chooses. A man does likewise with his silver jewelry, with the wages he earns, and with the income from his stock raising or farming. It is the man who represents the family in public and at ceremonials.

Visit Navaholand To see the Navaho properly, one must go into their own country—far afield, and often over dirt roads. Road construction and maintenance were long neglected on the vast, thinly populated expanses. Today, however, hundreds of miles of black-top highways have been, and are being, built on the main reservation, and even more of graveled roadways. Some Navaho may be found around the trading posts and stores, buying groceries, clothing and supplies, or pawning or selling their jewelry, radios, cameras, moccasins, rugs or blankets, belts, and miscellaneous items. Occasionally, one comes upon them by accident, herding their sheep or crowding the animals around a water hole or tank.

The typical Navaho dwelling, the hogan, is usually round or hexagonal, sometimes octagonal, constructed of logs and mud, or sometimes of rocks, with a central air vent in the ceiling. (*See* Richards 1970:8-9) Rarely are more than two or three together, and a traveler is likely to pass by without seeing them in daytime—so well do they blend with the natural setting; in the evening, one is surprised at the number of fires whose flickering light gives evidence of the Navaho dwelling or camp near at hand.

Near the hogan or under the shelter of a brush-covered ramada, Navaho women may be seen weaving rugs on an upright loom, which was adopted from the Pueblo Indians. Textile belts are woven on a loom made from a forked branch of a juniper tree. When in use, this is erected on a slight diagonal in front of the seated weaver. Small children will be playing nearby, or perhaps helping to card the wool. The older children and the husband are usually away, herding sheep or on an errand to the trading post. This picture is not so easily found today as the pattern of life is ever changing by acculturation. The Navaho rug is becoming a relatively scarce article.

Away from their homeland, Navaho Indians are seen at Pueblo ceremonies, especially at Jémez, Laguna, Zuñi, and in the Hopi villages. They come to trade and barter, to sell rugs and jewelry and to take home agricultural products and other Pueblo items. A few Navaho may be seen on the streets of Cuba, Santa Fe or Albuquerque. Their numbers increase as one goes westward; in Farmington, Gallup, Flagstaff, and other towns nearby they make up a considerable segment of the population. Part of the year, they are conspicuous in the southern Colorado towns where they go to work in the beet fields or engage in other work. In their "capital city," Window Rock, and places on the Navaho reservation, such as Shiprock, Chinle, Tuba City, Ganado, Fort Defiance, and Crownpoint, they are naturally predominant. It may be noted that each of these communities has a hospital or health center, and also a boarding school.

PHYSICAL APPEARANCE AND ATTIRE   The Navaho tend to be taller than the Pueblo Indians, and most of them are slender. They have long, somewhat raw-boned faces and a number of the men have mustaches. Back of the heads are flattened by cradleboards on which infants are carried. A typical Navaho woman might be described as having small arms, hands and feet, with thin legs; long face, nose and chin; and thick lips. The slanted, oriental eye is fairly common among women and children. Their particular style of walking and their manner of making gestures are identifying characteristics of Navaho people.

A few old Navaho men still may wear the attire of earlier days, at least in part. But in the main, clothing, like that of other Indian men, has come to be that of the western stereotype: blue denim pants worn with an ornamental belt, cowboy boots or heavy shoes; colorful shirts and kerchiefs, large felt or straw hats, or maybe a bright headband, coat or leather jacket. Particularly on special occasions, silver and turquois jewelry is worn. If the occasion demands, dress clothing, even tuxedos, may be worn.

The female attire has shown less change through the years. Until recently, most women and girls wore garments reflecting the style of the 1860's, when the Navaho women began to wear long, full skirts of calico or some other colorful material, and velveteen blouses—these from patterns that were supplied during the Fort Sumner days. A bright red woven belt and high-top laced shoes of tan leather would often complete the costume. Some years ago, bobby socks became popular and many Navaho women may be seen wearing them with saddle oxfords. Nevertheless, the traditional moccasins of deerskin and cowhide are still in evidence to some degree.

The Pendleton blanket, or one of similar manufacture or appearance, is a favorite of both men and women, worn about the shoulders or folded over an arm. These attractive, machine-made products often have been admired by newcomers to the Southwest as *Indian blankets*, which, indeed, they have become—by adoption only. (The Pendleton Woolen Mills of Portland, Oregon, long ago sent designers to the Southwest where they spent a great deal of time with the Navaho. They learned the symbolism and Navaho preferences. "Using this knowledge they then designed blankets in the Indian concept and in the colors and patternings the Indians most desired." (Eklund 1969) The Pueblos and other Indian peoples have distinct preferences also as to designs and colors.)

Entrance into a new era is observable as more and more Navaho people abandon their attractive clothing for the styles of their non-Indian neighbors. Professional dress designers have adapted the old style full-skirted garments and bedecked blouses of the Navaho women, and they market these gay frocks as "squaw dresses" or "fiesta dresses"; these have found favor among the young Navaho women and tourists alike.

The universal badge of distinction among the Navaho is the silver and turquois jewelry—rings, bracelets, necklaces, earrings, buttons and pins, hatbands, and even shoe buckles. But don't let this display of wealth deceive you. It may indicate something of the wearer's own prosperity, but most likely—especially if worn at a ceremonial or public gathering—it represents his borrowings from family and friends or from a nearby trading post operator. A Navaho frequently arranges to remove valuable belongings from pawn with a trader for display at special functions.

CONTEMPORARY LIFE

Herdsman vs, Farmer

Differences between the Navaho and the Pueblos are deeper than clothing, stature, or spoken tongue. The heritage of each is quite disparate. The Pueblo is a house-dweller and horticulturist, first and last; the Navaho is a herdsman basically and for that reason follows a shifting pattern of life. Kluckhohn has stressed the fact that the

Navaho has never been a nomad. (*See* Kluckhohn and Leighton 1962:38-39) Although the Navaho practice agriculture to some extent today, and engage in livestock raising, these sources of income are significantly augmented by miscellaneous revenues from other resources, such as timber (of which there are over 472,700 acres of commercial value), oil, gas, vanadium, uranium, coal, sand and gravel. The Navaho tribe is in big business, totaling in the millions, which requires employment of skilled attorneys, business men, and officials. Per capita personal income averaged around $772 in 1969.

Education   After decades during which the Navaho saw little reason to send their youngsters to the white man's schools, or to schools following ordinary white man's curriculums, their attitude has altered. Now, instead of resisting the federal efforts to live up to education stipulations made in the treaty of 1868, the Navaho have come to realize that the young should be trained to cope with modern demands. (*See* Smith, A.M. 1965, 1966, 1968) Consequently, the tribe and individuals as well exert their influence toward having adequate schooling for the young; and also they promote adult education.

Children from beginners through high school are enrolled in reservation schools. As they progress, they are taught skills and trades. Some of the schools are located in isolated regions, away from all other structures. Most of the pupils in these remote schools are picked up by bus and travel distances as much as fifteen miles, or more; and they may have to walk a mile or more from home to the bus stop. The majority of the children entering these schools are unable to speak other than their native tongue, Navaho. The BIA operates a five-year program in general education in several off-reservation schools. The Navaho Tribe has set up a multi-million dollar trust fund for scholarships for qualified Navaho high school graduates to attend colleges or universities of their choice. More than 46,000 young Navaho people now attend school regularly. (Anonymous 1972)

A community college was opened in January, 1969, in borrowed quarters at Many Farms, Arizona, a community of some 2,000 population. This is the only college established on an Indian reservation or to be sponsored by Indian people. Its success and growth resulted in the planning of a beautiful campus for the Navajo Community College in the Ponderosa pine forests north of Fort Defiance, near Tsaile Lake, on 1,200 acres of land provided by the tribal council. (Navaho Community College 1969) Loans totaling $2,530,000 were approved by U.S. Department of Housing and Urban Development for use in constructing the college; and a number of significant grants have been made by foundations and commercial organizations for its operation. The new site of the college was dedicated on 13 April 1971, with some two thousand people attending the ceremonies. The plans are conceived to reflect Navaho culture in design and construction. Target date for the completion of the first phase of construction and occupancy was set for April, 1972.

The college, whose president is a Navaho, early achieved correspondent accreditation status from the North Central Association of Colleges and Secondary Schools, and started working for full accreditation. Its program revolves around an Indian studies program, with the study work geared to the individual who does not have a great deal of education. It teaches what the Indian wants to learn—Navaho history, arts and crafts, and, among other things, driver's training. Any Navaho over eighteen years of age who applies for entrance is accepted. Of the spring enrollment for 1971, eighty per cent of the 571 enrolled strudents were Navaho; 10 per cent were Indians of other groups; and 10 per cent were non-Indian. About one-third of the thirty-five-member faculty are Navaho. On 4 May 1971, seventeen students were graduated from the college.

Modern Government   To this day, the Navaho continue their organization based on regulations promulgated by the Secretary of Interior. Modifications are made as occasion demands "by the governing body itself, with the consent and approval of the Secretary, rather than an institution based on a constitutional framework approved by the people it represents." (Young 1968:61) The governing body is composed of a chairman, vice-chairman, and seventy-four delegates elected on a land management district basis. Elections are held every four years; campaigning becomes active at these times. Voters, both men and women over twenty-one years of age, must register; voting is done by secret ballot. Women can and do serve on the tribal council. The term is four years. All officers are sworn in by a District Judge from Arizona or New Mexico.

Council meetings are held in the Council House at Window Rock, a structure built in octagonal shape like a huge hogan. Each member of the council has a desk with his or her name on it. Meetings are conducted entirely by the Navaho; Indian Service personnel are available for consultation but do not participate unless requested. A number of committees serve, such as the Advisory Committee (which is comparable to the Cabinet of the federal government), and smaller bodies, each attending to specific duties. A trained and uniformed Navaho police force is selected by the Advisory Committee. Surrounding the council chamber is a complex of administration buildings in which offices and necessary facilities are housed.

In 1969, the Advisory Committee, serving as the executive arm of the Tribal Council, directed the council "and all departments, divisions, agencies, enterprises, and entities of the Navajo Tribe to use the phrase 'Navajo Nation' in describing the lands and people of the Navajo Tribe." Furthermore, the Advisory Committee directed that "all resolutions of the Tribal Government be certified as being duly enacted at Window Rock, Navajo Nation (Arizona)." Perhaps in way of explanation, it was stated: "The Treaty of 1868 recognized the Navajo People as a sovereign nation and spelled 'Navajo' with a 'j'." This, incidentally, is in direct contrast with the feeling of the Navaho council members of a few years ago. At the council meetings then held, the federal government was entreated to spell the tribal designation with an "h," the Navaho saying that they were among the "first Americans," and that they preferred the Americanized spelling. The government took no heed of their pleas. Scholars agree with the older Navaho sentiment. (*See* Trager 1969)

A tribal Parks Commission was created in 1957, and it has recently become very active. One of its important duties is to protect the hundreds of prehistoric ruins that are located within the confines of the Navaho reservation. These are considered to be among the tribe's irreplaceable assets, and great efforts are made to protect them from vandalism and "pot hunting." A reward of one hundred dollars ($100) has been posted for information that will lead to the arrest and conviction of anyone illegally excavating in the ruins. Violators can be fined up to five hundred dollars ($500) or not more than ninety days in prison, or both.

Parks and visitor centers have been developed, guided tours have been organized, tourist accommodations developed over the vast reservation, and arts and crafts promoted. Annual fairs are held, as well as the many scheduled and unscheduled ceremonials, sings, rodeos, rug auctions, and other events. For information, visitors to Navaholand are directed to write to the Navajo Parks and Recreation Department, P. O. Box 418, Window Rock, Arizona, 86515.

Industrial and commercial developments on the reservation have had increasing impact on the Navaho people. A number of years ago, the Navajo Arts and Crafts Guild was initiated to encourage production of reservation items and to serve as a commercial outlet therefor. This is now located at Window Rock; it supplies Navaho arts and crafts productions to centers located at other vantage points on the reservation and elsewhere.

Electric power lines have been strung across the reservation and underground pipe lines for oil and gas and water crisscross the terrain. These have made possible large industrial undertakings. In 1960, the Navaho established the Navajo Tribal Utility Authority (NTUA) with headquarters at Fort Defiance to supply electricity, gas, sewerage, and water to the people and installations on the reservation. It is a multimillion dollar operation, employing some one hundred and eighty technically skilled Navaho.

The vast timberlands have been utilized, from simple sawmill operations to a sophisticated lumbering industry. First was a lumber camp at Sawmill, Arizona, which came to produce around twenty million board feet of lumber annually. Then, the tribal council appropriated eleven million dollars for new sawmill operations in the Chuska Mountains along the Arizona-New Mexico border. There, a whole new town, Navajo, New Mexico, has been established about twenty miles north of Window Rock. The plans are to cut approximately fifty million board feet a year for a decade, and then level off at about thirty-eight million board feet annually on a sustained yield basis.

Wisely, the Navaho elected five long-time western lumbermen to its board of directors and hired an expert manager for the new sawmill. The employment schedule there is about 325 Navaho; while some 150 work at the old mill. The Navajo Forest Products Industries now produces lumber and wood products for nationwide distribution.

In the mid-1950's, forward-looking companies concerned with the development of fuel components and power began to prospect in promising locations on the Navaho reservation. El Paso Natural Gas Company of El Paso, Texas, leased nearly 100,000 acres in the Burnham area, some fifty miles south of Farmington, New Mexico, with a view to possible strip-mining operations. Explorations revealed a potential of 519 million tons of strippable coal in the whole area.

The Utah Construction & Mining Company (now Utah

International, Inc.), headquartered in San Francisco, leased a twenty-five mile long strip of Navaho coal land and got a 50,000 acre-foot water allotment on the San Juan River from the New Mexico State Engineer. Currently, at Fruitland, New Mexico, huge draglines, one of which weighs four million pounds, strip away dirt and rock to a depth of as much as 120 feet to expose a low grade coal seam. This is then blasted for shoveling and hauling of the coal to the Fruitland power plant. In 1970, this mine was expected to produce around 8.5 million tons of coal per year—more than any other mine in the world at that time. At an agreed rate of fifteen cents a ton, the revenue—royalty and lease rentals—to the Navaho tribe was estimated at $1.3 million. (*See* Montgomery 1970b; 1970d)

The Navaho employed in the mine and generating plant benefit economically from this industrial undertaking, and from several similar or related projects. But the tremendous amounts of water required for cooling the generating plants arouse deep concern of far-seeing conservationists who realize that the mining of water may have detrimental results of increasing significance. Also, smoke and millions of tons of fly ash and chemicals fill the air and are deposited annually over a wide area.

A related multimillion dollar coal mining project under lease involves the Navaho and Hopi Indians, covering Black Mesa (the Navaho "female mountain") south of Kayenta and extending southwestward to the Hopi villages. There, the Peabody Coal Company of St. Louis, Missouri, arranged to operate on a 60,000 acre area where it is estimated that some 16 billion tons of coal occur at two main levels. Some 350 to 400 million tons of coal appear to be economically feasible for strip mining. The project is to furnish fuel for power generating plants at Mohave Station in southern Nevada and at Page, Arizona, on the Navaho reservation. Page originated in the 1950's as the construction camp for the building of the Glen Canyon Dam. The generating plant there is now under construction.

Huge draglines remove the ground cover of grass and piñon trees, and great shovels lift the thirty to forty feet of overburden and gouge out giant bites of coal. Water is being mined from sources built up during millions of years, from a depth of 2,000 feet or more below the top of Black Mesa. The water pours into a pipe of eighteen-inch diameter and is mixed with an equal part of finely pulverized coal for transportation along a 273-mile slurry line to the Mohave plant—thus being expected to move 117 million tons of coal over a period of thirty-five years. This pumping of water is calculated by certain water experts to result in the lowering of the watertable around Kayenta by one hundred feet. Water required for the thirty-five years' pumping is calculated to be 33,000 acre feet a year. It is purchased from the Navaho tribe at $7.50 per acre foot. An eighty-mile electric railroad, costing $40 million, is designed to deliver the coal from Black Mesa to the plant at Page. Water is to be derived from Lake Powell. (Montgomery 1970d)

Peabody's 1967 contract "called for a rental annually of $1 an acre the first five years of the lease and $2 an acre thereafter for the life of the lease on the 60,000 acre plot of mesaland." (Montgomery 1970c:A5)

All aspects of these monumental undertakings are envisioned as resulting in millions of dollars of income for the outside companies and subsidiaries, sizeable salaries for a small number of Indians and lesser sums for others. It has been estimated that in the period 1963-1970, some $4 million in tribal funds were expended in efforts to bring new industries to the reservation. BIA statistics for 1969 and 1970 show the Navaho labor force to be slightly over 38,000, and of these, nearly 45 percent were said to be out of work. New industries are credited with having produced 2,300 new jobs in the past five years. (Anonymous 1969b)

It is inevitable that the landscape of Navaholand will be altered, although present contracts call for restoration of the land to some degree. The natural beauty will be changed forever, as will be the centuries-old lifeways of the aboriginal inhabitants of the region.

Other undertakings are not so overwhelming or disturbing. At Shiprock, the Fairchild Semiconductor Division is the largest non-federal employer of Indians in the U.S.A. And General Dynamics Corporation has a plant at Fort Defiance. At Page, by the Glen Canyon Dam, is a Vostrom Electronics installation.

Early in 1969, a supermarket chain, FedMart Corporation, opened a large shopping center in Window Rock, with low cost prices—an innovation on the reservation. Other commercial ventures are starting where industrial areas are growing—Colonel Sander's Kentucky Fried Chicken, for instance, and banks and service enterprises. And with expansion of businesses, new housing projects are keeping pace. Some homes are privately financed. Over six hundred Low Rent Housing units have been erected under the Navajo Housing Authority; and Mutual Help units are being built with families achieving equity through participation in the construction. More than 2,000 Navaho have taken part in a home improvement program, adding needed space, a new roof, or completing sanitary facilities.

The Navaho have appointed a Planning Board to work toward a total program of land use, participation of local people in determining their role in the community development, to meet the needs of child care, delinquency, education, care of the ill and elderly, and in making their homeland better for future generations.

During April, 1971, the community of Piñon scored a first on the reservation with the opening and blessing of a retail cooperative called the DINE-BI-NAA-YEI Cooperative. It is a dues-paying member of the Arizona Grocers Association. Open six days a week in the remodeled old arts and crafts building of the Piñon chapter house, it is operated solely by and primarily for the Navaho people of Piñon, which is located on reservation Route 4, between Second Mesa and Chinle. Members pay a one-dollar fee. Expectations were that the enterprise would be grossing about one thousand dollars a day. Federal funds, those of the Navaho, and of others were utilized in this undertaking.

In June of 1971, the Navaho took a historic step toward more independence from the federal government with the signing of an agreement to take over the federal commodity food program on their reservation.

Many of the younger Navaho and government officials want innovations to come to the reservation, and their views are coming to prevail in tribal elections. Jobs, changes in traditional concepts, and urbanization become increasingly important factors. A BIA official has said "if the economy can be stepped up, we can see sizeable towns develop." And he remarked that the Navaho are "very rapidly urbanizing and modernizing." (Graves 1970:24 August) One of the Navaho men deeply interested in the welfare of his people has pointed out the need for services on the reservation and, like others, he realizes the ever-growing need for more water.

At the same time, economic growth on the reservation is viewed with concern by the "traditional" Navaho who want to continue living as they have in the past. The opposing points of view result in conflicts. This is not a new trait in Navaho culture, but certain conflicts result in mental illnesses which old practices no longer control. Although youthful suicides are all but unheard of among many Indian groups, such as the Pueblos, the Navaho now have an exceptionally high rate of suicide. (*See* Levy 1965; Levy et al. 1969:124-147) Speaking of this, Dr. Karl Menninger says: "Where one commits suicide, scores are in despair."

The poem at the end of this chapter, on page 142, gives a Navaho's arresting commentary on white man's progress vs. Indian tradition.

Off-Reservation Employment   An increasing number of Navaho take off-reservation employment each year. This may be seasonal, with the Navaho working for a few months and then returning home to spend the remaining months with his family; with the development of industries on or near the reservation, jobs become longer lasting. In addition, an ever-growing number are leaving the reservation and settling in industrial areas. For these, employment is relatively permanent. Many thousands now live in Los Angeles, San Francisco, Oakland, Denver, Chicago, Dallas, and other cities. Such resettlement has been successful only when the Navaho has had sufficient education, hand skills, and understanding of non-Indian culture.

During times of war or other national stresses, the Navaho—both men and women—have made fine records in the armed forces, and in supporting industries. Today, they are well represented in most branches of the armed services.

HOPI-NAVAHO LAND DISPUTES   Through the years, Navaho and Hopi dissatisfaction over the lands supposedly shared between them has increased. Each became more and more vocal about the matter, and press notices on the subject appeared frequently. During early 1970, the news media carried extensive accounts of Navaho claims and Hopi briefs that had been presented to the federal Indian Claims Commission (a body established by Congress in 1946 to adjudicate and settle, once and for all, Indian claims against the U.S.A. "for unconscionable acts in previous years that had injured or unjustly deprived Indian tribes of lands and resources."). (*See* Young 1968:75) After hearing pro and con arguments, the commission finally laid down boundary lines involving about thirty million acres, and ruled that the Navaho should have been compensated therefor in the 1868 treaty. The Navaho will not get the land—whatever the specific acreage is computed to be—but they are entitled to a cash settlement from the government. It is intended that much of the money the Navaho are to receive will be used for industrial development of the tribe.

With this much accomplished, the Navaho set out to have legislation introduced which would add 240,000 acres to their reservation. They are seeking land adjoining the southeast corner of the Navaho reservation and jutting out toward Gallup and Zuñi. The bulk of the acreage is US public domain held by the Bureau of Land Management, with a small amount of state land. Later, they look toward the checkerboard area, where they want to have several hundred thousand acres transferred to their reservation. It is a fact that Navaho have for some time been buying privately owned ranches east of the reservation. This has enabled them to get grazing permits on the adjacent public domain.

NAVAHO CEREMONIES   Among the Pueblo peoples, weather control—placing great emphasis on rainmaking—is fundamental in religious organization and ceremonial enactments under the control of priests. In contrast, Navaho religion centers in curing ceremonies directed by shamans following a system of imitative and sympathetic magic. All Navaho rituals are performed with certain aims in mind: restoring health, securing food, insuring survival. In the Navaho universe, two classes of personal forces are recognized, human beings and the Holy People, or supernatural beings—holy in that they are powerful and mysterious. The Navaho believes his universe functions according to certain set rules. If one learns these rules and lives in accordance with them, he will keep safe or be restored to safety. The Holy People have great powers over the people on earth; on the other hand, they may not only be supplicated and propitiated, but may be coerced as well.

The Navaho greatly fears death and everything connected with it. This intense feeling—a trait traceable to his Old World origin—stems from the fear of ghosts and witches of the afterworld. He fears the dead may return as ghosts to plague the living. Therefore, any dead person is a potential danger. Ghosts are believed to take the form of human beings, animals, birds, or whirlwinds, spots of fire, etc. They appear only after dark or at the approach of death. Ghosts may foreshadow general disaster as well as harm to an individual. When a Navaho sees a ghost or dreams of one, it is imperative that the proper ceremony be performed or the individual will surely die. If successful, such ceremonial cures are believed to have killed the witch, one way or another.

Disease and accidental injury are felt to result from an attack by the Holy People, and may be traced to some transgression on the part of a victim. A cure must be effected by a specific chant (a song ceremonial, the songs of which are accompanied by the use of a rattle), and by making sacrificial appeasement to the offended Holy Person, or by engaging the mightier power of a higher divinity to remove the witchery and evil influence of an inferior one. Should a given ceremony fail to cure the sickness, it merely indicates that the offense has not been properly traced and the source must be further sought. Numerous chants may be performed until the patient recovers, or dies. Death is considered to be beyond human calculation. When death of a patient becomes certain, the officiating singer (*xata·łi*), or "medicine man," who conducts a song ceremonial, withdraws before the inevitable.

Chants and Sandpaintings   In general, every chant has its own particular sandpaintings. These represent the divinities or some event connected with a divinity, as told in Navaho legends. More than five hundred different sandpaintings have been recorded, and fifty-eight or more distinct ceremonies—each with its own body of legends. Navaho mythology tells us that originally the drawings were made by the gods, or yé'ii, themselves, and were stitched into some kind of fabric. Actually, it would be more accurate to call these *drypaintings*, for pollen, meal, and other vegetal material, as well as pulverized clay and certain minerals may be used in addition to sand; and occasionally, the paintings are made on buckskin. Usually, the paintings are made on a background of clean sand. The details of the patterns are handed down by memory from one singer to another. Different colors are made by crushing rock, charcoal, or other material into fine powders and mixing them with sand or dirt for easier handling.

Each chant has certain songs, prayers, and herbal medicines which are held to be particularly its own, and the appropriate sandpainting is made inside the hogan where the ceremony is held, or out-of-doors on occasion. But regardless of which chant and paintings are being performed, the basic procedure is the same. Upon completion of the treatment, the patient leaves the hogan, the painting is destroyed in the same order in which it was made, and is deposited to the north of the hogan.

Navaho chants may be grouped according to their mythological associations, rituals they have in common, and as they are addressed to the same or related forces. The six main groups of song ceremonials are: *Blessingway* rites and ceremonials; *War* ceremonials (obsolescent), *Gameway* (hunting) rites (obsolescent); and the three curing ceremonials, *Holyway* employed for the attraction of good, *Evilway* (Ghostway) for exorcism of evil, and *Lifeway* for

SONG OF THE TWINS

That which is good,
May it be made as offering to him [the Holy Spirit Boy],
May it be made as offering to him;
    The young man who walks in the darkness,
May it be made as offering to him,
May it be made as offering to him;
The pretty black bead,
May it be made as offering to him,
May it be made as offering to him;
The pretty sparkling stone,
May it be made as offering to him,
May it be made as offering to him;
The pretty blue flower pollen,
May it be made as offering to him,
May it be made as offering to him;
The pretty corn pollen,
May it be made as offering to him,
May it be made as offering to him;
They will be exchanged for his mind, his voice;
May they be made as offering to him.
    That which is good,
May it be made as offering to him,
May it be made as offering to him;
The young woman of the dusk,
May it be made as offering to her,
May it be made as offering to her;
The pretty white shell,
May it be made as offering to her,
May it be made as offering to her,
The pretty sparkling stone,
May it be made as offering to her,
May it be made as offering to her;
The pretty blue flower pollen,
May it be made as offering to her,
May it be made as offering to her;
The pretty corn pollen,
May it be made as offering to her,
May it be made as offering to her;
They will be exchanged for his voice, her mind;
May they be made as offering to her;
    That which is good,
May it be made as offering to her,
May it be made as offering to her.

From: *Chants of the Creation Myth*, Museum of Navaho
Ceremonial Art.

curing bodily injuries. One of the Holyway curing group, *Beauty-way*, will likely be given if snakes have been offended. If lightning or thunder must be appeased, a *Shootingway* will be used. Where one has trouble from contact with bears, the *Mountain Topway* is the proper treatment. Sometimes a Navaho contracts illness from a non-Navaho, and then he needs to have the *Enemyway* performed. The Enemyway was formerly used in connection with war.

All Navaho rites are accompanied by social functions. One of the features of the Enemyway is the so-called squaw dance. Originally, the intention of this dance was to announce publicly the fact that the girls participating in the ceremony, and who asked the young men to dance with them, were of marriageable age. The young men came to sing and to look over the girls. And crowds gathered to watch the procedure. Today, squaw dances are popular with Indian and non-Indian audiences alike. Groups of Navaho often perform them publicly; and non-Indian people frequently participate. Since the man has to give the girl a present—commonly money—before she will release him from dancing with her, an innocent "victim" may afford the audience much amusement before he "catches on"; and he may accumulate considerable indebtedness to the girl. The squaw dance goes on all night long.

The *Blessingway* places the Navaho in tune with the Holy People. It is performed in approval of a newly selected headman, for an expectant mother, for men going away in their country's service or upon their return. Blessingway songs are sung in the girls' puberty rites and in marriage ceremonies.

Navaho boys and girls are introduced to full participation in ceremonial life by a short initiation rite which is usually held on the next to last night of the *Nightway*. The initiation ceremony and the entire Nightway are popularly known as the *Yeibichei*. The name comes from the principal figures in the initiation ceremony, who represent yé'ii. The Nightway is one of the few Navaho chants that has an attending public dance.

Nightway (Yeibichei)   The Nightway is a nine-day ceremonial, during which the patient is treated. It is a complex of ceremonies, having a name and an origin legend, carried out according to a certain ritual. Singing occurs for nine nights, sandpaintings are made on the last four days, and prayers and other symbolic offerings and rituals are tendered. On the ninth night comes the climax, a drama illustrating an elaborate myth. The Navaho ride in from far and near, make camp, build their fires, and arrange themselves for the night.

Necessary for the enactment of the Nightway are actors representing certain yé'ii: Talking God (who is also called Yeibichei, "Grandfather of the gods"), Born-of-water, and preferably twelve dancers, representing male and female deities in equal numbers. Monster Slayer, Calling God, Black God, Fringed Mouth, and others may also appear. With these are the singer and the patient.

The dancers impersonating male divinities have their naked torsos, upper extremities, and thighs whitened. Each wears a mask, collar of spruce, loincloth of some showy material, dark wool stockings with red woven garters and moccasins, a silver concha belt with foxskin suspended in the rear, ear pendants, bracelets, and many necklaces of shell, turquois, silver, and coral. In the right hand, each carries a gourd rattle painted white and sometimes decorated with spruce twigs; in the left hand is a spruce twig wand. The casque-shaped mask is painted blue, with a horizontal yellow streak at the bottom crossed by four pairs of perpendicular black lines. A fringe of hair crosses the mask from side to side over the crown of the head. Small eye holes are outlined by red triangles. From the front of the mask, a snout projects; at its base, is a fringe of fur. Two eagle plumes and a bunch of owl feathers are affixed to the mask.

Dancers who impersonate female deities are usually small men or youths. Sometimes women take part; and when they do, they dress in ordinary female costume with which they wear a mask like that of the men. They carry no rattles, but have spruce boughs in each hand. They have no foxskin and wear no blanket; and they dance a different step from that of the men. When men impersonate female deities, they sing in falsetto and wear an ornate kilt or scarf around the hips. Otherwise, they are dressed like the other dancers with whitened body, concha belt with fox skin hanging behind, dark wool stockings and moccasins, ear pendants, necklaces, and bracelets, but in each hand, they carry spruce boughs and their masks are different. The masks cover only the face and throat, and the hair flows free. The masks are nearly square, slightly rounded at the top, painted blue, but with white "ears" protruding at the sides; eye margins are black triangles, and black squares surround the mouth holes; from the bottom of a mask may hang a piece of red cloth, and at the top may be a fringe of short hair. At the center of the top is tied a piece of abalone shell with turkey, eagle, or woodpecker feathers behind it; beads, bits of shell, and other articles of adornment may be added.

The dancers are dressed and painted in the medicine hogan; then they go into an arbor across a cleared area in front of the hogan where they get their masks, wands, and rattles. The performance is in two parts: outside is dancing and singing; within the hogan is chanting, but no dancing.

The visitor will become conscious of soft singing, to the accompaniment of the swishing rhythm of rattles, coming from the hogan. After a time, the performers enter the dancing area. The singer leads the procession. He is followed by Talking God, then the dancers in single file, and Born-of-water in the rear. When all are in front of the hogan, the singer turns and faces the others, who halt. The patient, warned by a call, comes from the hogan. Patient and singer then walk along the line of dancers, from west to east. The singer takes meal from a basket carried by the patient and, as they pass each dancer, he sprinkles it on the right arm. Sometimes, the patient takes part in the sprinkling. Patient and singer then turn, sunwise, and retrace their steps to the front of the hogan and face the dancers. The dancers have taken up the sprinkling movements and continue them. Then, with shaking of rattles, and whooping, the dancing and singing get under way.

Born-of-water serves as clown. While the others are dancing, he engages in all sorts of capers, getting in their way, sometimes imitating Talking God, losing some item of attire and making a great to-do about it, dancing, and acting as buffoon in general.

Throughout the night, different acts are performed in an orderly and regular manner. The participants take short rest periods. It is said the most desirable number of repetitions of the dance is forty-eight, when four sets of dancers perform twelve times each. But many variations from the standard may be seen. After the dancers have finished their last song, singers inside the hogan chant the four Finishing Hymns; one or more assistants may aid the singer, sitting at his right. Those who are near the hogan may hear this singing, but few white people are privileged to witness the ceremony within a medicine lodge. As the last verse is sung, the singer overturns an inverted basket drum toward the west, making movements as though releasing winged insects from under the basket and driving them out through the smoke hole in the roof; he blows a breath after the invisible insects as they supposedly depart. During this song, an assistant to the singer has been applying meal to the lower jaw of the patient. Finally, an act of unraveling the drumstick is performed. While an assistant carries out this procedure, the singer gives final instructions to the patient. All are then free to depart. Certain taboos must be observed and definite rites followed. The patient must not go to sleep before sunset. The singer retires to the medicine hogan to sleep and must do so for four consecutive nights. (Matthews 1902)

Mountain Topway   The Mountain Topway—commonly known as the Mountain Chant—is usually held over nine consecutive days. The first four days are not of particular interest to the general visitor. On the fifth day, in conjunction with the curative rites, the first sandpainting is made in the hogan. Other paintings are made on the three succeeding days. On the ninth day, preparation goes forward for the nighttime ceremonies—the making of plumed arrows, wands, trees, and so forth. The final night is the big spectacle. A great woodpile is surrounded by a huge corral with an opening to the east. It is made of evergreen branches. As this corral is being finished—just after sunset—the head singer stands at the entrance, singing and shaking his rattle. As night falls, the Navaho spectators enter the sacred enclosure, build their small fires near the confining wall and settle themselves to watch the night's performances.

When the great bonfire is roaring, a warning whistle is heard from the outer darkness. A dozen lithe, lean men come bounding into the corral. They wear only breechclouts and moccasins. Their bodies are painted white. They carry feather-tipped wands which they wave to the four directions as they move around the fire. The heat is terrific, but they circle it twice. Then, they plunge toward the flames, close enough to burn the plumes from the ends of their wands. The next feat is for each to restore the feathers to his wands.

Because of this startling spectacle at the beginning, this ceremony is frequently called the fire dance. A dozen or so dances may follow—each with its chorus of male singers. Acts such as arrow swallowing, growing of the yucca plant, feathers dancing in a basket, and other skillful legerdemain may be performed. Very elaborate costumes are worn.

The final act in this ceremony is another fire dance around the renewed fire. Before the dancers appear, strange sounds are heard in the distance—the blowing of horns and shrill calls. As the sounds come closer, perhaps ten men advance through the eastern entryway into the corral. They wear only narrow loincloths and moccasins, and their bodies are covered with white clay, giving them a ghostly appearance. Each man, except the leader, carries a long, thick bundle of shredded juniper bark in each hand; and one carries an extra bundle for the leader to use later. The leader carries four small fagots of flaming juniper bark. All dance around the great central fire four times, waving their bundles toward the fire. On the east side, they halt; the leader advances toward the fire, kindles one of the fagots, shouts loudly, and tosses it over the east wall of the corral. Then, they move around to the south, the west, and the north, where similar acts are performed. But before the leader throws the burning brand to the north, he lights the bark bundles of the other dancers.

The entire group begins to dance wildly about the roaring fire. They run hither and yon, the breeze fanning the brands into long brilliant streamers of flame, which play upon the bodies of the participants. As the bundles burn, glowing fragments drop off; these are tossed about or thrown upon the other dancers. Every time a brand is applied to the flesh of one of the performers, the trumpeting sound is heard. The juniper bundles are relighted from the central fire in case they cease to burn. When a brand finally is consumed, the dancer drops the ash and runs out of the corral. One by one, they all disappear. (Mathews 1887)

The fire dies; dawn comes. Three more openings are broken in the corral wall. The Indians pick up their blankets and fire-blackened coffee pots, mount horses or pile into wagons or motor vehicles, and head for home. By the time the sun is well over the horizon, the cars are out of sight, but the horses and wagons are still drawing crooked lines across the countryside.

The fire dance is frequently performed alone at public exhibitions, such as at ceremonial events in Gallup, the Flagstaff Pow-wow, and similar exhibitions, where it makes a dramatic climax to an evening's program.

Most of the Navaho chants can be held at any time of the year, but the curing ceremonials are restricted to certain months. The Nightway and the Mountain Topway cannot be given until after the first killing frost; they are usually held in November and December. The Enemyway is generally performed after completion of the spring work and before the harvesting and marketing season arrives.

The Ramah Navaho (*see* pp. 110-12) do not hold some of the longer chants, such as the Nightway and Mountain Topway, but many of the shorter ceremonials are performed frequently. Local practitioners—who include singers, curers, prayer makers, diagnosticians, and witches—know about twenty different ceremonials. Around twenty adult men are classed as practitioners, but most of these are curers, who know only part of a ceremonial, as opposed to singers who know at least one ceremonial of five or more nights' duration. (*See* Vogt 1951:17) All who practice any form of divination are known as diagnosticians, "those who investigate to reveal." (Kluckhohn and Wyman 1940:15-16) A dozen or so of the Ramah men and women are diagnosticians.

Cost of ceremonials is borne by the patient or by his family. Today, that means as much as seven hundred dollars or more for a Yeibichei, and four hundred dollars for a squaw dance. A Yeibichei singer receives from seventy-five dollars to one hundred and fifty dollars in cash, plus one hundred dollars to two hundred dollars worth of goods, and small contributions from people going in to witness the sandpaintings. For a squaw dance, the singer may get twenty-five dollars for preparations and procedural instructions, plus a possible additional take from contributions during the ceremony. Those assisting the singer are also paid. Equipment such as baskets, herbs, deer skins, and the like, must be purchased. And, most important of all, those who attend the ceremonial must be fed. Thus, all Navaho ceremonials are expensive undertakings.

The Peyote Cult   During the difficult times that prevailed in the 1930's, the peyote cult gained a foothold among the Navaho and some of the other Southwestern Indians. Peyote, a hallucinogenic cactus, had been widely used among Mexican Indians in religious rites since prehistoric times. Spanish documents mention it early in the seventeenth century. Until the 1800's, peyote was eaten by Indian peoples privately to induce visions or as a trance-producing feature of group dancing. Then, toward the end of the nineteenth century, use of peyote became the core of a new ceremonial complex among the Indians of Oklahoma; it was highly developed by the Kiowa and spread to other Indians who used peyote in various rites.

In 1918, a number of the Indian peoples in Oklahoma incorporated a movement known as the Native American Church; peyote served as the means of spiritual communion between man and his deity—known to the Navaho as *pioniyo*. The Navaho, around 1940, began to practice the peyote cult with increasing vigor. They learned the peyote ceremony from the Ute Indians of southern Colorado, who are said to have used peyote for years.

In 1944, the name was changed to the "Native American Church of the United States," and in 1955, it was changed again, to the "Native American Church of North America," to include Canadian peyote groups. (Anonymous 1970a:12)

For a long time, the use of peyote by the Navaho was "an underground phenomenon, illegal by tribal law, the subject of fierce, though carefully hushed, controversy. Now, it is said to be surfacing as one of the Navaho's most significant cultural crutches in a troubled time. The cult displays a unique blending of traditional Navaho ceremonialism, fundamentalist Christian elements, and 'pan-Indian moral principles' " (Nabokov 1969:129*); it appears to be meeting the deepest spiritual needs of a transitional people. Estimates of the practicing Navaho membership in the Four Corners region run from one-third to 80 per cent.

The increase of peyotism seems due, largely, to the introduction of new and varied doctrines by missionaries of differing Christian denominations. In the majority of instances, the result was a partial Christianization, which left the Navaho (and other Indian groups) with a sense of insecurity regarding their traditional religion. One investigator, who made an in-depth survey at mission stations on the Navaho reservation, found that "a good deal of Christian mission work completely missed the idea that religion is involved in the whole life for any people who have come out of animism," as have the Navaho. It was noted that the Native American Church has positive values in its favor, for example, emphasis on family life and stress on fellowship. The investigator stated that, "Despite twenty-five years of work, and considerable expenditure, mission work for the church I was studying had made an unsatisfactory impact." (*See* Thrapp 1967:II:6)

Before the peyote cult reached the Navaho, nothing seemed to bridge the gap between the old ceremonial ways and the new patterns resulting from culture changes and the demands of the modern world. More and more, the ills which formerly called forth a singer to perform a Navahoway, or a curing ceremony, came to be met by Peyote Road rites.

A recent participant in a Navaho peyote ceremony has stated that peyote (*Lophophora williamsii*) when eaten, produces "relatively standard physiological effects, but markedly varying psychological ones, depending on the user's cultural background." He explains that:

Peyote's make-up of alkaloids—at least 15 at latest count, the most studied being mescaline—acts like a series of timed depth charges. First comes an unpleasant, stomach-unsettling sensation. Within a half-hour this dies, leaving a face starting to flush, pupils dilating, salivation increasing and a sense of exhilaration growing through the body, resembling the effect of swift intakes of pure oxygen. Then one moves into a period of withdrawal, of intense color awareness, of successions of hallucinations when eyes are closed, energies focused inward.

A few hours later, this levels off onto an intense plateau. Then whatever one is prompted to concentrate upon—here the cultural situation is a critical determinant—becomes uncannily luminous. During these hours, reflexes are heightened, occasional muscle twitching is common, time is overestimated, spacial perception is altered, hearing and sight yield intensified tones, ideas flow rapidly, but physical movement is awkward.

This final period . . . diminishes through the following day with no aftereffects . . . ." (Nabokov 1969:30*)

The performance of rites of the Peyote Road is a dusk-to-dawn affair which is conducted by an officiating priest known as the Road Chief. He is assisted by three other principals: a Drummer Chief who does much of the drumming, the Cedar Chief who sprinkles powdered juniper ("cedar") on the fire during the meeting, and a Fire Chief. With "Indian sage," the Road Chief prepares an altar on the floor of a hogan, shredding the sage while the Fire Chief, who sits on the north side of the door, tends the fire built in the center of the chamber of uniformly split wood. The sticks are arranged in V-shape, and flames rise upward from the tip. Then, the Road Chief arranges a nest of sage pods in the middle of the altar which he has fashioned in a crescent of earth known as the Peyote Moon. A large peyote blossom is carefully placed in the sage bed, representing the Peyote Chief, symbol of the spiritual medium of the Peyote Road.

After the altar has been prepared, the participants take the sacramental food, munching on peyote buds that have been sliced and dried, or sipping brewed "tea" made therefrom. The final period of effectiveness is entered toward midnight. Then, the Road Chief readies a kettle drum, inside of which are a few soaked coals and water "to 'strengthen' the drumbeats." The religious services then begin—a night of ceremonial praying, smoking, and singing, of confessing and weeping, which continue until dawn. Then, a traditional blessing of the peyote breakfast occurs, followed by a final prayer.

Such ceremonies take place on Thanksgiving eve and the night before Christmas and the New Year, at Easter, the Fourth of July, and on Armed Forces Day.

Insignia of the peyote cult consist of a cardinal red tie and socks, silver "water bird" ornament, and a rectangular box made of

*© 1969 by The New York Times Company. Reproduced by permission.

"cedar" for ritual paraphernalia—feathered fans, drum, eagle bone whistle, gourd rattles with beaded handles, and a horsehair-tipped staff. As one travels through Navaholand, the decals he sees with the letters "N.A.C." and a spread-wing bird motif affixed to car or truck windows indicate membership in the Native American Church.

State and federal laws are in conflict and confusion regarding the legality of use of peyote. A bill permitting the use of peyote for bona fide religious purposes was passed by the New Mexico Legislature in 1956. Four years later, the state of Arizona decreed peyote use legal for NAC members, and a few other states have taken similar action; federal tolerance of its ritual use depends largely upon a Supreme Court ruling of 1961.

It is recorded that: "On October 9, 1967, the Navajo Tribal Council adopted a declaration of basic Navajo rights which cancelled all previous laws denying freedom of religion inconsistent with this declaration."

Title 17, subchapter 21, section 641, of the Navajo Tribal Code, in re "sale, use or possession" of peyote, states:

It shall be unlawful for any person to transport peyote into Navajo country or buy, sell, possess or use peyote in any form, and any person convicted of violating this provision shall be guilty of a misdemeanor punishable by a fine not to exceed $100 or imprisonment not to exceed nine months or both; provided that it shall not be unlawful for any member of the Native American Church to transport peyote into Navajo country, or buy, sell, possess or use peyote in any form, in connection with the religious practices, sacraments or services of the Native American Church. (Anonymous 1970a:12)

The Navaho, like all other Americans, have been beset by the barrage of capitalized initials that are poured continually into governmental nomenclature, the news media, and everyday speech. Much of the time, those outside a particular organization have little or no concept of what various initials may denote. Then, when the Navaho, or others, select initials to indicate certain committees, groups, agencies, operations, and the like in their *own* language, the uninitiated are indeed perplexed. (Yes, the Navaho language has now been fully recorded, as set forth by Young). (Young 1961:430-500)

One reading periodicals, viewing TV, or listening to radios which report happenings in the Southwest frequently sees or hears comments on DNA. These initials are seldom explained. And small wonder. They refer to *Dinebeiina Nahiilna be Agaditahe*, Navaho for the Office-of-Economic-Opportunity-financed "Attorneys who contribute to the revitalization of the people." (Anonymous 1970g)

**OFF-RESERVATION
NAVAHO GROUPS**

Ramah Navaho

Not only visitors in the Southwest, but residents of New Mexico as well, are often surprised to learn that several groups of Navaho Indians have lands located away from the main reservation. The largest of these is the *Ramah Navaho*, numbering 1,380, of whom 1,075 reside in the community. Their land lies southeast of Ramah, New Mexico, both north and south of El Morro National Monument on State Highway 53, a few miles east of the pueblo of Zuñi. This is a belt approximately eighteen by thirty miles in extent, with elevation averaging around 7,000 feet, but ranging up to 9,000 feet in the mountains, where good hunting is offered. Although there are deep canyons to the north, most of the region consists of broad valleys covered with grass or sagebrush bordered by ridges forested with piñon and juniper. Nearly five hundred different kinds of plants have been identified in the area, and the Navaho knew the names of all but three of these. (*See* Vestal 1952)

Some of the Navaho and also a number of Apaches managed to escape from Fort Sumner during their exile. We are told that among the Navaho escapees were the parents of a man known as Many Beads, who went to live among the Chiricahua Apache. Many Beads had a son who was born among the Chiricahua and was but two years old when the Navaho captives began their trek back from captivity. Learning of this movement, the lad's parents also set forth for their old homeland. After a winter spent at Acoma, the family settled in the mountains near Fort Wingate. There they were joined by Many Beads, who accompanied them back to a place where they had dwelt formerly, at a spring near present Ramah (where Mormon missionaries in 1876 persuaded the Navaho to allow them to establish a small colony—which, in spite of a severe smallpox epidemic, was refounded in 1882 and has grown into a community of several hundred people). Another Navaho and his mother lived there likewise, and thus, we know of the two families in that locality about 1876; undoubtedly, others settled there, for the released captives strongly tended to return to their former homesites. The son of Many Beads became a patriarch of the community and longtime leader. (*See* Young 1968:43)

The Ramah Navaho have a political structure with characteristics of a band. It has long had a single headman. Through time, a number of factions have developed, following the conservative and progressive pattern of so many Indian groups. The former wish to continue their old ways, while the latter favor the ways of the white man. Of the total of 146,996 acres under control of the Ramah group, less than 200 acres are farmed, and livestock is grazed. In most ways, the ceremonial structure follows that of the other Navaho.

The people of the community constitute the Ramah Chapter; this has a president, and an elected delegate to the Navajo Tribal Council.

For their education, about one hundred youngsters of this Navaho group ride buses from their homes to the Ramah public school. For 148, dormitory space has been provided so that students can live in Ramah. The dormitory system operates in a modern facility consisting of four separate buildings that are divided into sections and attractively decorated; the grounds are well landscaped. Each building houses a different age group and sex. In January, 1970, the staff numbered twenty-seven being comprised mostly of Navaho and Zuñi people trained in the problems of children.

Although the Navaho long opposed the dormitory idea because it took the youngsters away from home, they came to realize the benefits not possible in the scattered, dirt-floor hogans: good food regularly served, running water, children and toys with which to play, as well as education.

Each section of the dorm consists of a room divided into sleeping quarters, a lounge area with television and desks, and a recreation area. The children sleep in bunk beds and each shares a dresser with another child. Each one performs a daily chore, attends classes and studies; otherwise, time is free to do as one wishes. Tutors are available to assist those having difficulties with their studies.

In addition to some four hundred school-age Navaho who do not live in the dorm or come to Ramah by bus, one hundred others ride a bus to the Fence Lake School; a few attend the school at Fort Wingate or the Intermountain School at Brigham City, Utah; and several go to school in Salt Lake City. In 1970, one hundred and twenty were enrolled in the Albuquerque Indian School. It is planned that more school and dormitory buildings will be built in Ramah.

Some years ago, a fine school building was constructed there and equipped for students of high school grades, the Gallup-McKinley County High School. Then, in 1968, the plant was abandoned and allowed to fall into disrepair. The students were sent by bus to schools in Zuñi or towns miles distant, and frequently to boarding schools in California, Utah or Oklahoma. The Ramah Navaho fought this action effectively and set about to establish a school of their own. Funds were secured from the BIA, OEO, and from private foundations.

The Ramah school board was incorporated in February, 1970, and a summer session was opened in June. The school board involved the Navaho people of the district; and the summer project brought a Neighborhood Youth Corps into the picture. Living in tents, the students started work aided by adult Navaho workmen from Ramah. A new roof was placed on the old school building and general repairs were made. The students entered into the creation of courses for their school; students and their parents were polled to determine what the people closest to the school felt it should offer. Then only was a teaching staff hired, a staff of broad and varied backgrounds. It is felt that upon being graduated from this high school, the young people should be able to understand and participate in Navaho culture, "be employable, and be able to go to college if they choose." (Bartel 1970:2B; Waliczek 1970) A number of vocational and cultural areas considered to be a part of the school's curriculum have been stressed. The director was to be a Navaho, and the initial non-Indian personnel to be replaced by qualified Indians.

The Edward Elliott Foundation of New York helped fund the summer school, and officers of the foundation are deeply impressed by the efforts of the Navaho to control their own school.

The Puertocito (Alamo) Navaho

Next in size of the off-reservation groups is the *Puertocito Navaho*, a band that has been separated from the main body for some one hundred-odd years. This group developed in part from Navaho slaves who ran away from their Spanish masters living in Socorro. They congregated at Alamo, or "at Field's place," about thirty-five miles northwest of Magdalena, New Mexico; from this location, they are commonly called the "Alamo Navaho." It is said that they were once part of the "enemy Navaho," and that they are called *Tsa Dei'alth*, or "stone chewers," for, when they fought, they got so angry that they chewed rocks. (*See* Harrington 1940:515-516)

The few who settled in the Field locality intermarried with Chiricahua and Mescalero Apaches and with Mexicans; they were joined by Navaho from other areas, some of whom fled there to escape Kit Carson, and others who fled from Fort Sumner. Between 1912 and 1920, allotments were made to these Puertocito Navaho, and purchased lands were added to their holdings by the federal government and the Navaho tribe. Their domain now embraces some 56,670 acres, and their population is about 920. The land is semiarid, with many deep arroyos and high mesas. Grass is in limited supply among the piñon and juniper growth.

In 1941, a day school was built and opened for the Alamo youngsters. Teachers did not like the isolation and student attendance was irregular; as a result, the school failed. A survey made in 1959 revealed the average adult education to be one and a half years. That year, a dormitory was opened at Magdalena so students could live there and attend the public schools. The graveled road to Magdalena was improved; otherwise, country roads and dim trails must be followed over the reservation.

Until the early 1960's, almost everyone lived in log-built hogans. Then, a house-building project was initiated and now most of the Navaho families have moved into new homes. Each faces the east, as do traditional hogans. In 1967, a Rural Electrification Administration power line was brought to the reservation, enabling the people to have modern appliances for the first time. The main water source, Alamo Springs, was improved and the beginnings of a running water system was started.

The political structure follows that of the main reservation. (*See* Euler 1961)

The Cañoncito Navaho

A third group, which lives some twenty-five miles west from Albuquerque, a few miles north of Interstate Highway I-40, is known as the *Dine'é Ana'i*, or "enemy Navaho." They derive from Navaho who had moved southwestward into the Cebolleta Mountains under Spanish pressure during the eighteenth century, and they remained there when the main body of Navaho moved to the west. Then, as those who had been confined at Fort Sumner trekked back toward their homeland, Chief Delgadito separated about four hundred people from the seven thousand who left Fort Sumner on 15 June 1868—fifteen days after the Treaty of 1868 was signed. These returned to their old territory in the Cebolleta region. Later, remnants of Sandoval's Cebolleta band received allotments and other lands in what came to be known as the Cañoncito reservation. Since those earlier days, other Navaho have married into the community. Today, they number close to 1,125. Their land holdings total 76,813 acres.

In 1969, the Cañoncito group initiated an annual rodeo. This is scheduled around the middle of July, and may follow a horse sale. The rodeo features bareback riding and bull riding, calf roping, team roping, and barrel racing. Winners of each event, based on average points, receive awards. Refreshments are sold.

Each of these off-reservation groups lives in accordance with the general pattern of Navaho culture. They all engage in farming and stock raising. Few arts are practiced; certain Cañoncito women make fine fabric dolls with characteristic adornments, and they fashion attractive beaded ornaments. A limited number of baskets are made by the Ramah Navaho.

The "Checkerboard Area"

In addition to the above off-reservation peoples, about 25,000 Navaho live in the so-called "checkerboard area." This extends eastward from the Navaho reservation to the Jicarilla Apache reservation, and south of that beyond the town of Cuba. Here the public domain (662,776 acres) has been allotted so that each alternate square mile is Indian land, with non-Indian sections in between—hence the designation checkerboard. The normal allotment to an Indian is 160 acres. The Eastern Navajo School has been built south of Huerfano Mesa—a modern community near the Blanco Trading Post—and that area is called the Eastern Navajo District by the government officers at Crown Point.

GREAT WIDE BEAUTIFUL

that's how I describe the Apache land
on which I live.
You see, I'm an Apache
living around wonderful rivers, grass and cactus.
I will long remember the times I had
with my mother when we walked across fields
among the dancing flowers. With a mother around
every joy is here.
We went through places where long ago
my people once lived
and now it is deserted
with trees, weeds, growing here and there.
Mountains are on all sides blue, green mixed together,
which makes a pretty color. . . .
And before us was a river flowing
and alongside it were grasses, trees
dancing among the breeze: then. . . .
Slowly we started home in the direction
where the sun was setting.
This place which I call home is really my home
and I hope it always will be.

By Lenora Palmer (White Mountain Apache)

From: *Art and Indian Children.* Curriculum Bulletin No. 7, 1970. Institute of American Indian Arts, Santa Fe, N. M.

.... THE APACHE INDIANS

The Apache peoples spread southward, as Athabascan bands, along the easternside of the Rocky Mountains. Each local group had a headman, who led by reason of prestige and good example, and a headwoman, whose function was to council her people in the ways of living, and especially to organize wild food-gathering parties among the women.

Our data on the Apaches have come mostly from documentary accounts written by non-Indians and from ethnological studies. It was said that the Apache dwellings were similar to the forked-stick hogan, and they had many culture traits akin to those of the Navaho of the Gobernador Phase. In their migrations, they picked up numerous Plains Indian characteristics, such as the type of dwellings (tipi), articles of attire and hair styles, and perhaps, elementary knowledge of horticulture.

Not a great deal has been known about the Apaches archaeologically, although the late Carl Lumholtz is said to have dug some sites in Chihuahua, Mexico, about the turn of the twentieth century (See Lister 1958 and Lumholtz 1902) and certain investigators have engaged in local studies (See Gerald 1958; Gunnerson 1960; 1969a; Gunnerson and Gunnerson 1970; 1971a, 1971b) These latter works have revealed that: "For two centuries or more, many Apaches were peaceful farmers, living in permanent villages on the eastern edge of the American Southwest and in the central and southern plains." In the Southwest, these Apaches "rapidly learned a new way of life that included dependence upon corn. They manufactured pottery, and constructed houses more permanent than the skin tepees in which they had originally lived." Working along the eastern base of the Sangre de Cristo mountain range, near Cimarron and Las Vegas, New Mexico, in 1967, the archaeologists made an exciting discovery; they uncovered a seven-room adobe dwelling that had been built around 1700 by the Jicarilla Apache, in Pueblo manner. (See Gunnerson 1969a)

The cultural material associated with the house structures indicated extensive trade with the Pueblos and western Texas peoples. The Apache evidently went on bison hunting expeditions. At another site, evidence was found of a type of dwelling not previously identified with the Apache—a circular pit about twelve feet in diameter and two feet deep, which had had a rock wall laid

115

up around it and roofed over. Spanish contact materials were found there. A large site near Las Vegas exhibited more of the ringed construction. Some 250 rings of rocks appeared to have been used to hold down the bottoms of tipis. There, residence was less permanent, and this indicates a shifting from location on the valley floors to low terraces (reflecting a need for more protection from unfriendly peoples, such as the Comanche). Trade items in these villages appear to date in the nineteenth century. (*See* Anonymous 1967)

In 1969 and 1970, investigations were made at the ruins of Pecos, for the pueblo had been an important trading center for Pueblo-Plains Indians in the late 1600's and early 1700's, and probably long before. Within the confines of the Pecos National Monument, nine areas were found that yielded Apache pottery. Other sites in the area will be discovered with further investigating.

The historical Apache were known as notable enemies whose hardihood was incredible. Meat was the favorite food, and where available, mescal was harvested and eaten in great quantities. When necessary, the Apache literally could "live off the land," eating berries, roots, seeds, cactus, or crawling animals (but never fish, or snakes—which they feared—or turkeys and dogs that ate them). They were extremely healthy before European diseases were introduced, and could go practically naked in zero weather.

Characteristically, the Apache has a splendid physique. Although individuals vary greatly, the people average above medium height. The well-formed head rests on a short muscular neck. The face is broad, with high cheekbones and strong nose. Apache men have rather sparse beards which they formerly plucked.

Little girls were given the same training as boys. Every day, they practiced with bow and arrows, slings and spears. They were taught to mount an unsaddled horse without help, and to ride expertly. At puberty, Apache youths were tested in all kinds of hardships by their elders. Girls went through extensive rites, of which more is written below.

The Apache men have high regard for their women; in days of old, particularly, they were respected, cherished, and protected. Chastity was rigidly enforced. Children were seldom spaced closer than four years. In times of warfare, wives were permitted to go on the warpath with their husbands. With the Apache, scalping was not a custom; they abhorred mutilation. When death occurred, sympathy was not extended by words. A killing obliged the next of kin to seek revenge. Great store was set by promises, and a liar was despised by all. The Apache felt that "without respect no human relationship (was) of any value." (Ball 1970:29)

Essentially, the Apache were a mountain people, traveling from ridge to ridge, but they were at home equally in the parched semidesert wastes by which they were surrounded; they were hunting and fighting people. As one writer has said summarily:

They moved about freely, wintering on the Río Grande or farther south, ranging the buffalo plains in the summer, always following the sun and the food supply. They owned nothing and everything. They did as they pleased and bowed to no man. Their women were chaste. Their leaders kept their promises. They were mighty warriors who depended on success in raiding for wealth and honor. To their families they were kind and gentle, but they could be unbelievably cruel to their enemies—fierce and revengeful when they felt that they had been betrayed. (Sonnichsen 1958:4)

They became primarily tipi-dwellers. Those who lived in the forested dells in the mountains erected shelters fashioned of slender poles which were covered with brush and grass—the wickiup. Two general types of these were used: one built on a tipi frame, and the true dome-shaped *wickiup.* Each was built with doorway toward the east. Adopting matrilineal descent, the Apache also took over matrilocal residence as a social pattern. (*See* Kaut 1957:39) Band exogamy was not required, but marriages between kinsmen were forbidden. A girl's mother and other female relatives constructed a dwelling for a newly married couple, not far distant from the maternal abode. The mother-in-law taboo is observed, and cousins of the opposite sex are not supposed to talk directly; they should have some sort of a screen between, or at least have their backs to each other. Kinship is reckoned bilaterally.

Rather than shaking hands, or kissing, as is common in many cultures, Apaches embrace upon meeting one another. The Apache is very modest, and the privacy of others is highly respected.

THE CHIRICAHUA AND MESCALERO

The Chiricahua and Mescalero Apaches are closely related, and they formerly occupied adjacent areas. It is commonly said that the Chiricahua territory lay to the west of the Río Grande, centering around Ojo Caliente, or Warm Springs, the water of which seeps from the foot of a little hill on the west side of the San Mateo range, north of Monticello, New Mexico; from there, bands, numbering around one thousand persons in all, ranged through southwestern New Mexico and southeastern Arizona, and over the northern parts of Sonora and Chihuahua in Mexico. By the seventeenth century, they were strongly entrenched in those regions and fighting to retain them.

More details have been given recently by James Kaywaykla, an Apache who was born near Warm Springs and who died in 1963 at the age of about ninety years. Early writers included the Warm Springs Apaches as Chiricahua, but Kaywaykla has said that the Apaches themselves recognized four bands; of these, only the groups headed by Cochise and by Chihuahua were true Chiricahua.

In the words of Kaywaykla, "Juh was chief of the *Nednhi* Apaches, whose stronghold was in the Sierra Madre of Mexico (their "Blue Mountains"). Gerónimo was leader, but not chief of the *Bedonkohes*, whose territory was around the headwaters of the Gila. Though closely associated, we were distinct groups." The Warm Springs Apache in their own tongue were *Chihinne*, or "Red People," so called because of a band of red clay which was painted accross their faces. (Ball 1970: xiv)*

The band was the political unit, with leader and followers. This system had no tribal chief, no council of leaders, and no device for decision making. The bands were not local groups; "they were not resource holding units, and exercised no control over a specific portion of land." (Basehart 1970:92) For another thing, bands "grew, lost members, disappeared, and new groups developed," resulting in "a continual but gradual redistribution of the population." (Basehart 1970:93) This was difficult for the white officials to comprehend; they needed some or fixed point of reference.

If a band was small, the members usually formed a single scattered encampment; larger bands might have several camps. The core of a band was a "relative group," primarily—but not necessarily—kinsmen.

The Apache women of these bands wore two-piece dresses made of calico; skirts were long and full, and long blouses were worn outside of the skirt belts. Each woman carried a knife, and some had ammunition belts and rifles. Apache girls had their hair arranged around two willow hoops, worn over the ears. Some of the older women dressed their hair in Plains Indian manner, parted in the middle, with two braids. The attire for warriors consisted of calico shirt, a muslin breechclout supported by a belt, one or more

---

In the Days of Victorio: Recollections of a Warm Springs Apache, James K. Kaywaykla, Narrator, by Eve Ball, Tucson: University of Arizona Press, copyright 1970. All quotations reproduced by permission.

cartridge belts, moccasins, and a headband to keep their long hair out of the eyes. To distinguish themselves, the Warm Springs people wore a band of buckskin, colored yellow with sacred pollen of cattails, over the right shoulder and tied to the belt under the left arm. Buckskin shirts and beaded robes of the women were used for ceremonial attire. Blankets, too, were used. Some men wore large, loose deerskin coats in winter.

The moccasins had high tops that could be drawn up for warmth, or could be folded below the knee for protection against thorns and rock. Kaywaykla has said: "In those folds we carried our valuable possessions, valuable primarily in the sense of usefulness. Sometimes these included extra cowhide soles, for soles wore out quickly and had to be replaced. We carried the endthorns of a mescal plant with fiber attached for sewing the soles to the uppers. The soles were tanned with the hair left on, and they projected beyond the toes and terminated in a circular flap with a metal button sewed to the center. This piece turned back over the toes for additional protection. Because we frequently had to abandon our horses to scale cliffs, the moccasin was our most important article of dress." (Ball 1970:17-18)

In Kaywaykla's youth, Victorio (who succeeded Mangas Coloradas, after Cuchillo Negro had been leader for a time) was their chief; among the notable leaders were Nana and Loco, et al. Leaders were men of influence rather than wielders of power.

When the U.S.A. assumed sovereignty over New Mexico in 1848, the Mescalero utilized the country to the east of the Río Grande, extending from northern Mexico to the region south of Santa Fe; a branch dwelt on the plains in western Texas. Natziti was the head chief, a contemporary of Victorio. The Apaches all knew their territory intimately; they had no specially built strongholds but survived by ranging rapidly in and out of wild, rugged places. When they camped, they never stayed close to the edge of a water body, for "the water belonged to all creatures, not man alone." They selected a campsite in a grassy location or a wooded area and carried water from the source to the camp.

Horses were well cared for, never ridden to death. The Apache did not travel at night, nor did they fight during the nighttime unless forced to do so by soldiers or others.

Harassment and encroachment by the Spaniards, conflicts with the Comanche during the latter part of the eighteenth century, then Mexican domination and the American occupation of the mid-1800's with its increasing pressures and controls; such vicissitudes were more than these free souls could accept. Their original friendliness toward foreigners ceased. Striving to hold their ancestral lands, their life ways, and their very lives brought forth the fierce emotions of the Apache. Naturally, they raided the newcomers' settlements and drove off their animals—especially horses, mules, and burros, which increased their mobility and speeded their getaway. They killed when it seemed necessary, and came to be the most dreaded warriors of the Southwest.

As the westward expansion of the white men heightened, the Apache were pushed from their holdings and the game upon which they depended was driven away. Having no place to go, they turned southward into Mexico, from where raids were made across the border. After the Mexican and U.S. governments combined efforts to quell the Apaches, life for them became extremely perilous.

In 1863, about four hundred Mescalero Apache were taken to the concentration camp, Bosque Redondo or Fort Sumner, on the Pecos River. (*See* McNitt 1970) Colonel Carleton planned to put all of the Apaches there . . . and make farmers of them! When the Navaho, enemies of the Apaches, were rounded up and confined there, too, the situation became unendurable. Smallpox contracted by the Navaho from the soldiers contaminated the water being used by the Mescalero. Seeing the Navaho dying by the hundreds, the Mescalero took what they could carry and fled to one of their old campsites on the Bonito, above Fort Stanton—which had been established in 1855.

Victorio outwitted Colonel Carleton and kept his band from being sent to Bosque Redondo. By an Executive Order in 1870, the government promised him a permanent reservation for his Chihinne band at Warm Springs. The decimated group assembled there, and an adobe building was erected for their headquarters across the Cañada Alamosa from Warm Springs.

At the same time, Cochise, the Chiricahua chief, who had gathered his band near Warm Springs, was to have a reservation about his stronghold. Neither promise was kept. As a result, Cochise resumed raiding. In 1872, the Chiricahua were separated from the Mescalero by establishment of reservations for each group.

Because another Executive Order had come through, returning the Warm Springs (Chiricahua) reservation to the public domain, Victorio was commanded to move his people to a high mountain valley of the Tularosa River in westernmost New Mexico—a place impossible during the winter. Severe cold, starvation, and death forced the government agent to let the Apache return to Warm Springs for a short time. Other leaders, including Gerónimo, brought their bands to camp in the vicinity.

During 1877, Gerónimo had been joined by bands of Apaches from Mexico, and numerous raids were made in southern New Mexico and Arizona. Victorio received orders from the agent at San Carlos to come there and bring his people. For their compliance, all of the leaders were arrested. Gerónimo and seven other headmen were already there, chained in a corral. Victorio, Nana, and Loco were not confined.

San Carlos was considered to be "the worst place in all Apacheria." (Ball 1970:5) The Apaches were quartered at old Camp Goodwin, which had been abandoned by the cavalry because of many deaths from malaria. Summer temperatures allegedly got as high as 140°. "There was no game, no food except the occasional meager and unfit stuff issued to them (by the Indian agent). The insects swarmed about them and almost devoured the babies." (Ball 1970:50)

During the summer, Victorio saw his people suffer and die. Finally, joined by Nana and Loco, plans for flight were carefully arranged; they evaded the cavalry for weeks, but were eventually captured and imprisoned. The Army fed them until November, 1877, and then returned them to Warm Springs. (Ball 1970:52)

Then came the insidious orders of Carleton—the orders of a man determined to exterminate the Apaches. Victorio was to take his people to San Carlos again . . . that horrible place! If they did not go, the orders stated, every man, woman, or child, found off the reservation was to be shot without being given a chance to surrender.

Nana, who was considered to be the "fiercest and most implacable of all Apaches," (Ball 1970:71) and his followers had no intention of returning to San Carlos. They could have joined Juh in Mexico, but it was decided that the most feasible thing at the time was to join the Mescalero, from whom permission was obtained. In December, 1878, Nana took his Warm Springs band to Blazer's Mill on the Tularosa River in south-central New Mexico, then the headquarters of the Mescalero Apache reservation. Sixty-three were there enrolled, received ration cards, and were issued rations. They were allowed to settle in the remote and rather inaccessible Rinconada canyon—where Nana had previously (and secretly) sent most of his young men and horses. Brush arbors were built and covered with hides; wood, water, and game were abundant. (Ball 1970:25-27)

Victorio, too, came to the Rinconada encampment—with a bounty on his head—for a warrant had been issued for his arrest. The arrival of soldiers at Blazer's caused him and his men to make their way to their sacred mountain in the San Andres, where they could not be captured.

Loco started to take his band to San Carlos on the Gila River. At the east end of Cook's Peak (north of Deming, New Mexico), they were attacked by US Cavalry and several Apache were killed before Loco could convince them that they were going to San Carlos voluntarily. When the soldiers were convinced, they escorted the Apache band toward the Gila. A snowstorm forced them to turn north to Fort Apache, and Loco's group was taken to Camp Goodwin. Victorio learned of these developments, and was prepared to aid Loco, should he decide to flee to Mexico.

Nana decided to lead his people to Chihuahua by way of the Big Bend country in Texas; several other small bands joined in the dangerous journey. Victorio dashed from place to place, drawing the cavalry away from the traveling ones. It is said that Victorio took about four hundred people with him, seventy-five of them warriors; some were Mescalero and Lipan. (Ball 1970:75) In 1880, they headed north again.

Gerónimo made peace with General George Crook in 1882, but this lasted only three years. Then the Apache were forced to assemble again, and raiding was resumed. In 1886, Gerónimo brought his people forth to surrender. As a result, he was imprisoned and sent to confinement in Florida, where the Chiricahua and all associated bands were transferred.

Later, a home for them was sought in Alabama; finally, they were taken to Fort Sill, Oklahoma, "to round out a term of twenty-seven years as prisoners of war. In 1913, they were released and given the choice of taking up residence on the Mescalero Indian Reservation in New Mexico (northeast of Alamogordo) or of accepting allotments of land in Oklahoma." (*See* Opler 1942:viii) Some one hundred took the allotments, but the majority of the Chiricahua joined the Mescalero. Henceforth, the development of these groups may best be considered as the Mescalero-Chiricahua; however, scholars have been able to gain specific data from Mescalero, Chiricahua, and related informants, and thus to establish their respective past history to some degree.

In their social organization, an extensive bilateral reckoning of kinship is found among the Apache. (*See* Goodwin 1942) The Mescalero, for instance, did not require band exogamy, but marriages between kinsmen were forbidden; consequently, unions outside the band were most common. Marriages tended to be easily broken, especially during the early years of a union. Polygyny was allowed, but was rarely practiced. More usual was "serial monogamy," wherein "a married man might go to another area, perhaps on a raid, extend his residence there, and eventually marry again. The social network of an individual Mescalero was both extensive and flexible, permitting him to activate ties with a wide range of cognates and to initiate new affinal bonds to meet the demands of a specific situation." (Basehart 1967:284) Marriages with outsiders were frowned upon by the Mescalero—particularly when they resulted in the loss of a Mescalero to another group.

The ordinary house type of the Chiricahua was the dome-shaped wickiup of brush. Mother-in-law avoidance was followed, as with the Navaho. Like the Navaho, too, the Chiricahua regarded birds, insects, and coyotes as once having been people; mankind, then, is but following in the footsteps of those who have gone before. No one account of the creation of human beings seems to have existed. (*See* Opler 1942:1) Mythical personages are closely related to those of the Navaho; they bear similar names, but they have differing positions of importance in some instances.

If death were to occur in a dwelling, it was deserted; the name of the deceased was not spoken. Other death customs included hair cutting and wailing. If a funeral party were seen or a newly bereaved family encountered, a Chiricahua would avoid a meeting or join in the wailing for the dead. A successful war expedition was always followed by a victory dance.

The area east of Tularosa of U.S. Highway 70, became the Mescalero reservation, and today it covers some 460,000 acres. There the Apache have adjusted themselves to the life of their fellow Americans by becoming farmers, ranchers, loggers, machine operators, nurses, ministers, artists, carpenters, clerks, accountants, policemen, and firefighters. They were the first to offer the U.S. Forest Service a trained and organized unit of firefighters to help put down forest fires in the Southwest.

Currently, attire is much like that of any western citizen. Most of the Apache men have adopted "western wear" for everyday: colorful shirts, denim pants, cowboy boots or shoes, and fitting accessories. Most Apache men have their hair cut, and they commonly shave. Some of the Apache women still wear a one-piece dress of Mother Hubbard style, or a loose hip-length blouse overhanging full skirt. Now, the tendency with the young is to wear non-Indian clothing. Moccasins are seldom worn except at ceremonial events. The Mescalero dye their deerskin moccasins a yellow color; these are made with the peculiar up-turned toe and circular element which serves as protection against cactus spines and other prickly vegetation.

The Mescalero operate several profitable industries, including a store and Summit enterprise, a woodyard and Christmas tree market, the Ruidoso recreation area with fishing and skiing developments; they practice soil conservation and engage in cattle raising. They have an incorporated Cattle Growers Association with a manager under contract. A board of directors elected annually controls the operations. Not all members of the tribe are stockholders in the corporation, but all stockholders are tribal members. Over 4,500 head of cattle are run on more than seven hundred sections of the reservation. An annual tour-type sale attracts buyers to the Mescalero auction from far and near. In 1969, some $300,000 worth of cattle were disposed of in less than an hour. A herd of good horses, with forty-five breeding mares, is also maintained.

The bulk of the Mescalero income is derived from timber sales and is deposited with the United States Treasury. Individual income is realized from cattle and wages, and a limited amount from small farm assignments which are made by the governing officers.

A federal charter declares the Mescalero a federal corporation. They operate under a constitution and by-laws, governed by the Mescalero Tribal Business Committee. Officers of the tribe are a president, vice-president, treasurer, and secretary; the council is composed of these and other members—numbering eleven in all—elected by eligible voters of the tribe; women may, and do, hold office as well as men. All positions and operations are supported by the tribe. They have criminal and civil codes and police themselves, as well as administer their self-government.

In recent years, the Mescalero have shown a steady increase. Reduced to 630 in 1915, they numbered about 1,740 as of 1 January 1970. This figure includes the Mescalero, those of Chiricahua ancestry, and remnants of the Lipan and other bands.

THE JICARILLA   During their early days in the Southwest, two divisions of the Jicarilla Apache were recognized. The *Hoyero* (also spelled *Ollero*), or "mountain people," and the *Llanero*, or "plains people." (*See* Harrington 1940:511) At that time, they ranged from the Chama valley eastward across what is now central and eastern Colorado into western Oklahoma, and at least as far south as present day Estancia, New Mexico. In their easternmost contacts, the Jicarilla took over certain elements of Plains Indian culture, as did the Mescalero who roamed the eastern plains.

Among the features adopted was the style of moccasins and leggings worn by the Jicarilla; natural deerskin of the moccasins was whitened, rather than dyed yellow, and the toe was without the protective up-turned feature of other Apache groups. Soles were of rawhide or cowhide. The hip-length leggings, suspended from a belt, were distinct from those worn by other Apaches. They were made from a single piece of dressed deerskin, hair side out, with the addition of a cuff, fringe, and tabs—which may represent survival of the large cuff tabs in style on the northern plains one hundred to one hundred and fifty years ago. The bottom of the cuff was cut into four tabs, each with very short self-fringe, while the cuff top had fringe about two and a half inches long. The entire legging was colored with yellow ochre, and decorative stripes commonly were added in other colors; red and green were favored. Then, a band of beading was worked on the skin with simple design units, a row of beading across the cuff being characteristic.

The men parted their hair in the middle, plaited it into two braids, which were wound with strips of deerskin and worn in front over the shoulders. At one time, they wore bangs across the forehead on a line with the cheek bones and tied their hair in a knot at the back of the head, like the Navaho and most of the Pueblo men. The favored ornaments worn by the men were large earrings of the old Navaho type—a silver circlet with a loose silver bead dangling at its lower circumference. They also wore short bead pendants suspended from the pierced earlobe. A kerchief was commonly tied about the neck, with ends falling on the chest, "cowboy fashion."

Deerskin garments of Plains type were worn by the Jicarilla women; they never adopted the Mother Hubbard style of dress taken over by other Apache women.

The Jicarilla Apache were a problem to the white men during the mid-1850's, (*See* Taylor 1970) and were among those pacified by Kit Carson in 1868. Following this event, they were first placed on the Mescalero reservation, and then in an area just to the east of the Navaho—putting them, it would seem, in or near the territory that had been occupied by their ancestors. In each instance, such hard fighting between the Jicarilla and other Indians resulted that they had to be moved again.

The north half of the present Jicarilla reservation was established in 1887; the south half was added in 1908; together, they include nearly three-quarters of a million acres of varied plain, semidesert, mountain and forest land dotted with small lakes. These holdings extend south from the Colorado border for approximately sixty-five miles to the vicinity of Cuba on N.M. Highway S-44. Altitude varies from 6,400 to 8,200 feet above sea level. The agency headquarters is at Dulce on Highway S-17, some twenty-seven miles west of Chama.

Within the last few years, the Jicarilla have improved their water and sewer systems; they have built many modern homes on the reservation and have remodeled old ones; a church has been erected. Several families live in new trailers. Many new miles of paved roads lead to and traverse the Jicarilla holdings. As of 1 January 1970, the census recognized 1,742 tribal members—a growth of 1,157 since an epidemic of influenza reduced them to 585 just fifty years ago.

Apache men are good stockmen. The Jicarilla own some 20,000 head of sheep, around 1,500 cattle, and, too many horses. Lamb and wool sales net significant income annually; cattle produce less revenue. Hundreds of gas wells have been drilled on the reservation, and more than one hundred producing oil wells. Royalties from these wells make up an important part of the Jicarilla income. New industries that will employ people dwelling there are being attracted to the reservation. Raw materials and products of agriculture, livestock, and forestry, all-year recreation activities, great power potential, and favorable market conditions are among the inducements at hand.

New Mexico has figured importantly in movie making the last few years, largely through undertakings of state agencies. Now, the Jicarilla have provided a good example of Apache acumen. On their own behalf, the initiative was taken to promote commercial motion pictures. Making contact with the Harvest Productions of Los Angeles, the Jicarilla agreed to finance the movie, *A Gunfight*, up to $2 million. Portions of the film were shot near Santa Fe, interior scenes were made in Hollywood, and other portions, including a bullfight, were made on location near Ocuna, Spain.

One of the Jicarilla men, who had been tribal accountant for nearly twenty years, resigned to become program affairs director for the BIA's Jicarilla agency. He and another of his tribesmen, the agency superintendent, went to Spain to help coordinate European sales of the film. They, incidentally, financed the trip from personal funds. European salesmen had already offered $1,750,000 for the movie. The first $2 million of profits is designated for the Jicarilla tribe (but as this book goes to press, only a few thousand dollars had been received, and interest losses were mounting). (Sandoval 1971)

The picture, released in the spring of 1971, featured such stars as Kirk Douglas and Johnny Cash, and an Italian actor, Raf Vallone, for the bullfight scene.

Another Jicarilla accomplishment of note is the construction of an Olympic-size, heated indoor swimming pool and recreation area at Dulce. It was jointly funded by HUD and the tribe, the cost of $1.5 million being met on a fifty-fifty basis. With this underway, many of the Jicarilla—adults and children alike—began learning to swim. Arrangements were made with personnel of a camp on the Brazos River, near Chama, for two groups of twenty-one each to take four weeks of instruction. Tribal officials were included; some prepared themselves for lifesaving and instructor's certificates. The facility was dedicated on 7 January 1972.

The Jicarilla govern by means of an eight-member council of male and female members who stand for election every two years, in accordance with an adopted constitution and by-laws. A president, vice-president, secretary, business manager, director of the tribe's Game and Fish Department, and an executive committee are chosen by the council. According to the constitution, only business surplus can be distributed on a dividend basis, as with any other corporation. Funds of their corporation have been allocated for training of personnel and the construction of facilities to assist firms providing the greatest economic benefit to the Jicarilla.

More than two hundred Jicarilla derive individual income from tribal employment; over fifty have positions with the BIA and a few with the U.S. Public Health Service; others have miscellaneous sources of revenue. Education in general receives major attention, and up-to-date school facilities are provided. In 1956, the Jicarilla tribe placed one million dollars in an Albuquerque bank to finance education for children and adults who want to learn new jobs, and to aid worthy students who do not have sufficient money of their own.

As a result of having shown such sound operation of their 742,303 acres of land, permitting balanced programs in range use, outdoor recreation, and game management, the Jicarilla were honored, in the spring of 1970, by a Department of the Interior Conservation Service Award—that department's top honor. In a letter to the president of the Jicarilla council, the Secretary of the Interior offered "recognition of the significant progress of the (tribe) not only in conservation and improvements of their natural resources, but also in the variety and intensity of the management of their own affairs, and their cooperation and involvement with other federal and state agencies." (Anonymous 1970c)

THE WESTERN APACHES

The major Western Apache divisions embrace the White Mountain, Cibecue, San Carlos, and northern and southern Tonto groups that now dwell in southeastern Arizona. Although each division has certain distinctions, such as linguistic dialects and religious and social practices, they share basic characteristics. Their terrain is cut by high mountain barriers which rise to well over 11,000 feet, from lowland areas of some 2,600 feet elevation. These natural barriers tended to isolate one band from another, so that each came to have fairly well-defined territories. No political affiliations existed between the various groups, in the past or at present. They were relatively peaceful until forced to develop a raiding pattern by foreign peoples, Indian and non-Indian. As with other Indian peoples, treaties were made and broken.

The family constitutes the Apache economic unit. This includes the normal pattern of those adhering to a matrilineal system, where children are born into the clan of the mother: grandparents, married daughters and their husbands, unmarried sons, and children of the daughters. Each family is bound together by certain rights and duties. The clan system—which still operates to a degree—cuts across groups and bands. Marriage within one's clan is forbidden. In the Apache clans, cousins are called "brother" and "sister." Marriage between cousins is taboo. Families live in relatively large groups with the home of the mother being the family center. Mothers and daughters are very close and they carry on many tasks together. When a son marries, his obligations henceforth are to the family of his mother-in-law; he is to protect and work for the domestic circle into which he marries. If a man's wife dies, he may remarry. Frequently, he marries a sister of his deceased wife. Marriages now are in accordance with the white man's practices.

In their chosen locale, livelihood did not come easily. Primary foodstuffs consisted of wild game and fruits, seeds and nuts of indigenous plants; some corn, beans, and squash were raised. Conflicts grew through the years, culminating in a terrific battle between the Anglo-Americans and the Apache in 1862. Mangas Coloradas, a Nednhi Apache, had come to the fore, and was then an elderly man; he was wounded in battle, but recovered. He was ready for peace and, being tricked by a promising overture, he went to an army camp in New Mexico where he was murdered in January, 1863. His son, Mangus, became leader. An intensive and treacherous campaign against the Apache was waged by the army and by civilians. Scores of Apache were killed, but Victorio and other leaders retaliated. It is said that the U.S. government spent some $38 million from 1862 to 1871 in its effort to exterminate the Apaches.

General Crook, who knew the Indians well, then was assigned the task of "taming" all of the Apache bands in Arizona. A few swift campaigns resulted in subduing the Western Apache and the Yavapai, with whom extensive intermarriage had taken place. They were placed on reservations at San Carlos and at Fort Apache. Crook hired Apache men as scouts, and programs in agriculture and livestock raising were initiated. Uneasy peace reigned for several years; no consistent Indian policy was followed. As related above, at one time the Chiricahua were forced to dwell among the Western Apache, as were the Tonto and some of the Yavapai. Of course, this was unsuccessful. In large part, Apache scouts led to the downfall of the Apaches—for they knew the haunts and practices of their people, and how to lead the soldiers to them.

Through all the tumultuous decades, the Chiricahua and associated bands were hardest hit by their foes. On the other hand, the Western Apache fared much better. It is said that they had a population of about 4,000 in the 1860's and that in 1890 their census enumerated 4,138, and they still occupied their homeland, an area reaching from Flagstaff and Showlow to the Santa Catalina, Rincon, and Whetstone Mountains on the south, and from the Camp Verde-Superior alignment on the west almost to the New Mexico border on the east. (*See* Baldwin 1965:52)

In November, 1871, the original White Mountain reservation was established; it included the present Fort Apache and San Carlos reservations. In 1897, the area was divided and separated into the Fort Apache and the San Carlos reservation, respectively.

Over the years, their acreage was continually reduced by white men who hungered for the valuable resources of the Apaches—minerals and grazing lands especially. By 1920, leases held by whites amounted to approximately five-eights of the San Carlos reservation, and the lands were being destroyed by illegal grazing of thousands of unregistered cattle. The San Carlos lands were not allotted, and it is said that "due to the peculiar topographical conditions of the reservation with its small patches of ground suitable for farming and its scattered watering places in the grazing areas, individual allotments would never be practical." (Arizona Writers' Project 1941:33)

Agents interested in the Apache welfare came on the scene by 1923, and the overgrazing situation began to change. Leases were gradually terminated and the lands returned to the Indians (the last outside grazing leases ran out in 1948). (Anonymous 1969d) Indian organization, or participation in Apache interests was started in 1924 with development of the resources of tribal and individual potentialities, "which consisted of cattle interests, small gardens, and a home security or social system." (Arizona Writers' Project 1941:33) Until 1932, these efforts were carried on by community meetings. Then, a Business Council was organized. Its plans were sound, with result that progress was constant. A self-supporting program was inaugurated and meetings held by various groups; grazing fees per head of all cattle sold were established, permitting the San Carlos to build up and maintain one of the largest cattle ownerships as a self-supporting economic venture, without required assistance from tribal or federal funds.

The Apache ability to understand the fundamentals of self-government by actual practice led to almost unanimous acceptance of the Reorganization Act of 1934 and a favorable vote on their constitution; the latter provides for the election by the Apache of a tribal council as the governing body. "This was followed by acceptance, with some amendments as applying particularly to this tribe (San Carlos, White Mountain), of the Law and Order Regulation as approved by the Secretary of the Interior November 27, 1935, and the immediate functioning of the reservation under these new regulations. The Indian Court, working with the Indian Council, claims they had been using practically these same regulations for several years, which resulted in little or no confusion in the change-over to an approved and regulated method of court procedure." And the San Carlos took over "the responsibility and duties of this splendid piece of legislation with little change in their economic or social standards and procedure," (Arizona Writers' Project 1941-34) with gratifying results. Law infractions are handled by native judges, with court order kept by native police. Court procedure is similar to the white man's.

Other programs administered include general administration,

construction and maintenance of roads, employment assistance, forestry and range conservation, soil and moisture conservation, irrigation, plant management, education, and welfare.

Agency headquarters of the 1,648,000-acre reservation located in Gila, Graham, and Pinal counties of Arizona is at San Carlos, southeast of Globe. Apache living on the reservation number about 5,000. Their sources of livelihood come primarily from livestock, mining, and timber activities. The tribe operates general stores at San Carlos and at Bylas, on U.S. Highway 70; and a few privately owned businesses are permitted on the reservation. A number of the San Carlos are employed at the copper mines in Globe, Miami, and Superior. Some work on a seasonal basis for highway contractors on road construction projects; others are employed by the BIA in various capacities on the reservation. Out-of-door recreation facilities have been developed, offering hunting, fishing, camping, horseback riding, etc.

A combined BIA-public school for grades one through four is in operation at the agency headquarters. From the fifth grade up, San Carlos children attend the Globe Public Schools and the fully accredited Globe High School. A Catholic elementary school in San Carlos takes children through the second grade.

Unfortunately, recent years have seen adverse changes occurring among the San Carlos people. During 1973, Joel Nilsson, a general assignment reporter for the *Arizona Daily Star*, lived for a month on their reservation and looked at all facets of San Carlos life. He found unemployment responsible for many ills. This fluctuated between 25 and 40 per cent. Almost two thousand of the Indians were on one kind of welfare or another; over 900 of some 1,000-odd reservation homes were determined unfit to live in; about 20 per cent of the Indian population had alcoholism problems, and the rate of suicide was rising. Although Apache law states that students must stay in school until the age of eighteen or until they have completed high school, about seventy youngsters in the sixteen-eighteen bracket were not attending school.

A struggle for leadership within the San Carlos group and questionable fiscal practices caused serious conflicts and added to the difficulties. (Anonymous 1973)

The White Mountain Apache live on the Fort Apache Indian reservation in Navajo, Apache, and Gila counties of Arizona. This adjoins the San Carlos reservation and comprises an area of some seventy-five miles east-west and forty-five miles north-south, with an acreage of 1,656,698, or 2,601 square miles. Holbrook lies eighty-five miles north of the reservation headquarters, which is at Whiteriver, about four miles north of Fort Apache (site of a former military post). From the semiarid southwest corner of the reservation, where the elevation is about 2,700 feet, the terrain ranges upward to 11,459 feet at the northeast (Mount Thomas). Nearly half of the population lives in permanent cabins or modern homes; others occupy wickiups which are generally modified somewhat from the original structure pattern—a small entrance hall with door is common. Clan ties are maintained.

Like the San Carlos, the White Mountain Apache operate as a tribe under provisions of the Reorganization Act of 1934; they have a constitution. The council consists of a chairman and vice-chairman who are elected by popular vote for four-year terms; and nine members, two of whom are elected by popular vote of the Cibecue, Oak Creek, and Grasshopper districts, two similarly by the Carrizo, Forestdale, and Cedar Creek districts, and two by the East Fork, Turkey Creek, and Seven Mile districts, and three members by the Canyon Day and Whiteriver North Fork districts. Excepting the latter district, these are elected for terms of two and four years; those receiving the most votes serve for the longer period, and the others for the two-year term; the exception elects two members at alternating elections for four-year terms. The council has authority to appropriate tribal funds for the welfare and benefit of the tribe and for the development and protection of the reservation and its resources—with the approval of the Department of the Interior.

The White Mountain Apache entered into the cattle business to a limited extent, about 1900 with the introduction of cattle from Mexico. In 1917, some 800 head of grade Herefords were brought from Mexico to Fort Apache. From this beginning, the White Mountain Tribal Herd was increased by the purchase from time to time of cows and bulls, and the present herd of fine stock numbering 2,200 head was developed. Issues were made to individual Indians. This enterprise operates a tribally-owned ranch of nearly 138,000 acres on the southeast corner of the reservation.

Individual livestock owners are organized into eight livestock associations for management and sales, but all cattle are individually owned and branded. A stockman is chosen for each district to perform the duties of the old-time foreman; each district has a three-man board of directors. A manager is in charge of the tribally-owned cattle, and a general livestock manager looks after the individual members' stock, which number 15,000 Herefords.

This is one of the most competitive cattle spreads in the American West. The cattle industry alone puts between $30,000 and $40,000 back into the tribal coffers annually.

Various other enterprises are operated, each with a managing board of directors; one is the Fort Apache Timber Company which employs some one hundred and ten members of the tribe; this produces an annual income exceeding $3,000,000. Another undertaking, the White Mountain Apache Enterprises, consists of summer homesite leases, five stores and service stations, several boat dock concessions with boat rental, first class tourist facilities, a liquor store in McNary, and the Apache Flame. The White Mountain Recreation Enterprise, which includes the largest privately owned recreation area in the West (with several lakes and 300 miles of trout streams), controls game management, fishing and hunting licenses, campgrounds, and game wardens.

The White Mountain Apache, like the Jicarilla, were cited by the Secretary of the Interior in April, 1970. Their citation was in recognition of an "outstanding conservation program"—this being for the "preservation of the Arizona (Apache) trout, which had faced extinction until the Apaches began their preservation work in 1952." (Anonymous 1970c) Efforts of the White Mountain Apache increased the number of trout and prevented further hybridization.

These Apache are also engaged in an intensive program to provide housing, training, education, and employment opportunities for their 5,300 members. Approximately 2,500 members are now attending school from Head Start through universities. School attendance of children between the ages of six and eighteen is enforced by the council. In 1956, a scholarship program was initiated for the aid of tribal members interested in continuing their education beyond high school. The majority of students are in public schools, nearly one-fourth attend BIA schools on the reservation, and about one-fourth are in mission schools. An outstanding summer youth program is carried on each year.

Health facilities are provided by the U.S. Public Health Service, with a hospital in Whiteriver and clinics in the various communities.

Law and order is maintained by a Special Officer and a force of ten policemen. All offenses are handled by the Tribal Court, with exception of the ten major crimes which, as among the other Southwestern Indian groups, go to the Federal Court. (Young 1961:284)* Tribal police have the same official status as officers in any other community, and they cooperate fully with county, state, and federal law enforcement agencies. The Tribal Court was established in 1940; it consists of one Chief Judge and two Associate Judges. Cases coming within the jurisdiction of the court are heard daily and, where evidence is sufficient to convict, penalties are assessed according to the existing Law and Order Code.

RELIGIOUS BELIEFS AND CEREMONIES

The Apache awareness of deity and their attitude toward a supreme being have been little understood, and less promulgated.

In general, the Apache recognize a supreme deity of impersonal character to whom no sex is attributed, but who is thought of as the creator—a deity that may be identified as *Yusn*, as *Ussen*, or Giver-of-life. This omnipotent one is the source of all supernatural power and is "the maker of world and man," but since the creation, little direct contact has prevailed between Giver-of-life and man.

However, supernatural power reaches mankind and exercises strong control over worldly affairs. In contrast to this, it is noted that the "Giver-of-Life is remote and nebulous to the Apache mind. . . . The power of Giver-of-life becomes translated into specific ceremonies. It is these ceremonies which warmly and intimately impinge against Apache life . . . and dominate Apache religious thinking. Giver-of-life may be mentioned in the opening prayer of a rite. Thereafter, however, the attention shifts to the specific power whose aid the ceremony is attempting to win." (Opler 1935:66*)

At every point in life, the Apache seeks supernatural aid in meeting his problems and conducting his affairs. These aids from the supernaturals are manifest as ceremonies that are markedly similar in pattern, though they differ widely in detail. Nearly all of them are initiated with ceremonial smoking, then throwing of pollen to the four directions, prayer, and singing.

The Apache, we are told, think of power

as a mighty force that pervades the universe. Some of it filters through to the hands of man. But to become manifest to man, power must approach him through the medium of certain agencies and channels, must "work through" something. The most conspicuous of these agencies are certain natural

---

*These include murder, manslaughter, rape, assault with intent to kill, arson, burglary, larceny, robbery, incest, and assault with a deadly weapon. An eleventh crime is embezzlement of tribal funds.

*Opler (1941:281) says *Yusn* [Ussen] is from the Spanish *díos*—thus a Christian transfer of deific name.

phenomena such as the lightning or sun, and a number of animals, principally the bear, snake, owl, and coyote . . . but there are scores of possibilities. (Opler 1935:66*)

An Apache may accept or reject the power offered to him. Every Apache man or woman is a potential recipient of supernatural power. If the power is accepted, the recipient, it is said, " . . . is given directions for conducting a ceremony; he is instructed in the songs, the prayers, the four ceremonial gifts he must ask in return for his services, and the taboos, if any, which he must observe himself and impose on the one for whom he is working." (Opler 1935:67-68) One may be given as many as five different ceremonies. Thus, it is "that an Apache becomes 'loaded up with powers.' " A man's power is not public property. (Opler 1935:68; *cf.* Ball 1970:11) Often, no one other than a person's own family may know of his ceremony. Ceremonies may be transmitted from one person to another, as from elder to younger people. When a ceremony is taught to someone outside the family circle, a fee is always charged by the teacher.

As do the Navaho, the Apache account for death, disease, and disaster as power manipulated by malevolent persons, or power itself seeking to do harm. Appropriate terms are applied to such agencies, as for beneficial supernatural powers.

The ceremonials of the Apache have not had the same publicity as have those of the Navaho. But ceremonies are performed as cures, to set things right, or to ward off possible evil. The majority of Apache ceremonies are curative rites which are carried out by shamans who have obtained supernatural power from a great number of sources, chiefly from the potent Mountain Spirits, supernatural beings called *Gáhan* or *Gáhe*. All Apaches consider the ceremonial circuit as clockwise; and few are the things not connected with the number four.

Once a shaman has been engaged to conduct a ceremony to cure an ill person, the procedure is to dress and paint the bodies of several men—usually four—to represent the Mountain Spirits. These dance into view, approaching the patient, or the camps from which the illness is to be exorcised; and by dancing, giving forth distinctive calls, and making gestures, the objective is attained. Songs are sung by the shaman while the dancers are being prepared and while they are performing. The songs function as messages to the supernaturals and acquaint them with an aid required by the shaman.

*All quotations from Opler 1935 are reproduced by permission of the American Anthropological Association from *American Anthropologist,* Vol. 37, No. 1 (1935).

The Mountain Spirits are considered to be numerous and they inhabit many mountains. Like all supernaturals and ritual objects, they are associated with colors and directions. Therefore, the Mountain Spirits of each cardinal direction are represented by a leader, and a particular color is attributed to him. Although the associations vary somewhat, the most common color representations are said to be:

> Black Mountain Spirit is the leader of a single file
> from the east;
> Blue Mountain Spirit is the leader of a single file
> from the south;
> Yellow Mountain Spirit is the leader of a single file
> from the west; and
> White (or Grey) Mountain Spirit is the leader of a
> single file from the north.

The blue, or turquois, color and the cross are used extensively in ceremonial symbolism. Pollen represents growth and vitality. (*See* Opler 1938a:154-155) Abalone is considered as pollen also—perhaps "water pollen."

Studies have revealed that not such a wide gulf exists between the Navaho and Apache basic cultures as was once thought. As might be expected, the major Jicarilla cycle of mythology closely parallels the Navaho. For instance, the Jicarilla puberty ceremony is similar to that of the Navaho. It is not tribal, but is held by a girl's family or clan when she is ready for marriage.

The Jicarilla observe a bear dance upon call of a curer, or shaman. The name is taken from a Ute Indian ceremony which has nothing to do with bears. In fact it is a Holiness rite (*See* Opler 1938b:27-44), performed within a brush corral, as is the Navaho Mountain Topway. Small fires are lit around the interior of the enclosure. A medicine tipi is erected at the west end. Where the Navaho would drum on a basket to set the rhythm, several Jicarilla men rub notched sticks together, resting the end of a rasp on a basket. This appears to be an element derived from the Ute. It produces a resonant, powerful sound which is very effective. While the main ceremony—the most sacred part, in which dry paintings (sandpaintings) are made—goes on in the lodge, women select partners and dance with them outside, somewhat after the manner of a Navaho squaw dance, except that no payment is made; one steps out when he tires of dancing. A dramatic entrance occurs when a group of masked dancers accompanied by sacred clowns comes onto the scene. Certain cautions have been advised by people who have attended the bear dance; it is suggested that visitors should not attempt to witness the ceremony unless they know the Jicarilla well, and have adequate information regarding situations that might arise.

On 4 July, the Jicarilla hold a feast, without attendant ceremonies. Annually, a two-day celebration is held on 14 and 15 September, near Horse Lake. This reenacts the yearly reunion of the two divisions of the tribe—the mountain people and those of the plains. On the fifteenth, they perform an imitation of the ceremonial race that is run at Taos during the San Gerónimo fiesta. At night, a round dance is held. The friendship between the Jicarilla and Taos Indians is so close that each attends the other's feast, or *fiesta*, in large numbers; Taos people participate in the Jicarilla race, and a few of the Apache take some part in the ceremony at Taos.

Unlike other Southwestern Athabascan peoples, the Mescalero do not tell an emergence legend in the course of which reference is made to the creation and to the origins of the major ceremonials. Instead, they have utilized the *coyote cycle* to introduce these elements. This cycle is a connected series of episodes that describe the travels and adventures of a trickster, the attributes and characteristics of which are sometimes human, and again, those of an animal. Coyote is a type character that reveals a remarkable self-portrait of the Apache—a shrewd and powerful satire of his culture and of human foibles. (Opler 1938a:214)

The Apache have a common custom of referring to something else than that which is mentioned, to something which resembles it, as for example, calling an owl's ears a "hat"—much to the merriment of all. In speech, direct reference is not made to a bear; to do so would "run the risk of seeing the bear shortly afterwards and of catching the sickness (a painful disease that might be contracted)." (Opler 1938a:217)* To throw food about or to handle it carelessly is thought by the Apache to be very dangerous and unlucky. Bones are not thrown around; they are placed in a neat pile and disposed of at once. To do otherwise "is to invite the loss of hunting skill and shortage of food." (Opler 1938a:217)

With the Mescalero, the girls' puberty ceremony is their most important public observance; and this was true of the Chiricahua. (*See* Opler 1938a:143-151) Two ceremonies are held for girls who go through the performance. Much symbolism is worked into the rites.

At that time, Sun and Earth are important agencies. First, a large brush tipi is erected, representing the universe. It is said to be constructed of "old age staffs and gray hair"—to give long life to the girls for whom the ceremony is held. A girl being inducted to womanhood represents White Painted Woman, the Apache priestess who officiates with the Sun's representative; she is the model for all Apache womankind. The rites of induction, throughout, symbolize the recreation of White Painted Woman (comparable to Changing Woman of the Navaho). At the end of the rites, the tipi is taken down. All is in charge of the "medicine man," or shaman. Second is the sun greeting ceremony. This takes place early in the morning of the first day of the observances, and again early in the morning of the final day.

MESCALERO APACHE SONG OF THE GOTAL CEREMONY

The black turkey gobbler, under the east, the middle
*   of his trail; toward us it is about to dawn.*
The black turkey gobbler, the tips of his beautiful tail;
*   above us the dawn whitens.*
The black turkey gobbler, the tips of his beautiful tail;
*   above us the dawn becomes yellow.*
The sunbeams stream forward, dawn boys, with
*   shimmering shoes [sandals] of yellow.*
On top of the sunbeams that stream toward us they
*   are dancing.*
At the east the rainbow moves forward, dawn maidens,
*   with shimmering shoes and shirts of yellow*
*   dance over us.*
Beautifully over us it is dawning.
Above us among the mountains the herbs are
*   becoming green.*
Above us on the top of the mountains the herbs are
*   becoming yellow.*
Above us among the mountains, with shoes of yellow
*   I go around the fruits and the herbs that shimmer.*
Above us among the mountains, the shimmering fruits
*   with shoes and shirts of yellow are bent toward him.*
On the beautiful mountains above it is daylight.

From: *Gotal: A Mescalero Apache Ceremony*, by P. E. Goddard (1909:216)—an adolescence rite for girls.

At night, the Gáhan—those supernatural beings who live in the mountain caves and beneath the horizon in the cardinal directions—

appear as masked dancers. For each four dancers, a shaman is present to dress and decorate them. He performs a ceremony while they are being painted and attired. The painting of the upper portions of the body is accompanied by a song, and the mask and headdress are held toward the four cardinal directions before they are worn. The dancers must be painted differently for each of the four nights of the ceremony. These dancers approach a large bonfire, around which they dance. They come in single file from each of the four directions. They come four times, swaying and uttering a peculiar call. Each carries painted wands which are brandished vigorously.

The headdresses are spectacular. They are made of thin strips of wood, arranged in various patterns: crosses, fans, circles, and so on. They are colorfully decorated and further embellished with tin ornaments and downy plumes. The upper, ornamented part of the headdress is supported on a length of small sapling bent to fit around the head. This is covered with black cloth which falls over the dancer's head and is gathered in to cover it closely. Tiny eyeholes are cut in the front. Above these, shiny buttons or brass paper fasteners or metal discs are attached, which give the mask a fantastic appearance in the firelight. This striking headdress has led to incorrect designations of the dance. It is spoken of as a "devil dance," or "crown dance," whereas it is actually the mountain spirits dance. Since these mountain spirits, or Gáhan, are helpful beings who introduced the dance to the Apache as a curing ceremony, one sees how serious a misnomer is this. Portions of this dance are often presented at public celebrations, such as pow-wows, the Nizhoni Dances in Albuquerque, programs at the Institute of American Indian Arts in Santa Fe, and the like—where they are received with great enthusiasm.

Among the Gáhan personators is one called the Grey One, who may take the place of White Mountain Spirit. He is a clown who caricatures the movements of the other dancers; he goes through all sorts of capers, amuses the public in general, and serves as messenger. This character compares with Born-of-water of the Navaho. While the Gáhan dance, rites are conducted in the big tipi by the shaman, the girls participating, and the women attending them. On the fourth night, the girls dance throughout the night. At first daylight, they leave the tipi for a rest period, returning at sunrise.

Finally, the girls take part in a footrace, running to the east around a basket filled with ceremonial paraphernalia and back to where deerskins have been laid out on the ground in front of the tipi. The shaman and his assistants sing four chants and during each chant the girls run. Each time, the basket is moved nearer to the deerskins. During the last chant, the girls stop at the basket and each takes a feather from it. They then circle round the basket and run far to the east. When they return, they enter their own tipi. During these races, the ceremonial tipi is dismantled. Then, gifts are thrown to the spectators and the ceremony ends. The girls, however, must remain near their tipi for four days and nights. They must observe certain taboos. After this period, they return to everyday life. (*See* Ball 1970:37-43, 207n2); (*see also* Breuninger 1970)

After this ceremony, the girls, theoretically, are ready for marriage. Traditionally, the shaman will give instructions to the young men whenever they present themselves and request it. For instance, a youth may bring to the shaman a gift of pierced blue stone with an eagle feather through it. Then, night after night, until the young man has learned, the rhythmic beat of drums can be heard at the shaman's wickiup. Thus, the songs and dances are perpetuated and the unrecorded ceremonials preserved. A few of the minor ceremonies last a short time only. The major ones are given over a period of from one to four days. Some have their own set of songs, others have prayers with words similar to songs. The songs and prayers must be used in proper sequence. Many ceremonies have their own paraphernalia: charms, certain plants or animal parts. These contain power and are used for drawing out sickness from a patient. Pollen is the most important ceremonial offering; white shell, turquois, jet, and catlinite are sacred and potent, and each has directional significance; eagle feathers are important in religious rites.

Curing ceremonies are usually held for one person only, but a few rites can be given in time of epidemics to ward off the disease from all. Other ceremonies for the good of the community, holy rites, may be held in the spring and summer when lightning, snakes, and other harmful agents are present.

In olden times, after a young man had chosen a girl for a wife, it was required that he get the consent of his people; then he made his desire known to the girl's parents. Generally, his father or uncle would do the honors for him, after which came the real proposal. Presents were offered to the girl and to her family. Wealth was counted chiefly in horses and dressed deerskins; in the night, the suitor would tie one or more horses near the girl's wickiup. A single animal was considered a poor offering. If the girl took the horses and fed and watered them, the indication was that the proposal had been accepted. If the animals were not cared for, the proposal was rejected.

Wedding ceremonies were observed by a feast and celebration that lasted three days. During that time, the betrothed couple seldom saw or spoke to each other. Formerly, after a marriage, the young couple built a wickiup near that of the wife's mother; today they may live with whichever family group is more convenient.

The Mescalero hold the puberty ceremony at the beginning of July, the erection of the tipi taking place on the morning of 1 July. This is the only instance in which a Mescalero ceremony is conducted on a fixed calendar date, a fact that derives from an old government order which forbade the holding of ceremonies at any other time of the year.

Among the Western Apache, the puberty ceremony for girls was one of their major observances, when the mountain spirits appeared. In addition to its ritual importance, the occasion was an important social event. Wealthy families held the full four-day ceremonial, while poorer ones had a one-day event. Today, these ceremonials continue, but they have lost much of their significance and influence. They are usually conducted during the 4 July celebration and the reservation fair of the Fort Apache in August or September. The Gáhan attire and accoutrement are similar to those of the Mescalero, but the wands that are brandished and the headdresses are decorated in such manner as to make them distinctive, one group from the other.

The Western Apache still recognize and respect their shamans, but they have very limited influence, especially on the younger generations.

NEW WAY, OLD WAY (NAVAHO)

Beauty in the old way of life—
The dwellings they decorated so lovingly;
A drum, a clear voice singing,
And the sound of laughter.

You must want to learn from your mother,
You must listen to old men not quite capable of becoming
    white men.
The white man is not our father.
While we last, we must not die of hunger.
We were a very Indian, strong, competent people,
But the grass had almost stopped its growing,
The horses of our pride were near their end.

Indian cowboys and foremen handled Indian herds.
A cowboy's life appealed to them until economics and tradition
clashed.

No one Indian was equipped to engineer the water's flow onto a
    man's allotment.
Another was helpless to unlock the gate.
The union between a hydro-electric plant and
Respect for the wisdom of the long-haired chiefs
Had to blend to build new enterprises
By Indian labor.

Those mighty animals graze once more upon the hillside.
At the Fair appear again our ancient costumes.
A full-blood broadcasts through a microphone planned tribal action.
Hope stirs in the tribe,
Drums beat and dancers, old and young, step forward.

We shall learn all the devices of the white man.
We shall handle his tools for ourselves.
We shall master his machinery, his inventions, his skills, his medicine,
    his planning;
But we'll retain our beauty
And still be Indians!

By Dave Martinnez

From: *The Writers' Reader*, 1962-1966. Institute of American Indian
Arts, Santa Fe, N.M.

4 the Ute indians

In the state of Colorado, only the Ute Indians dwell today as organized groups. They are descendants of a people who once claimed about half of the area of the present state, two-thirds of Utah, and bits of northern New Mexico as their domain. They required a large geographical area to sustain themselves.

The Ute, who called themselves *Nünt'z* ("The People") had a food gathering-hunting economy; they wandered on foot, collecting plant foods and hunting game. Their struggle to survive took much of their energy and precluded extensive social development. All social behavior was defined or controlled by the family, often through an older member. Defensive war and the social bear dance were the only activities requiring the cooperation of a tribal unit larger than the family.

No overall political organization was ever achieved by the

Utes. They were divided into small bands, each with its own chief. Each band was an independent group. Among the larger bands whose names have come down through history were the *Uncompahgre*, or *Tabeguache*, whose central home was in the area around present day Gunnison and Montrose, Colorado; the White River and *Yampa* bands of northwestern Colorado; the *Mouache* who roamed along the front range of that state; the *Capote* who lived in the San Luis valley; and the *Weminuche* who occupied the San Juan basin of southwestern Colorado. The *Uintah* lived in eastern Utah.

After the Ute acquired horses from the Spanish immigrants, they were able to add greatly to their store of essentials. They became bison hunters and tipi dwellers. From 1630 to 1700, the seven bands consolidated into the Ute Confederation, and were able to transform from primary family units to warlike bands.

The Ute bands often fought with other Indians and sometimes among themselves. Generally they were friendly with the white men who invaded their mountain domain to trap, trade and prospect for minerals. But they were unprepared for the onslaught that was to follow. After the trappers, traders, and prospectors came the white miners and settlers who crept ever westward, until they occupied various areas on Colorado's eastern slope. In 1863, the federal government called a council of all the Ute bands; it was held in the San Luis valley. Fearing trouble between the whites and the Indians, the government wished to persuade the Utes to move out of these areas and to remain west of the Continental Divide. The government negotiators found it difficult to deal with the numerous chiefs. Finally, at government insistence, an Uncompahgre leader named *Ouray* (meaning "arrow") was designated as spokesman for all the bands. At first, Ouray and other Ute leaders declined to move away from the San Luis valley and the other areas which the government wished them to leave.

Reduction of Ute Holdings   Gradually, however, the Ute ceded most of their lands to the federal government to be used by white men for farming, ranching, mining, and the building of railroads and towns. Under a treaty made in 1868, the Utes promised to remain west of the Continental Divide. The treaty provided that virtually all of Colorado west of the Divide would be kept as a reservation for the Ute, with agencies established in the area of Gunnison and on the White river.

Before many years the treaty was broken by the whites. Gold and silver were discovered in the San Juan Mountains, and white miners invaded the Ute lands. A new treaty was negotiated in 1873, under which the Ute gave up the region in which minerals had been found.

The Mouache, Capote and Weminuche bands were consolidated on a strip of land along the Colorado-New Mexico border, fifteen miles wide and 140 miles long. There the Southern Ute reservation, with an agency near present day Ignacio, Colorado, was established in 1877. Almost all of those Ute people came to live in or near the Pine River valley. Principal leaders were Buckskin Charley of the Mouache, Severo of the Capote, and Ignacio of the Weminuche.

The Weminuche considered that region as their own, and from the beginning of this arrangement they resented the location of the Mouache and Capotes among them. It was impossible for them to get along with the other two bands. Heeding the counsel of their chiefs, the Weminuche declined to farm, which was the intent of the government agents.

In 1879, the Yampa and White River bands, whose agency was on the White River near modern Meeker, Colorado, became restive. Goods and payments that had been promised by the government had not been delivered; and the insistence of the agent (N. C. Meeker) that the Ute become farmers even to the extent that he had their race track plowed up, led to eruption. Before the trouble ended, twelve white employees at the agency, including Meeker, had been killed. Troops under Major T. T. Thornburgh that were enroute to the agency were attacked and thirteen soldiers were killed before the Ute withdrew. We read of these happenings as the "Meeker massacre" and the "Thornburgh ambush."

Ouray, who became the most prominent of all Ute leaders, died near Ignacio while visiting the southern bands in 1880. As a result of the Meeker incident, pressure mounted among the whites to have all the Utes removed from Colorado. In 1881, the White River and Uncompahgre bands were exiled into eastern Utah to a reservation that previously had been established for the Uintah. By 1882, two-thirds of the Colorado Utes had been removed from the state.

As part of their scheme to make farmers and cattle raisers of the Ute by settling them on reservations, the federal government offered to allot each family land in the Pine River valley area. Those who accepted allotments got 160 acres of land, apiece. The Mouache and Capote bands, merged as the *Southern Ute Tribe*, remained on these lands. When Chief Severo died, Buckskin Charley became chief of both these bands. They gradually accepted the change from a nomadic life to an agricultural one. After the allotments were made to individual Indians in the Pine River valley, other reservation lands were returned to the public domain and were opened to homesteading by non-Indians. For many years the Southern Ute have lived as close neighbors of non-Indian farmers and ranchers (Spanish-Americans and Anglos).

The Weminuche, however, in 1895 chose to move to the arid, barren western end of the reservation, rather than accept allotted farm sites in the fertile river valleys to the east. With division of the original reservation, the Weminuche became today's *Ute Mountain Tribe*, with their own social organization and reservation. They have lived as stockmen, isolated to a great degree from non-Indians. On their western holdings, the "Ute Strip," the Weminuche eventually were furnished with an agency built at a point known as Navajo Springs, south of Sleeping Ute Mountain. About 1917 the agency was moved a few miles to the north, where a new community called *Towaoc* (meaning "all right" or "just fine") was established.

THE MODERN UTE PEOPLES

In securing up-to-date data for inclusion in this book, an effort was made by the author to obtain modern illustrative material. In very kind manner, I was told that: "The Ute Mountain Tribe is isolationist by nature and prefers to be left alone if at all possible. I questioned tribal officials as to whether they would permit publication of pictures of themselves, their homes or their ceremonials. They responded that they would prefer not."*

Although members of the Ute Mountain and Southern Ute groups speak the same Indian language, Shoshonean of the Uto-aztecan family, and have the same physical characteristics, they are two distinct entities. Each has its own tribal government and conducts its business independently of the other. Both groups were impoverished until recent years.

In 1950, however, the Confederated Ute Tribes (the two Colorado groups and the Northern Ute—those who had been exiled to eastern Utah and live on what is known today as the Uintah and Ouray reservation) won a $31 million judgment from the U.S. government as a result of claims for lands wrongfully taken in the

---

*I am indebted to the office of the Superintendent, Ute Mountain Agency, Towaoc, Colorado, for two mimeographed leaflets containing much of the information presented in this section: "The American Indians of Colorado" and "A brief history of the Colorado Utes." Other information was received in personal letters. (For general facts of the Utes of 1868, *see* Fowler and Fowler 1971:38-76, 110.)

mid-1800's. The Ute Mountain Tribe received about $6,266,000 in judgment funds after attorneys' fees were paid. The Southern Ute received around $5,500,000. And about the same time the land claims were awarded, natural gas was discovered on Southern Ute lands. Since then, oil and gas discoveries have enriched the Ute Mountain treasury also.

Following these events, both groups spent much time in studying ways in which their new wealth might best be spent for the benefit of their people. These studies resulted in rehabilitation programs which have brought about great improvements in living conditions. The people now live in modern homes. Health and sanitation standards have been raised. New roads have been built and old roads repaired. Tribal lands are being improved through good conservation practices. The children of the two groups have shared in the good fortune. They attend public schools, and scholarship programs of the tribes help young people who wish to attend colleges or vocational schools.

TRADITIONAL OBSERVANCES   The old Indian way of life is fading on each of these reservations, but two annual events stemming from the ancient heritage of the Utes still are observed. These are the bear dance—the traditional welcome to spring—and the sun dance—a religious ritual that originated with the Plains Indians. The bear dances usually are held in April or May, and the sun dances in July or August. Since these are tribal festivals, rather than performances for tourists, the dates are not set far in advance. Each fall the Southern Ute hold a tribal fair to which visitors are welcome; and both they and the Ute Mountain Ute hold rodeos that are open to the public.

RECENT RE-ORGANIZATION   Upon petition of the tribal councils concerned, and approval of the Department of the Interior, the Consolidated Ute Agency at Ignacio was split into the Ute Mountain Agency at Towaoc and the Southern Ute Agency at Ignacio. The change became effective on 29 December 1968. The agency staffs and other BIA personnel assist the tribal organizations in the fields of resources management (including soil and moisture conservation, land reclamation, irrigation, forest and range management, and realty problems), in community services (including welfare, education, and law and order), and in administration. The tribes receive certain assistance in health matters from the U.S. Public Health Service.

Joint objectives of the tribal organizations and the BIA are to give the Indian people greater economic security, to develop Indian resources to maximum productivity, and to help Indians take their place in American community life. It is said that both of these Ute tribes are making progress toward these objectives.

THE UTE MOUNTAIN UTE

The Ute Mountain reservation is located in the extreme southwest corner of Colorado, with a small extension into New Mexico. Most of the reservation lies in Montezuma county, Colorado, with the remainder in La Plata county, Colorado, and San Juan county, New Mexico. The location in general is high, deeply dissected tableland; the climate is semiarid to arid. A small number of Ute Mountain tribal members live in southeastern Utah on allotted trust land; although the allotments are not within the reservation itself they belong to the Ute and are considered as part of the reservation.

The reservation proper was established in 1895 by dividing the original Southern Ute Indian reservation. The established reservation is tribal trust land and has never been allotted to individual members. The total tribal holdings amount to 591,670 acres. These include tribal trust acreages of 448,030 in Colorado, 107,520 in New Mexico, and 2,328 in Utah, or 557,878 acres in all. Indian trust allotments add up to 9,459 acres in Utah, and 40 acres of government-owned trust, totaling 9,499. Tribal fee simple title lands total 24,293 acres. In addition, the tribe owns grazing permits on 132,695 acres of U.S. Forest Service and Bureau of Land Management holdings. The majority of the land is used for livestock grazing. A number of oil and gas leases are on tribal lands.

An elected tribal council with seven members has governed the Ute Mountain group since 1940, when a tribal constitution was adopted. The hereditary chief of the tribe, Jack House, although no longer an elected member of the council, has continued to have much influence in tribal affairs.

While the English language has come to be spoken, the common tongue is Ute. Much non-Indian attire is worn generally, but many of the women customarily wear shawls or blankets.

Reservation employment for wages consists of work for the tribal organization or the BIA. Self-employed activity is limited to stock raising with a very little farming. Revenue for the tribal organization comes from petroleum royalties and rentals and interest on tribal funds deposited with the U.S. Treasury.

The health of the population is good. Health care has been emphasized by the tribal government for a number of years, and is similar to health practices in general.

In the early 1950's, the average academic level of the Ute Mountain Ute was about fourth grade. Now the average is about sixth grade and is slowly rising. Younger children finish grade school, but the majority fail to complete high school. Concerted efforts by the tribal council, the tribal education committee, the BIA, and the public schools are helping, for more students reach the twelfth grade every year. Individuals are showing serious interest in vocational training, and several have taken advantage of programs offered by the BIA, OEO, and MDTA (Manpower Development and Training Act).

As of 1 August 1970, the tribal rolls of the Ute Mountain people listed 1,164 members; from this it has been estimated that the enrollment as of 1 January 1970 was 1,146 members. Of these, 778 live in Colorado, practically all in the community of Towaoc, the only reservation community. Some three hundred live in Utah. Descendants of small bands that always claimed the Blue Mountain region of Utah, and who refused to move to the Colorado reservation, reside on individual allotments of land at White Mesa in the vicinity of Blanding, Utah. The allotments were made in the 1920's and 1930's. There are some two hundred of these Blanding Ute —who are usually referred to as the Allen Canyon Ute.

Eighty-six Ute Mountain enrollees live on other reservations or off-reservation. Their closest ties are with the Southern Ute and the Northern Ute.

Inasmuch as other Indians, Spanish-Americans, and Anglos also reside on the Ute Mountain reservation the actual population was 1,187 as of July, 1970. Other Indians living in areas adjacent to the reservation bring total residency up to about 1,250 persons. Average family size is 4.7, and the average age in the tribe is sixteen years.

The council members of this reservation recognize that jobs are greatly needed. They are seeking industrialists to locate labor-demanding enterprises on the reservation. Presently, only few industries exist. Major resources include oil and gas from the San Juan basin, and "a spectacular extension of major archaeological ruins of the Mesa Verde type." The reservation adjoins the Mesa Verde National Park. Some timber is owned by the Ute Mountain Ute, but its economic value is uncertain. (Anonymous 1970b)

**THE
SOUTHERN UTE**

The Southern Ute Indian reservation also is in southwestern Colorado, occupying parts of La Plata and Archuleta counties. It has retained the fifteen-mile width of earlier times, but the length has been reduced to seventy-three miles. Within the boundaries of the reservation is some non-Indian land. The opening up of the reservation years ago to non-Indian homesteading resulted in an intermingling of Indian and non-Indian land holdings. In the 1930's the federal government returned to tribal ownership those acres contained in the Southern Ute reservation that had not been homesteaded. Of the present total of 818,000 acres within the exterior boundaries, some 307,000 acres are Indian land. Tribal trust land amounts to 299,443 acres; 4,967 acres are individually owned trust land.

The reservation lands vary from stream valleys to high mesas, with the most of the area at an elevation of between 6,000 and 7,000 feet. The climate is temperate and semiarid.

Since the reservation's establishment the people have relied on an agricultural economy based on cattle and sheep production, supplemented with some cash crops. Homes are built on irrigated farms in or near the Pine River valley. The land-base limitations and the general low economic level of agriculture in southwestern Colorado tend to prevent self-sustaining agriculture by a majority of the tribal members. For that reason, increasing tribal emphasis is being placed on development of employment-income producing enterprises in the fields of tourism and light manufacture.

In late 1971, a deluxe tourist center was opened at Ignacio. It includes

a 38-unit motel with meeting and banquet rooms, a pool, a lounge, a museum of Indian lore, an arts-and-crafts shop where guests may watch Indians at their native crafts, facilities for the display of motion pictures or slides, and a hall capable of accommodating four hundred.

In its auxiliary services, the tribe will supply fishing tackle and take its guests to the tribe's own Lake Capote for fishing. During big game season, guides will escort hunters on Southern Ute lands, and unexplored Indian ruins will be made accessible to guests.

Young members of the tribe were trained in tourist complex operations by restaurants, a motel, a hospital and the food service department of Fort Lewis College in Durango, 25 miles north of Ignacio. (Anonymous 1971b)

Aside from the dominant self-employed activities, wage employment is almost entirely of the service type, with the tribal organization and BIA being the principal employers.

In 1936 a tribal constitution was adopted, and since then the Southern Ute have been governed by an elected tribal council of six members. Their last chief, Antonio Buck, Senior, son of famed Chief Buckskin Charley, died in February, 1961. His position had been largely honorary, and the tribe has not chosen a new chief.

Revenue for the tribal organization is from petroleum royalties and timber sales and interest from tribal funds on deposit with the U.S. Treasury.

Enrolled membership of the Southern Ute is approximately 760, of whom about 600 are residents of the reservation; the remainder live in areas some distance from the reservation. Although Ute is the common language, most speak English. They dress as do their neighbors, for the most part, although a few of the women continue to wear shawls or blankets.

With the reorganization of agencies in 1968, the Southern Ute agency set up sixty-seven permanent positions, including twenty-nine people in school dormitory operations at Ignacio. This agency also provides some services to the Ute Mountain agency, such as plant maintenance when required. The latter agency has a staff of fifteen permanent employees.

THE NORTHERN UTE

The Northern Ute people live today on the Uintah and Ouray reservation, with agency headquarters at Fort Duchesne, west of Vernal, Utah, on U.S. Highway 40, approximately one hundred fifty miles east of Salt Lake City.

The reservation contains 1,008,192 acres of land situated in the Uintah basin of northeastern Utah. The elevation ranges from 4,655 to 9,200 feet above sea level, and the terrain varies from semidesert to forested mountains. In this environment, excellent hunting and fishing are provided.

On lands where the Uintah originally had been confined, the Uncompahgre and White River bands were moved by the federal government in 1881. Today about 1,200 full-blooded Ute of a total population of 1,600 reside on the reservation.

In 1952, the BIA closed the boarding school in Whiterocks. A few students attend off-reservation boarding schools. The six hundred school-age children are in public schools in the Uintah and Duchesne school districts.

Public Health facilities are located in Roosevelt, Utah, seven miles from the tribal headquarters. A clinic with full-time doctor, nurse, and dentist on duty is operated for walk-in patients. If patients are to be hospitalized, they enter a new County Hospital in the same building as the clinic.

The tribe has been very active in its economic development program. Its cattle enterprise is second to none in the state of Utah.* During the last two years, two hundred jobs have been opened on the reservation. The same period has shown a decline of about 23 per cent in the tribal welfare rate, and similar declines in the unemployment rate and arrest record.

The Ute Fabricating Company is a cabinet mill initially employing fifteen full-time employees, with an additional thirty men in training. A housing program under HUD was set to build one hundred fifty three-bedroom houses, eighty-six of which were to be completed by October, 1970.

The Ute people here have no intention of waiting for things or opportunities to come to them. Being developed in the center of the reservation is a multimillion dollar motel, restaurant, and recreational project called the "Bottle Hollow Complex." For this Bottle Hollow enterprise—so named because when federal troops were stationed at Fort Duchesne in the early 1900's, they hid their empty whiskey bottles in a gully near the site where the motel complex is being constructed—they have made sound and practical plans. Seventy members of the tribe were started in training for resort jobs, from desk clerk to lifeguard. Seventy more were to be trained as replacements.

The complex is in hexagonal form, employing a familiar symbol in Indian design. Fifty-two motel units form two large hexagons, one containing in its open center a six-sided swimming pool. Most of the furnishings of the motel—from beds to restaurant tables—are hexagonal. Included in the plans are an arts and crafts shop, service station, a combined restaurant-convention center, and a hexagonal plaza. Fishing, boating, and water skiing are made possible at a nearby reservoir.

Employees are given intensive courses in Ute history, English language skills, and the art of dealing with tourists. As these frequently cause problems for their Indian hosts, a former director of a hotel management school, and other instructors, were engaged to assist the Ute in learning how to keep even tempers. (Anonymous 1971d)

The Northern Ute participate in tribal dances throughout the

*The office of the Superintendent, Uintah and Ouray Agency, Fort Duchesne, supplied most of the information in this section.

year. Most common are the bear dances held in springtime. A traditional celebration is held on 4 July, with war dances and social dancing at Fort Duchesne. In the summer, the sun dance is held. The public is invited to all dances, but no pictures may be taken at a sun dance.

A few years ago, a group of mixed-bloods voted to sever relations with the Northern Ute Indians and with the federal government. These are known as the Affiliated Ute Citizens of Utah.

As with the Navaho and other Indians, the best way to learn more about the Ute people is to visit their homelands. Ignacio and Towaoc, the principal towns on the Colorado reservations, and the Roosevelt-Fort Duchesne area of the Utah Utes, are easily reached by good highways. The people will be found to be friendly and courteous if visitors are. Books on the Ute Indians are listed in the bibliography.

UTE BELIEFS AND CEREMONIES The Ute bear dance, which is still performed by members of the Ute bands, has been mentioned. To gain information regarding this observance the reader is referred to an account given by a participant of the annual bear dance held in March, 1893, by the Southern Ute group. Mr. V. Z. Reed was an intimate friend of the then war chief and several other prominent members of the tribe, and was allowed to make a study of the dance. He could find no tradition antedating the dance itself on which the ceremonies were founded, but he believed the bear dance to be one of the oldest of all the Ute ceremonies. (Reed 1896:237) Indians came from far and near to participate in the dance. All except the smallest children danced.

Veneration of the bear, in one form or another, tinges many of the Ute ceremonies. The bear is regarded as the wisest of animals and the bravest of all except the mountain lion; he is thought to possess wonderful magic power. Feeling that the bears are fully aware of the relationship existing between themselves and the Ute, their ceremony of the bear dance assists in strengthening this friendship.

The bear dance was formerly held in March—when bears recovered from hibernation—under the direction of some one person. In olden times this was usually a medicine man or chief, who had a number of assistants. Then, too, preparations lasted for two or three months.

A site was selected for the dance, and an enclosure, or *a-vik-wok-et*, "cave of sticks," erected. It was circular, from one hundred to one hundred fifty feet in diameter, and represented a bear cave. Its one opening faced the south or southeast, toward the sun. The walls of timbers and pine boughs were built to a height of about seven feet; the enclosure was open to the sky.

Within this structure at one side, a location was selected for the stand of the musicians, and a concave hole was dug into the earth—simulating a cave. Over the hole a box or drum with an open bottom was arranged, and *moraches*, or "singing sticks," were placed with one end on the lap of a rhythmist and the other end against the box. Up and down the notched sticks, bones or pieces of timber are rubbed, making a rasping sound which the boxdrum amplifies. Reed described the sound as resembling muffled cymbals.

In his day, twenty or more musicians who had been specially drilled for the ceremonies sang and played their moraches. They were joined by others when old or familiar songs were sung; the singers were always men. The music, resounding in the little cave, is thought to be transformed to thunder, which arouses the sleeping bears in their mountain caves. The duration of the dance—four days and one night—was fixed by the time required by bears to recover from hibernation.

With the conclusion of the fourth day's feast, all ceremonies of the dance are over. The bears are felt to have fully regained use of their faculties, have found mates, have been provided with food, and it is felt that they will gratefully remember their Indian relatives and repay them by assisting in the practice of magic.

At the time of his participation in the bear dance, in 1893, Reed stated that in former times the dance was more exactly observed than at that date. As one witnesses a bear dance of the present time, he may compare the observances with those of many decades ago. (*See* Emmitt 1954:34-40) The bear dances—traditional welcome to spring—continue on, although the time of celebrating has been altered somewhat, and the length of the ceremonies shortened so as to better meet the demands of modern life patterns.

The sun dance, a great summer ceremonial performed by Plains Indian groups, such as the Kiowa, Cheyenne, Sioux, Omaha, and others, was adopted by the Utes, adapted to their purposes, and continues to the present. The author had the privilege of attending the sun dance held near Ignacio, Colorado, July 1962, as a family member.

The fundamental object of the ceremony seems to be the over-coming of certain cosmic elements. All Indians performing it divide the ceremony into secret rites of one to four days' duration and a public performance. The secret rites include smoking, fasting, praying, and the preparation of objects that are to be used upon the altar or worn during the public performance.

On the last day of the secret rites a great lodge is built in the center of the camp circle, the selection of the site being the office of a special individual and attended with formal procedures. The ceremony of the sun dance abounds in symbolism, no rite being performed except in a prescribed manner. Of the sun dance in general, its ritual relates that once, in a period of famine an individual wandered forth with a female companion in behalf of his tribe, encountered a deity, fasted, learned the ceremony, returned to the tribe, caused the ceremony to be performed, and thus brought relief from famine through the appearance of the buffalo. The ceremony accordingly may be regarded as one of rebirth or reanimation.

It has been said that more than any other ceremony or occasion, the sun dance furnishes the Indians an opportunity for expressing emotion in rhythm, and for becoming more closely united.

Like the Navaho, the Ute people have taken over peyote ceremonialism.

SPEAK TO ME

O trees, say something.
One day you move back and forth,
Another day you are still.
How can I tell
What you are thinking, feeling?
Please speak to me.
Lovers carve names in you.
That must be painful.
I sit beneath your branches on sunny days,
When the wind blows and
Your leaves whisper and fly away,
Waiting for you to speak to me.
Are you angry at everybody?
Do you feel pain or delight?
Oh trees, please speak to me.

By Calvin O'John, Ute-Navaho

From: *The Writers' Reader,* 1962-1966, The Institute of American Indian Arts. Santa Fe, N.M.

SOUTHERN UTES AND COLORADO RIVER INDIANS

Fig. 1   A Navaho singer in characteristic attire. He wears a shell-disc and turquoise necklace and a die-stamped and embossed concho belt and has a bowguard (kehto) on his left wrist. His hair is arranged chongo style and held in place by a colorful kerchief. Across his chest is a hand-tanned band supporting a quiver, which is worn at the back; these are commonly fashioned from mountain lion skin. A bow extends from the quiver.

Photo from Elita Wilson Collection

Fig. 2 A Taos war dancer. His attire was adopted from the Plains Indians (the feathered war bonnet is not native to the Southwestern Indians). The drummer, who provides the dance rhythm with a single-headed drum, wears his hair in the style of the northern Pueblos of the Tiwa and Tewa groups. The beaded moccasins are also typical of the Plains Indians.

Photo by Elita Wilson

Fig. 3 A dance team from the eastern Keres pueblo of Santa Ana enacts a Buffalo dance at an off-reservation celebration. The dance leader is at the left; a drummer stands behind the buffalo maiden. Each buffalo dancer wears a painted buckskin kilk, with tin tinklers at the bottom edge; the waist in encircled by a red textile belt and band of bells; strings of shells are wrapped around the wrists and armbands adorn each arm. A gourd rattle is held in the right hand and a feathered bow in the left; the neck-chest ornaments are fashioned of shells, tied down to hold them secure during the highly animated movements of the dance. A real buffalo head with horns is worn as headdress.

Photo by Elita Wilson

Fig. 4   The Tcirkwena, or Skipping Dance. From the San
Xavier district of the Papago Reservation.

Photo by James Griffith

Fig. 5   An eagle dance, performed in the plaza at Laguna.

Photo by B. P. Dutton

Fig. 6 Gáhan dancers representing the supernatural Mountain Topway Spirits. Note the type of drum and drumstick used.

Photo by Elita Wilson

Fig. 7 A Black Mountain Navaho dance group, performers of the Mountaintop Way at a ceremonial observance at Gallup, New Mexico.

Photo by Elita Wilson

Fig. 8   Apache and Navaho Indians under guard constructing barracks at Fort Sumner (Bosque Redondo), 1864-1865. They were paid $0.25 per day for their labor, and keep was provided.

Photo courtesy Museum of New Mexico, John Gaw Meem Collection

Fig. 9   These Navaho twins were born at Fort Sumner during the time their parents were being held there, but they survived through all the vicissitudes that the Navaho experienced, and they were living on the reservation at the time of the centennial observances in 1968. When the Long Walk was reenacted, these two rode along part of the way on one of the wagons.

Photo courtesy Navajo Tribal Museum

Fig. 10   Black-robed friars and others mounted on horses, rayed circular elements, and various examples of Navaho art at Canyon del Muerto, Arizona.

Photo by B. P. Dutton

Fig. 11   A Navaho singer and his assistants making a sandpainting in the hogan of a patient who is being treated with a Nightway ceremonial for an illness.

Photo courtesy Laura Gilpin, Santa Fe

Fig. 12 Hopi men painting katsina in a chamber decorated with Navaho rugs and a large double-headed drum. The figure between them is the highly favored Hemish katsina, a potent fertility figure. Men properly attired are commonly chosen to represent these personages at the Home dances that close the ceremonial season, when "the gods" go to their home in the San Francisco peaks in late summer.

Santa Fe Railway photograph, Elita Wilson Collections

Fig. 13 A Nightway depiction dating from soon after the Pueblo Rebellion of 1680. On display at the Museum of Navaho Ceremonial Art, Santa Fe.

Photo courtesy Harry L. Hadlock

Fig. 14 A Navaho summer home in Monument Valley, with the family living near their fields.

Photo courtesy Laura Gilpin, Santa Fe

Fig. 15   A rectangular kiva built among dwellings at the pueblo of Jémez. Red chili is drying on the viga ends. A closed conical oven is seen at the angle of a house and the ceremonial chamber (which is entered by means of two tall ladders).

Photo by B. P. Dutton

Fig. 16   The Hopi often set up equipment for outdoor living during the warm days, as seen here at Upper Moencopi.

Photo by B. P. Dutton

Figs. 17 & 18   A Hopi woman making piki.
Left, putting batter on a stone griddle with a
whisk of her hand; the batter is in a Hopi
bowl. *Right*, removing a sheet of paper-thin
bread from the griddle; she places it in a
Hopi basket, layer on layer.

Photo by Suzanne de Berg

Fig. 19   A Papago woman puts tamales
into a steaming pot. The structure in the
background is an earthen oven in which the
bread is baked when many are to be fed.

Photo by Earl de Berg (1971)

Fig. 20   The Pueblo of Taos, north plaza, with Mount
Wheeler (the highest elevation in New Mexico) in the
background.

Photo by B. P. Dutton

Figs. 21-29   Navaho women and girls in styles of dress commonly worn during the past century. Many carry articles that signify their respective skills and household tasks. Photographed at the time of the centennial observance of the Navaho nation's return from the Long Walk and captivity at Fort Sumner.

Photos courtesy Navaho Tribal Museum

Figs. 30-38 Navaho men and boys who participated in the centennial activities commemorating the Long Walk to Bosque Redondo at Fort Sumner and the century of progress since 1868. The pictures show typical clothing worn during the century, including some accoutrements used especially on significant cultural occasions.

Photos courtesy Navaho Tribal Museum

Fig. 39   A pottery bowl is molded into shape by a Hopi woman from First Mesa, Arizona.

Photo by Suzanne de Berg

Fig. 40   A Mohave effigy jar.

Photo by Leslie Buckland

Fig. 41 A Hopi woman placing rods for the foundation of a basket. Fibers are kept pliable in moist sand.

Photo courtesy Elita Wilson

Fig. 42 A Pueblo man from Hopiland, with hair cut at sides only and worn chongo style. He is weaving a ceremonial sash; the decorated portion is in brocade weave, showing a convention- alized katsina mask, Broad Face.

Photo by Elita Wilson

Fig. 43 Scenes in Papagueria. Papago Indian cowboys cut out horses in one of their corrals built of mesquite poles.

Photo courtesy BIA, Branch of Land Operations,
SMC cartographic Section, Concho, Oklahoma

Fig. 44 A lettuce harvest on the Colorado River Indian Reservation.

Photo courtesy BIA, Branch of Land Operations,
SMC Cartographic Section, Concho, Oklahoma

5 the Southern Paiute

Linguistically the Southern Paiute belong to a Numic-speaking group of the Shoshonean branch of the UTO-AZTECAN stock. It was said by J. W. Powell that the name Paiute properly belonged exclusively to the "Corn Creek tribe" [Pah-vants] of southwestern Utah, but that the term had been extended to include several other Shoshonean-speaking peoples. (Hodge 1910) In general "Southwestern Paiute" has been applied to Ute-Chemehuevi groups. Since we are writing of the Southwestern Indians of the Four Corners States, attention is given only to those Paiute peoples of northwestern Arizona and southwestern Utah, although others of Paiute classification live in southwestern Nevada and parts of southeastern California.

Archaeological investigations and linguistic evidence have shown that "these Numic speakers spread across the Great Basin into the northern portion of the Southwest some time shortly after A.D. 1000, replacing prehistoric Pueblo or Pueblo-like peoples who had earlier lived in the region. In extreme southern Nevada and southwestern Utah, archaeologists have excavated the distinctive ceramic remains of the Southern Paiute in direct association with those of the Pueblos made around A.D. 1150. The Paiute pottery was brown or reddish-brown, conical with pointed bottoms, and often decorated with rows of 'finger nail' incisions. This is easily distinguished from the highly decorated black-on-white, black-on-yellow, or polychrome pottery of the Pueblos." (Euler 1972a:2)

It is probable that Southern Paiute people learned to raise corn and certain other products from the Pueblo Indians, making it possible for them to initiate a semisedentary living pattern. Rude defensive features found at some of the mid-twelfth century pueblos suggest that strife may have arisen between the two groups, causing the Pueblos to leave the region and the Paiute to add to their holdings eastward. Primarily, the Paiute were wild plant gatherers and hunters of rabbits and mountain sheep—for which they used long bows and arrows and long nets. Their homes were probably temporary camps and, to some extent, along permanent streams where they could farm. Excavations have brought forth grinding implements with which seeds, piñones, corn, and meat were ground and pounded. These milling stones differ from those used by the Pueblos. Southern Paiute-Hopi relationships appear to have existed on a friendly basis from around A.D. 1300-1600; trade was a major factor in their contacts.

The Southern Paiute were little disturbed by the Spaniards, with whom they came in slight contact during the sixteenth and seventeenth centuries. Father Escalante, who traversed their territory in 1776, seems to have been the first European who attempted to describe them systematically. He went through southern Utah a few miles north of present day Cedar City, and met a seed-gathering party of Southern Paiute Indians. (Bolton 1950; Euler 1972a) Later he encountered the Kaibab group.

In the same year, Father Garcés visited southern Paiute people known as the Chemehuevi, who dwelt near the Mohave on the lower Colorado River. It has been noted that Garcés "made it clear that the Chemehuevi, in the 18th century anyway, did not distinguish themselves from the Southern Paiute in the Las Vegas, Nevada, area immediately to the north." (Euler 1972a:18)

After the U.S.A. annexed New Mexico and California, the Paiute domain was encroached upon steadily, and some of the

Indians were placed on reservations. The majority, however, remained scattered through their country. Friction between the Paiute and the whites was minor until the 1840's, when it increased greatly. (Euler 1966:44-74)

Recently, it is said, only about 1200 Southern Paiute still survive. A shabby settlement in Cedar City, Utah, bespeaks their current state, "too few to wield political power, too poor to pay for legal advice." The government cut them off from federal benefits in 1956, and it has been noted that:

> Without birth certificates, Social Security numbers, or land deeds, they couldn't collect welfare or negotiate loans. For that matter, they didn't even know how to qualify for hunting and fishing licenses to seek food in the mountains and streams of their forefathers.

> At the same time the federal government emancipated the Paiutes, it declared they were unable to manage their own affairs and directed [a bank] . . . to sell their reservations. (Anderson 1971)

The Indian Peaks band sold their 10,000-acre reservation for $40,000.

The few women here who made basketry—a craft already on slim grounds—encountered further calamity. Due to extensive use of pesticides by farmers or government agents who sprayed the vegetation, including the requisite materials for basket making, several of the basket makers became ill from drawing contaminated willow twigs through their teeth. As a result, they were forced to go as far as central Nevada to find DDT-free materials. To make the trip, the older women at least had to depend upon someone with a car to take them. This and other factors have resulted in the decline of basket production. (Fowler, C. 1971)

The Kaibab Paiute Just north of the Grand Canyon in Arizona, bordering on Utah, the small Kaibab group is located. As late as 1869 this branch of the Southern Paiute had scarcely seen a white man. They were seminomadic, with a hunting and food-gathering economy. They did some fishing, so their food consisted of fish, jackrabbit and other small game, piñones, and seeds that were ground into flour for bread. Their dwellings were brush shelters erected upon poles planted in the ground, or upon an interlocking pole tripod conical in shape. Shelters were very temporary and frequently in summer none were used.

The geographical location kept these a poor, unorganized people, unable to resist the white man's settlements pushing into their domain and usurping their water. For years, they lingered in their original habitat near the new villages being founded by Mormons in northern Arizona and southern Utah. Cattle, sheep, and farming of the white man caused the destruction of their native foods, making life increasingly difficult. Gradually they attached themselves to the Mormon communities. As they were peaceable, of high moral character, and industrious, their willingness and efficiency made them necessary to the white farmers. Apparently the Paiute had little or no religious organization, and as a consequence the Mormon efforts toward conversion met with some success.

Mormons who settled in the 1860's at Moccasin Spring—the water of which the Paiute had used exclusively for centuries—forced the Kaibab group to move and become nomadic; they made their base in and near Kanab, Utah. Some time later, but prior to establishment of the Kaibab Reservation in 1907, Mormon church officials negotiated a deal with the squatters at Moccasin Spring, whereby one-third of the flow of the spring was granted to the Paiute and they were permitted to farm a small tract of land, watering it from the spring. (Euler 1972a:84, 87) Thus the Indians came to practice a little agriculture, with some irrigation. The BIA issued cattle to them at the time the reservation was established. A good herd was built up, but soon disseminated. Another herd, purchased in 1916, had become reasonably successful by 1930, but the depression that followed and the war of the 1940s lowered the Kaibab Paiute to a state of mere existence.

Foremost of the Paiute arts was basketmaking, including conical baskets for carrying burdens, parching trays for roasting seeds, water jars, hats, and semi-basketry cradles for babies. As elsewhere in the Southwest, basket making is passing from the scene. Pottery production was always minor. Formerly, extensive use was made of animal skins for clothing and, to some degree, shelters.

A social event—the round, or circle, dance—was held, and games were played.

In time, the Paiute reluctance to accept a changing way of life was overcome. Progress has come rapidly. Numbering 136 (in 1972), the Kaibab Paiute continue to live in small groups on their 120,413 acres of reservation land west of Fredonia, Arizona, on U.S. Highway 89. All commonly dress in western garb today.

The Kaibab Paiute operate under a tribal constitution adopted in 1951, with a council of members of either sex elected annually. The officers are: a chairman, vice chairman, secretary-treasurer, tribal judge, and chief of police. The council meets each month in

Fredonia. The chairman is the only salaried employee of the tribe.

Their tribal headquarters is at Moccasin, in the west-central part of the reservation.

Under provisions of the Indian Claims Act passed by Congress in 1946, the Kaibab and several other Southern Paiute groups filed suit against the government of the U.S.A., "claiming restitution payment for all their aboriginal lands that had been wrongfully taken from them by the Government or agents thereof." (Euler 1972a:92) The case was not decided until 1970, but the Indians won and a judgment was received. With a land claim settlement of slightly more than a million dollars, the Kaibab appear to be destined for better times. It has been said:

Today, some fourteen families, comprising sixty-two people, live in the small settlement of Kaibab, two miles from Moccasin Spring. The remaining seventy-four individuals live nearby. While a few still live in small, frame houses, ten other families reside in attractive and recently completed "self help" concrete block structures. The main roads are paved, thus easing transportation problems especially in the snowy winter months. A spacious tribal administrative building was officially dedicated on June 2nd, 1970, providing adequate offices and meeting facilities for the tribal council and other employees.

Reservation lands are not yet used to their full economic potential. Until recently, approximately 10,000 acres of grazing land were leased to non-Indian ranchers but the remainder was not in any type of production.

There are two private enclaves within the Kaibab Reservation boundaries. One of these, 400 acres, comprises the Mormon settlement of Moccasin. The other tract, of 40 acres, is the National Park Service facility of Pipe Springs National Monument, an early Mormon "fort" around a small spring.

The Kaibab Paiutes receive medical and dental care through contract services with physicians and dentists in nearby communities, a program financed by the U.S. Public Health Service. There is also a resident P.H.S. community health worker on the reservation.

Paiute children—and of the total population of 136, forty-four are under the age of 16—attend a one room public school in Moccasin. From the sixth grade through high school, however, they are bussed to Fredonia, twelve miles to the east. Approximately 10 Paiute children are not in high school and four others are attending college. (Euler 1972a:92-94)

Opportunities for producing individual income on the reservation are limited. A few Indians are employed by federal or state agencies. Other than for those, stock raising provides some income, and men for the most part derive wages from work on nearby ranches owned by white men.

Expecting the land claims funds to alleviate some unemployment, the Kaibab Tribal Council has allocated 15 per cent of the total claim payment to per capita distribution. "This amounts to slightly over $1,000 per individual. An additional 15% has been budgeted for a 'family plan.' These funds are distributed by the council to enable families to pay off past debts, obtain household furnishings, and other immediate family needs. Both of these budgeted items are being released to the Paiute at the present time. The remaining 70 per cent of the land claim monies are being budgeted as follows: Education, 10 per cent; Tribal Enterprises, 35 %; Community Development, 15%; and Administration, 10%. None of these funds has as yet been expended. (Euler 1972a:94)

The Shivwits Indian Reservation

In the very southwestern corner of Utah, on a desolate 27,000-acre reservation, a Paiute people called the Shivwits are located. They were only beginning to have contact with the whites by 1870. When their land was offered for sale some years ago through a Salt Lake City bank, no one who wanted to buy it could be found. (Anderson 1971)

Theirs is plateau land, through which the Santa Clara River flows. U.S. Highway 91 leads through the reservation from Saint George, Utah, to the Arizona and Nevada borders. Between 150 and 200 are on the census roll. They live in brokendown shacks.

THE CHEMEHUEVI INDIANS

Chemehuevi is the Yuman name for a group of Indians who were a part of the true Paiute, and were associated with them and the Ute in one linguistic subdivision of the Shoshonean tongue. (*See* Fowler and Fowler, 1971:5,7) They called themselves *Tántáwats*, meaning "southern men."

Anciently, they lived in the eastern half of the Mohave Desert, and it has been estimated that there were between 500 and 800 of them. They lived in small huts of Paiute type, usually low shelters covered with dirt and of temporary nature. Their means of subsistence was seasonal plant-gathering and hunting, with a few attempts at growing meager crops near springs. (Stewart 1967:14) They made excellent baskets. In 1776 no Chemehuevi lived on the Colorado River below Eldorado Canyon. Later, they settled on Cottonwood Island, about fifteen miles north of Davis Dam, in the Chemehuevi valley, and at other points on the Colorado River. Here they were under strong Mohave and Yuma influence (these are discussed in the following section).

It is reported that although the Chemehuevi continued to stress basketry, they began to imitate the Mohave in making a few pottery vessels, quite in the Mohave manner. The men started to wear their hair in Mohave fashion, rolling it into thin "ropes" that hung down the back. They took over the use of tule rafts and log rafts, and "the Yuman practice of ferrying goods and children across the river in large pots." The Chemehuevi had known the practices of interment and of cremation; they followed the Yumans in cremating bodies and possessions of the deceased in a special rite, and in a mourning ceremony wherein images of the dead were housed in a special structure. (*See* Drucker 1937)

Another source states that, "Once on the river the Chemehuevi seem to have become a more definite political entity, with a chief called the *towintem*, who had more authority or at least more influence than Chemehuevi leaders had previously possessed." Their religion took on Mohave characteristics; they began to sing song cycles which told of mythological events, in the Mohave manner. And "like his Mohave counterpart, the Chemehuevi shaman dreamed his power to cure." (Stewart 1967:16) The Chemeheuvi also adopted certain Mohave modes of making war.

On 2 February 1907, the Chemehuevi Indian Reservation was created by the Secretary of the Interior, and became the home of the Chemehuevi. It was located roughly halfway between Parker, Arizona, and Needles in San Bernardino county, California. Then, in 1940, the river bottom lands totaling about 7,776 acres were sold to Los Angeles Metropolitan Water District and deeded back to the U.S. government for control. The Chemehuevi were paid $108,342 for the land. Eleven allotments—the only ones ever made on the Chemehuevi reservation—were assigned within the river bottom area. They were all sold and the land is now under water. The balance of the reservation—approximately 28,000 acres—was not productive without expensive irrigation facilities.

With the construction of Parker Dam on the Colorado River, which was completed in 1938, virtually all of the arable acres came to be inundated by the water of Lake Havasu. Insofar as was known in 1970, only one Chemehuevi was living on the reservation. The others were moved to the Colorado River Indian Reservation,and became enrolled members of the Colorado River Indian Tribes. It is estimated that the membership includes 600 Chemehuevi.

The Chemehuevi observe no tribal or religious ceremonies. Recently it was found that only one old basket maker remained of the tribe.

AS ONCE, SO WERE WE

We are the native Americans;
This was our land from sea to sea.
Our thoughts were all thoughts,
As once, so were we.

But time seemed to change
When the white man came;
Came he, mighty in strength,
As once, so were we.

"Never mind," said my father,
"The world will go on."
And he chanted and prayed
and sang his death song:

The Earth is my Mother,
She will always be near.
The Sun, my Father,
I have nothing to fear.
The Moon is my Sister,
Standing with me at night.
The Stars are my Cousins
Who guide me in flight.
The Great Spirit is my God
Of life and of love.
We will soon be with Him
In His land up above.

By Raymond Hamilton, Mariposa-Paiute-Tuolumne

From: *The Writers' Reader*, Fall, 1966, The Institute of American Indian Arts, Santa Fe, N. M.

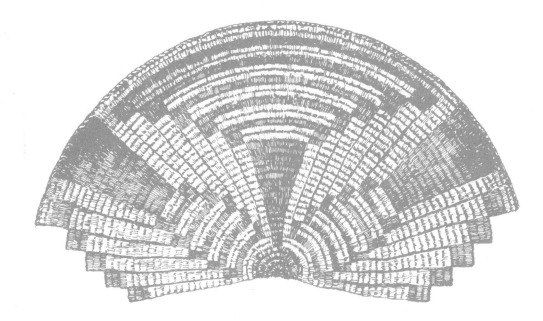

6 the ranchería peoples

In contrast to the Pueblo peoples, the great majority of aboriginal dwellers of southern Arizona (and northwestern Mexico), although equally sedentary, did not live in compact, closely built settlements. Their houses might be scattered at some distance from each other, thus forming loose settlements here and there on the farmlands, or *rancherias*. A group occupying these locations might shift from one ranchería to another during the course of a year. They were all agriculturists, with farming their major activity. Among these peoples, as among the Pueblos, many similarities obtained. Especially in their economy were they alike; in community structure they were more disparate. Most of them spoke languages belonging to the UTO-AZTECAN stock, such as the Pimans and Cahitans. But, other than these, the Yumans belonged to another linguistic family, the HOKAN-SIOUAN. Their range was to the northwest of the other ranchería peoples.

THE COLORADO RIVER
.... INDIAN TRIBES

The Colorado River Indian Reservation was established by Act of Congress, and approved by the President on 3 March 1865. The boundaries were subsequently fixed and determined by Executive Orders dated 22 November 1873, 16 November 1876, and 22 November 1915.

The reservation lies in a valley along the lower course of the Colorado River. Although surrounded by mountains, the valley is definitely desert with an elevation of approximately 400 feet above sea level. Characteristic vegetation of the valley consists of cactus, mesquite, and *chaparral*, or dense thickets of thorny shrubs; arrowweed grows along the river. Average rainfall is about four inches per year. No snow falls in the valley, but the surrounding mountains are sometimes capped with light snow in the wintertime. The average humidity is generally 15 per cent, but at times it runs between 55 and 60 per cent. The mean temperature averages 71° F., ranging from an average minimum of 56° to an average maximum of 86°, the average extreme maximum temperature being 97°. In December and January the average low temperature is 39°, and in June, July and August, the average high temperature is 110-113°.

The first expenditure of federal funds for irrigation development in the U.S.A. was made for work on this reservation in 1867, with fifty thousand dollars being spent. All the work was done with shovels and baskets by about five hundred Indians. Because of faulty design and an unusually high water level in the river, the canal washed out as soon as the gates were opened. In 1874 another canal was completed; it too met with failure. Additional appropriations followed for canal construction, pumping facilities, engineering studies, and construction of Headgate Rock Dam, a diversion structure that was placed in operation on 4 July 1942.

In 1873 the first school on the reservation was opened.

During World War II, the War Relocation Authority built camps on the reservation and relocated approximately nineteen thousand Japanese there. These camps were closed and the Japanese removed in 1944. A year later, sixteen Hopi families were relocated on the Colorado River Indian Reservation. During subsequent years, one hundred and fourteen Navaho families and three Havasupai families were colonized on irrigated lands on the reservation. The program was ended in 1952.

The Colorado River Indian Reservation is approximately 264,250 acres in size, with 225,914 acres located in Yuma county, Arizona, and 38,366 acres situated in San Bernardino and Riverside counties, California. The reservation agency is headquarters for the Fort Yuma Subagency, Yuma, Arizona (located on the Fort Yuma Indian Reservation, California), and for the Indian reservations of Fort Mohave (Needles, California), Chemehuevi, and the Cocopah around the mouth of the Colorado River (Somerton, Arizona).

THE FORT MOHAVE RESERVATION

This reservation is situated along both sides of the Colorado River, being partly within Mohave County, Arizona; San Bernardino County, California; and Clark County, Nevada. The land generally extends from a point across the river from Needles to a point about fifteen miles north of that city. The part west of the river begins some five miles north of Needles and is divided into two areas—one in California and one in Nevada. The northerly part of the lands is an integral area, while the southerly part, east of the river, is a checkerboard area, the sections alternating. The terrain is desertlike with brushy first bench land and river wash areas as well as portions of the river channel.

Agency headquarters is in Parker, Arizona, and the Mohave tribal offices are in Needles. The Fort Mohave Reservation was established by Executive Order, 19 September 1880. Another order of 1 December 1910 enlarged the reservation, but one of 2 February 1911 revoked that order and added other lands to the reservation. Then an act of 8 July 1940 granted the right to take specific Mohave lands within the reservation that would be needed for construction of the Parker Dam and Reservoir, up to the 455-foot contour line. "At no time did they intend or authorize a taking for any other purpose. Nevertheless, when the trustee later issued an order designating the Mojave* lands needed for the authorized purpose, no mention was made of the 455-foot contour limitation. Instead, the specified lands were erroneously described by metes and bounds, thereby resulting in an unauthorized seizure of several thousands of acres of Mojave land." (*See* note on following page.)

Then, we are informed:

Very recently, the Indian Claims Commission declared that title still resides in

*See the Linguistic Notes of p. xxix.

the Fort Mojave Tribe in regard to the several thousand acres of land to which reference has been made.

There are two categories of Mojave land included in the several thousand acres thus seized without authority: (1) Indian lands occupied and fenced by the Fish and Wildlife Bureau of [the] Department [of the Interior] far exceeding the area flooded by Parker Dam and in no manner required for that purpose; (2) Lands which have been flooded for which no compensation was paid. (Fort Mojave Tribal Council 1970*)

The present reservation of 38,382 acres is owned in undivided shares by tribal members, and is held in trust for them by the federal government. A total of 511 people live on the reservation. That their claims to title have not had due recognition or protection from the federal government is observable through one injustice after another that the Indians have suffered for more than the past three decades.

In 1962, when a case arose between the Indians and the U.S.A., the U.S. Attorney, purportedly in behalf of the Indians, abandoned their cause and argued against them. Primary results were that the Indians lost possession of lands (which many think should be returned to them) and a legal barrier has been interposed, denying them redress in present claims—which have received no support, apparently, from the Justice Department. The Indians state that:

Seizure by the United States, trustee of Fort Mojave Indian Property, has transpired throughout the entire reach of the Colorado River as it traverses or borders upon the Fort Mojave Indian Reservation. That seizure stems in part from acquisitions by the Bureau of Reclamation in the name of the United States which have cut off entirely or gravely impeded the Mojaves' access to the Colorado River to which they are legally entitled. Loss of access is tantamount to imperiling for all time the full economic potential of the Mojave lands.

There are at least seven substantial areas in which the right to access of the Mojaves to the Colorado River has been seized in its entirety or gravely impeded, all as stated above. In all, there are approximately 12 miles of land lying on both sides of the Colorado River where the irreparable damage to the Indians as described above has taken place.*

The Secretary of the Interior, as the principal agent for the U.S.A. and trustee for the Indians, was beseeched to "take speedy and adequate steps fully to assert on behalf of the Mohave Indians their rights of access to the Colorado River which have been seized from them without authority." (Fort Mohave Tribal Council 1970*)

*Letter of 27 October 1970, as follow up of an urgent telegram sent about six weeks before to the Secretary of the Interior.

THE MOHAVE PEOPLE   The Mohave and Yuma peoples spoke a different language from that of the Chemehuevi, being of the Yuman linguistic group of the HOKAN-SIOUAN family. It is said that the Mohave called themselves *Tzi-na-ma-a* before they came to live along the Colorado River. "Mohave" is taken from a native word, *hamakave*, referring to Needles, and signifying "three mountains." (Swanton 1952:356) These people came to dwell on both sides of the stream, mostly on the east side, between Needles and the entrance to Black Canyon. Theirs was a rancheria type of life. Early Spanish explorers mentioned their villages. Oñate met them in 1604-1605, and Garcés found their settlements in 1775-1776. (Galvin 1967:v, 12ff.) No Spanish towns or missions were established in the Mohave territory. The Mohave were said to number 3,000 in 1680 and 1770.

The earliest Anglos to enter Mohaveland were fur trappers and fur traders. They came from 1826-1834, but their visits had slight effect on Mohave culture. It was the coming of others, after the midcentury, that caused uneasiness among the Indians. In an encounter with soldiers in 1859, many of the Mohave were killed. From 1900 on, they apparently decreased steadily, and their enrollment shifted from one Indian agency to another.

The Mohave of Old   In their initial state the Mohave subsisted by small scale farming, gathering of wild plant foods, trapping, and hunting and fishing. A hunter never ate what he killed. Floodwater irrigation was utilized in the production of corn, melons, pumpkins, and several wild herbs. When floods did not occur and crops failed, the people ate mesquite beans; they ate beaver, but would not eat turtles, snakes or lizards as did the Chemehuevi and other desert dwellers.

The Mohave had hereditary chiefs in the male line—men of honor and dignity—but their functions are said to have been obscure. Much more influential were the brave men, war leaders, and shamans. Their enemies were the Cocopah, Pima, Papago, and Maricopa. Friendly peoples were the Yuma, Chemehuevi, Yavapai, and western Apache.

Homes of the Mohave were built of logs and wood, with roofs thatched with arrowweed and covered with sand. They were usually about twenty by twenty-five feet in size, and the door was always to the south because of the frequent cold north winds of the desert.

The Mohave attire generally was similar to that of other lower Colorado River peoples, but had its own characteristics. Both men and women commonly wore loincloths, covering the upper body only in inclement weather; they went barefoot and bareheaded. A woman's dress was made in two parts—separate back and front aprons of willow bark strips hung from waist cords. The front piece fell to the knees; it was donned first, with its cord tied in back. The calf-length back apron which was thicker was tied in front; it lapped over at the hips but left the outside of the thighs somewhat bare. A short underapron was worn at all times beneath the front apron; it was made of fine willow bark.

The breechclout of the men was held in place by a belt, the ends forming a short flap in front and a longer one in back—to the knees or below. These were made of willow bark strips in a checkerboard weave. When an upper garment was worn—a privilege of only a few—it was of rabbitskin strips held together with cords, obtained by trade from the Walapai Indians, or a wool poncho bartered from the Navaho. Sandals were worn by men and women only when traveling. No leggings were worn, nor hats. Sometimes men tied downy feathers or quills to the crown hair of their heads.

These people were long famous for the artistic painting of their bodies. Some tattooing was also done, though it is rare now.

Crafts and   Pottery was made by the Mohave in at least three distinctive forms.
Implements   A strong association was felt between their pottery and their agriculture. A harvest of food was not complete until bowls had been made for cooking and storing it. The men and women worked together. Clay had to be tempered with crushed sandstone, and the pottery vessels were built up by the coiling process; they were decorated with a yellow ochre pigment, which turned to a dull red upon being fired—by means of an open wood fire.

Mohave basketry was very poor, both in quality and in its paucity of types; none is made today. The only true basketry receptacle made was a flat tray, slightly oval in outline, some eighteen inches broad at the wider end, and two feet long. These were made of slender willow twigs twined at intervals with split willow twigs, and a rim was fashioned of a thick willow branch bound on with long split mesquite root strands. The trays were used for sifting chaff from ground mesquite pods or corn, or for cooling parched seeds. A netted structure supported by a framework of sticks served as a carrying frame. A headring used for carrying was made of willow bark; women used these to bear the forehead band of the carrying frame, or to support pottery or other burdens carried on the head, including the baby cradles when carried lying flat on the head. Otherwise cradles were held horizontally on the hip, never on the back.

When imported glass beads became available, the Mohave accepted them eagerly. To this day they do beautiful beadwork.

Gourds in a variety of shapes were used for carrying water and storing seeds. Globular gourds were made into rattles, with a wooden handle inserted in the stem end and fastened with gum of greasewood and arrowweed. Two parallel rows of tiny holes formed a decorative cross on the body of the rattle.

The Mohave used slim shinny sticks with moderate curve. Their bows were shaped like a shallow *D*, nearly straight for most of the length and tips curved toward the string. The bow staves were made of willow or screw bean (*tornillo*), or mesquite. Length of a bow depended upon the height of the man who carried it—the ideal length being from ground to the chin. Hunting bows were shorter than war bows, averaging three and a half to four feet. The Mohave had great interest in warfare; they were brave and had notable leaders, or war chiefs. Their fighting was primarily hand-to-hand, when they could charge upon their enemies with war-club and bare hands, or the bow and arrow. (Spier 1955)

Dream Life   In addition to their concrete day-to-day living, they set great importance upon their dream life; and even today they passively drift away without external inducement, such as drink, drugs, dancing or costume garments. From these dreams—which to the Mohave are regular visits with their ancestors—come their decisions and their principal motivations. Religious interest revolves around funeral ceremonies, in which they cremate their dead with rites and loud wailing; the meager supply of personal belongings is burned with the owner.

Changes in Attire   After a time, the basic agricultural products were expanded to include beans, cantaloupes, and wheat. With the improved economy, other changes took place. The older women wear long, full dresses of bright print, with scarves on their heads. When a death occurs in the family the women may cut their hair which, otherwise, is worn long and straight. The older men dress as most westerners, with denim pants, western shirts, boots, and large hats. The younger men and women and the children dress as do their white contemporaries.

*The People and
Their Ceremonies*

The Mohave men are inclined to be tall, large-boned, and lean. The women are not so tall and are prone to be stout; they have good-natured faces. Skin color is of a noticeably yellow hue. The people are responsive, energetic, and smiling.

Most of the ancient Mohave ceremonies have become extinct. A bird dance has been preserved, and is colorfully performed by a small group, carefully costumed, at celebrations and public gatherings. Several times during the decade of the 1960's and into the 1970's, this group presented its dance at the Intertribal Indian Ceremonial in Gallup, New Mexico.

Altogether, the present cultural picture is in sharp contrast with that of the past. (*See* Brennan 1966)

*Political and
Economic
Development*

The Chemehuevi, the Mohave, and the Hopi and Navaho Indians enrolled at the Colorado River Agency, Parker, Arizona, and living harmoniously together on the Colorado River Reservation constitute the Colorado River Tribes. They number 1,620, of whom 1,120 live on the reservation. They accepted the Indian Reorganization Act, have a constitution, and hold elections on the first Saturday of December every second year. The adult members vote, using the secret ballot. Their council, which governs the reservation, is made up of nine male and female members; it meets the first Saturday of each month at 9:00 a.m., in Parker.

They have six active committees, each with its chairman. Tribal operations relate to tribal government, enrollment, and claims; the improvement of social, economic, and political status; and the assuming of greater responsibility in the management of their own affairs. Programs under way include Community Action, Community Development, Headstart, and NYC (Neighborhood Youth Corps). They have their own code of law and order, tribal police and tribal court.

A new tribal administrative office building and a library have been built about a mile south of the agency. Across from these is a recreation center with a large building where fairs, socials, carnivals, and other events are held; there, too, is a baseball field and bleachers, an outdoor basketball court, and an outdoor stage for shows and contests. North of Parker the Indians are in the recreation business in a big way; they operate the Bluewater marina, with *cabañas*, trailer park, restaurant, gift shop, a boat launching pad, and judges' stand for boat racing. The Indians are attractive, gracious, and efficient hosts and hostesses. They are exceptionally progressive and farsighted, and are making great progress in their program to become entirely self-sufficient.

The winters here are so mild that fishing, boating, and picnicking continue throughout the year. (*See* Brennan 1967) Several motorboat races are held during the spring, and a two-day rodeo in November. Hunting is good on the reservation (ducks, geese, quail and doves), as is fishing. Permits are issued for these sports.

It is the general mission of the Colorado River Agency to administer Indian affairs within its jurisdiction, in cooperation with the Indian people in planning, executing, and coordinating the BIA's extensive and varied programs. These cover education, welfare, law enforcement, soil and moisture conservation, range management, irrigation, extension, forest management, road construction and maintenance, realty, credit, plant management, development of local self-government and tribal undertakings, industrial development, employment assistance and vocational training.

Land and Water   The most important single program, probably, has to do with the maintenance of subjugated lands and the development of more such land. In this, the operation of an extensive irrigation system, carrying water diverted from the Colorado River on the Arizona side, and hydrographic investigation, surveying, construction of facilities, drainage and seeding activities are said to be of paramount importance. The Indians have shown marked ability to take advantage of the latest advances in farming, such as use of modern equipment, methods, fertilizers, and insecticides. Several packing sheds operate in Parker during various harvesting seasons.

The U.S. Supreme Court has ruled that the Indians have "perfected water rights from the Colorado River" and permission to grant long-term leases to non-Indians: twenty-five years for residential land, ninety-nine years for recreational and commercial land. (Brennan 1967:18) Fifty thousand acres are now farmed by the Indians for themselves or lessees, and 107,000 acres are guaranteed a first-class irrigation system for the future. Market crops of alfalfa, barley, cantaloupes, carrots, cotton, corn silage double-cropped with maize, lettuce, and small grains are reported in truly fabulous yields and all the year round. Ten thousand sheep are wintered and cattle are fattened for market in feed lots. All prospects point to brilliant success, according to the most modern standards . . . if the Mohave can withstand the machinations and rapacity of the white men and the governmental agencies which they control.

Recently, like so many other of the Indian peoples, the Mohave and the Chemehuevi have developed a new awareness of their former cultural products. In 1970, upon learning of a collection of Mohave beadwork and pottery and Chemehuevi baskets which had been assembled by a pioneer storekeeper in Parker, Arizona, and was being auctioned off in Phoenix to settle an estate, members of the two Indian groups mortgaged their best land to raise fifty thousand dollars with which to purchase part of their heritage. They had to bid against dealers and collectors who were willing to pay as much as two hundred dollars each for the five hundred pieces which are irreplaceable today; nothing like them remained on the reservations. A Chemehuevi woman remarked that their basketry never had been made for sale, "but for use in this world and the next." She said, "It would never do to bury a Chemehuevi without a basket." (Anonymous 1970d) The items that they were successful in purchasing were for their tribal museum. The Indians' intent was to elicit as much information as possible regarding them from their old people, and to have the collection available for research purposes.

Employment, Housing, and Education

Many of the Indians on the Colorado River Reservation work for the BIA and the U.S. Public Health Service. The latter maintains a fully staffed hospital and field clinic at the agency for the people of the reservation; it can be used by the public in emergencies only. Positions for the Indians include clerks and office workers, carpenters, janitors, bus drivers, cooks, hospital aids, tractor and dragline operators, oilers, truck drivers, surveyors, stakemen, rodmen, engineering aids, ditchriders, mechanics, linemen and groundmen on the power crew, road grader operators, policemen, accountants, teachers, and nurses.

Quarters for the majority of the BIA employees have been furnished at or near the agency, at nominal rentals. They range from very good to poor, but all are equipped with coolers. Living accommodations in Parker are very scarce, and are generally more expensive. Electricity, natural gas, and bottled gas are all available in the area.

The public school system maintains a grammar school and high school in Parker for both Indian and non-Indian children, and a grammar school at Poston, seventeen miles from Parker, for Indian and non-Indian children. The schools are considered very good; they are accredited; and they have good hot lunch programs. Transportation is provided for all pupils living out of town. Very active programs are provided for the youngsters in 4H, FFA, sports, and recreation.

An increasing number of Indian boys and girls from this reservation attend college. Several have won scholarships, and several others are assisted by grants from the tribes or the federal government. These students are said to encounter about the same problems as other college students, and they make about the same grades as average students.

Law Enforcement Indians and non-Indians cooperate in law enforcement. Offenses committed by non-Indians on the Indian reservations of Arizona are handled by state or county officers exactly as if they had taken place in any non-Indian community. This applies also in most civil cases. Offenses committed by Indians on reservations within Arizona are handled through two courts: (1) if the offense committed is one of the eleven major crimes, it is handled through Federal District Court by the FBI and assistant U.S. Attorney General; (2) if the offense is of the misdemeanor type, the offender is arrested by the tribal policeman or BIA special officer and prosecuted by tribal court. All civil cases wherein the defendant is an Indian and the tort originated on the reservation are handled by tribal courts.

THE YUMAN (QUECHAN) PEOPLE *Yuma* is said to be an ancient Pima and Papago Indian term for the Indians that comprised one of the oldest groups of the old Yuma-speaking stock. Although commonly called "Yuma Indians," these people actually are *Quechan*, who speak a dialect of the Yuma language. "Quechan" derives from *xam kwatcan*, or "another going down" [on the legendary trail by which they came]. (Johnston 1970:64) Their prehistoric domain "stretched from the Pacific coast in the region of the present international boundary eastward through the mountains, across the southern portion of the less arid south-central valley of California to the Colorado River and beyond into the western portion of the elevated area of Arizona north of the Gila River." (Ezell and Ezell 1970:170) In early historic times they occupied both sides of the Colorado, fifty or sixty miles from the mouth thereof, at and below its junction with the Gila. Fort Yuma was in the approximate center of that territory.

The first explorer to mention the Yuman people by name was Father Kino, in 1701-1702. Later Spanish travelers spoke of them increasingly. They numbered between 3,000 and 3,500. With the treaty of Guadalupe Hidalgo in 1848, most of the Yuma lands passed to the control of the U.S.A.; the Gadsden Purchase

(1853) completed the transfer. Fort Yuma was established and relationships between the Yuma and the whites became close.

The Fort Yuma Reservation   The Fort Yuma Reservation was established by Executive Order of 6 July 1883, amended 9 January 1884, and included approximately 48,608 acres in the reservation proper. Then, on 4 December 1893, through agreement between the Fort Yuma Indians and the U.S.A., all land not considered irrigable was returned to the public domain. Congress ratified that agreement, and the present reservation of 8,661 acres was established. In 1912 the reservation was allotted to the Fort Yuma Indians.

The elevation of the reservation lands varies from one hundred and twenty five feet along the river to one hundred and forty feet along the All American Canal. On the hill where the subagency headquarters is located, the elevation rises to two hundred and sixty seven feet above sea level. The land is very good for farming, and it produces high yields when proper practices are followed.

In the Yuma country the climate is very dry, and all farming is done by irrigation. Annual rainfall amounts to approximately three inches, sufficient to support desert flora only. The evaporation rate is very high. Mean annual temperature is 71.9°F. The summers are long and hot, with a maximum temperature of 125°, and the winters are short and mild with a minimum of 22°.

The Quechan have been battling federal authorities on the issues of land and water for many years. Irrigation canals bisect their reservation; they run full of water—into non-Indian hands. One of the Quechan men recently said: "We have a one-inch pipe that brings water into our reservation. At the end of the line, there just is no pressure. We have had to stand by helplessly while several houses there have burned." Despite the ample water in the canals, the Indians cannot get more for their own use. (Mangel 1970:42-43)

Living on the Fort Yuma Reservation are some 1,007 Indians, and an additional 619 enrolled members live off the reservation. As the Quechan Tribe they adopted a constitution and bylaws on 28 November 1936. A council of seven members governs the group; these are elected to office by popular vote.

THE COCOPAH PEOPLE   The Cocopah represent the only remaining group of a series of important Yuman-speaking peoples that occupied the delta of the Colorado River in aboriginal times. All originally dwelt in Mexico—

until the U.S.A. border extended into their territory. The name Cocopah is said to derive from Mohave *Kwi-ka-pah*. (*See* Bahti: 1968:63) They were first mentioned by Europeans about 1605 when they lived in nine rancherías near the river's mouth. These rancherias were inhabited by related people. In 1771 the Cocopah occupied all of the southern one-third of the delta, but four years later they had been pushed to the west side of the river. Garcés reached them in December of 1775. Later, they occupied scattered settlements on both sides of the stream; and in 1900 it was estimated that about six hundred resided on each side, in three major divisions.

Those most favorably located practiced small-scale farming, with corn, beans, black-eyed peas, pumpkins and melons, primarily. Cultivated foods were supplemented by wild ones: seeds, roots and fruits; fish, game and eggs. Nearly all vegetal foods and some fish—derived from the Colorado River and the Gulf of California—were dried and stored for winter. The Cocopah hunted singly on foot, but group hunting came about with the use of horses. Rats and dogs frequently were eaten.

The dwellings were of various types, ranging from thatched temporary structures to more permanent mud-and-wattle houses. Small granaries were constructed with floors elevated above ground.

Until recently shamanism was practiced extensively, primarily for curing the ill. Everything was dream-directed. Women were tattooed and men's features pierced for ornaments; this was believed to be necessary to prevent wandering of the soul after death. Religious activities revolved around death ceremonies, and the dead were cremated. The name of a deceased one was never spoken.

Socially, a loose division of labor was observed. Adult men and women with established families bore the main responsibilities. Men were responsible for the planting, hunting and fishing; women did most of the gathering; and everyone participated in the harvesting. Children had only occasional chores.

Some pottery was made for domestic use, but this industry died out a number of years ago. Loom weaving was practiced and crudely woven cylinders of basketry were made—these were without bottom or top and were set upright on the ground and filled with beans and other items. Shell beads were made to some extent.

The Cocopah engaged to a considerable degree in warfare, mostly of the club and bow and arrow variety. War activities were carried on for hundreds of years, with formalized war patterns and leadership . . . yet the concept of leadership was not expanded to their political and social systems. It has been said that:

Disintegration of Cocopa culture and economy probably began with the disruption of war in the 'fifties, which removed a major field of interest for which, apparently, no substitute was found. Then came the river boats, and an appetite was created for American goods and foods. Finally, after 1900, when the irrigation companies began harnessing the Colorado, the Cocopa served as a source of cheap labor, and a wage economy was inaugurated. During the years between 1905 and 1907, when the Colorado was flowing into the Salton Sea, the Cocopa were left high and dry in their delta habitat. Not only was there no water for their farms, but that same lack prevented the growth of wild plants, and reduced the fish and game supply. It was a question of move or starve. (Kelly, D.S. 1950:167)

Lacking leadership of political, religious, or social nature, their economy and culture declined rapidly. As a people today, the Cocopah are impoverished to an almost unbelievable degree. They live under sub-sub-standard conditions. It is estimated that probably no more than three hundred of them live on each side of the international border. (Johnston 1970:64)

An article written by the senior editor of LOOK (2 June 1970), and factually illustrated, reveals circumstances of the present day Cocopah. Riding along the dirt bank of an irrigation canal, he noted that:

The canal itself, conduit for the valuable water flowing to farmers inland, is neatly cemented and fenced, sharp contrast to the shanties lining its side. The desert grit cuts your eyes and seeps into your mouth and nose even after the car windows roll shut. The kids wipe uselessly at running noses with their sleeves. (Without adequate shelter, clothing, diet or medicine, Indian children remain the number one victims of the respiratory infections that other Americans no longer consider dangerous.) (Mangel 1970:39)

This article is not exaggerated; anthropologists have found conditions to be as set forth here.

The writer described one of the houses as a nine by twelve foot shelter made of flattened cardboard cartons; the six-foot high roof, made of the same materials, was held down by two old automobile tires. Income of the dweller therein was $67.00 a month from welfare. Other residents were found to be living under similar conditions. Cocopah unemployment is cited as "an incredible nine out of ten men."

It was further reported that:

Welfare keeps them alive, with a family income of about $1,000. Among the adolescents, virtually everyone I met had quit school. They desperately seek release from boredom and poverty. Indians have the highest suicide rate in the nation. Two young Cocopah killed themselves the month before I arrived. One was 16, the other, 18. Both had left school years before.

Timidity clouds the Cocopah future. Penniless, disorganized, they are uncertain of their own direction or of where to turn for aid. The BIA, under new and tougher local leadership, is beginning to stir, but slowly. (Ten houses—abandoned when a Marine air base was closed—have been trucked in to one of the three different sites that comprise the Cocopah reservation.) The bedrock problems of schools and job training and employment remain untouched. Cocopah men and women, like Indians elsewhere, are slow to leave the reservations for jobs even if they have the skills and the perseverance to withstand employer prejudice (33 Indian men went to Yuma two years ago to enroll with the Federal employment office; not one has yet been offered a job). The public schools to which most Indian children today are assigned clearly are failing them (eight Indians from one local school attempted junior college in the past few years; none could handle it). (Mangel 1970:41-42)

YUMA CURING SONG

Your heart is good.
[The Spirit] Shining Darkness will be here.
You think only of sad unpleasant things,
You are to think of goodness.
Lie down and sleep here.
Shining Darkness will join us.
You think of this goodness in your dream.
Goodness will be given to you,
I will speak for it, and it will come to pass.
It will happen here,
I will ask for your good,
It will happen as I sit by you,
It will be done as I sit here in this place.

From: *Ethnography of the Yuma Indians,* By C. Daryll Forde

The Cocopah Reservation An Executive Order of 27 September 1917 established the Cocopah Reservation, setting apart 528 acres for use of the Cocopah Indians; and Public Law 87-150 of 17 August 1961 granted 81 acres of public domain to them. Of the 609 acres, about one hundred are used for small subsistence plots and some for growing cotton. All reservation lands are held by the tribe. Individual plots are assigned for family farms and homesteads. A few of the Cocopah and the Quechan farm for a living, but most of them work for other ranchers or are employed as wage earners in and around the city of

Yuma. Water is currently plentiful, and irrigation water is supplied at a reasonable cost.

Approximately ninety-five Cocopah Indians are enrolled on the Cocopah roster. A number of Cocopah are not eligible for enrollment because of their Mexican birth. Those born in the U.S.A. are citizens and eligible for enrollment. Membership in the tribe and residence on the reservation is open to all Cocopah, whether enrolled or not. Enrollment originally was a matter of individual family choice.

Cocopah government is under the control of a five-member council, elected to office by popular vote. Elections are held in even numbered years on the second Friday in July. The council meets monthly, every second Friday at 1:00 p.m., at Somerton, Arizona.

.... THE PAI

It is said that the native northeasternmost Pai Indians considered themselves as one ethnic group—"the only true human beings on earth," or, in the prevailing notion, "The People." These Pai occupied an area in northwest-central Arizona, "between the Colorado River on the west and north, its Little Colorado tributary on the east, and on the south a line through the San Francisco Peaks, Bill Williams Mountain, Picacho, and down Chino Creek, the Santa Maria River, and Bill Williams Fork." We are told:

These Indians not only spoke a common language but shared a common culture at the time they were first seen by Europeans. During the long period of Spanish and Mexican sovereignty in the Southwest, this group always was designated in Spanish as *Cosninas*, a hispanicized form of the Hopi term for these people, *Ko' ho'-nin* [Cohonina]. The Spaniards, few of whom beside Fray Francisco Garces achieved direct contact with the Pai, preserved the native Indian concept of the "tribal" or cultural unity of this group.

When Anglo-Americans invaded the Southwest and conquered its native peoples, accidents of geographic patterning of their contacts with the Pai led them to conceive of this ethnic group as two "tribes." For a century, therefore, Anglo-Americans have written and thought about "Walapais" and "Havasupais" while the Indians in question continue still to think of themselves as simply Pai. (Dobyns and Euler 1960:49)

"Walapai," or "Hualapai," is said to come form the native Yuman word, *Xawálapáiya*, meaning "pine tree folk." (Swanton 1952:365) It appears that the first mention of them was made in 1776 by Father Garcés, but it is possible that other Spanish explorers encountered them earlier. At any rate, they were never directly affected by the Spaniards. It has been stated that the major effects that Spanish colonization had on the Pai were:

1. an intensification of Pai trade and social intercourse with the Western Pueblos, with a corresponding shift in Pai reference group orientation toward the east, and 2. the beginning of deterioration in some native Pai handicrafts caused by the importation of Spanish goods, which led eventually to substitution of European-made artifacts for native products on a very large scale. In 1776 Garces found the westernmost band of Pai already using Spanish belts, awls, and other implements they had acquired from New Mexico indirectly via Hopi middlemen. (Coues 1900, II:320)

Beginning in 1826, hostilities arose between the Pai and the whites; first with French-Canadian and Anglo-American trappers, and then with slave raiders from the Territory of New Mexico.

About 1842, the Pai, who for some years avoided all possible contacts with the whites, bridled their fear of non-Indian expeditions and began to engage in military actions to preserve their independence and integrity.

After the Southwest was acquired by the U.S.A., a new era of exploration and colonization opened. Captain Lorenzo Sitgreaves, in 1851, encountered eastern Pai bands northeast of Flagstaff, Arizona, and in the upper Truxton Canyon area; and one of his guides (Leroux) was attacked by the Cerbat Mountain Pai band. (Dobyns and Euler 1960:50) Six and seven years later, Lt. E. F. Beale traversed the country of the Pai, and mention was made of a Pai band at Peach Springs, Arizona.

The western bands became known to the federal troops as "Walapai," from the *Hawhala pa'a* band—the one Garcés had noted in 1776. By the close of the War of the Rebellion, "a number of small prospectors' camps were scattered along the western slopes of the Cerbat and Hualapai Mountains where two mining districts had been organized." (Dobyns and Euler 1960:53)

Mining developments, establishment of military posts, and freighting roads wrought increasing changes during the nineteenth century. In 1866, "a typical race-prejudiced frontier type" killed the principal chief of the southern Pai bands. Those bands and the western Pai responded in accord with their time-hallowed traditions and exacted vengeance on the whites, precipitating "the Walapai War". (Dobyns et al. 1957:61)

Unfortunately for the Pai, the western bands went over to the offensive just after the end of the civil conflict in the United States, when men who had found a taste for military life during the war years sought to justify their continued employment in a reduced but still oversized military establishment with far too many senior officers. In the summer of 1867 the river steamers deposited at Fort Mojave contingents of veteran regulars under Lieut. Colonel William Redwood Price to undertake the subjugation of the western Pai bands, labeled "Walapai" and thought of as a tribe.

Lieut. Colonel Price pursued a policy of harrying the elusive western and southern Pai bands as often as possible with the aid of detachments from the post at Fort Whipple, seeking to precipitate a decisive battle. Acutally, the Pai won all the pitched battles fought, choosing their ground carefully, and accepting battle commitment only when they enjoyed equal or superior firepower and superior tactical position behind good rock cover. Price's scorched earth tactics eventually brought the "Walapai" to admit defeat and sue for peace. Effective peace was re-established in 1869, the western and southern Pai admitting Anglo-American military superiority. (U.S. Senate 1936, *in* Dobyns and Euler 1960:53-54)

The social relationship between the conquerers and conquered peoples was yet to be fully clarified, however, for the Pai had still to experience the full range of Anglo-American culture and society. . . .

In 1871 the Pai began to learn that the U.S. Bureau of Indian Affairs considered itself the government agency in charge of administering their transition from native life to subordinate cultural and social status in the United States. A one mile square reservation for the western Pai was set aside in that year.

Committed to the general policy of removing conquered Indians from their ancestral lands to a distinct Indian Territory, the Bureau sought army aid in moving the western Pai to the Colorado River Indian Reservation. The Pai had been placed under the charge of the agent of that reserve in 1873, and in the spring of 1874 the army forcibly moved the western Pai under its direct control to La Paz in the Colorado River Jurisdiction, in the Pai version of the "Long Walk" or "Trail of Tears." The eastern Pai bands, already differentiated from the western groups by pre-contact experiences, safety during the Walapai War, and continued isolation from mines and military posts, were further distinguished from the relocated Pai by their escape from removal. The one or possibly two bands now called Havasupai, the Pine Springs Band, and some of the Peach Springs Canyon Band Pai waited out deportation in the isolated fastnesses of the Grand Canyon and its southern tributaries such as Cataract, National, and Prospect Canyons. (Dobyns and Euler 1960:54-55)

On the low-altitude river flood plain location, the Pai suffered extensively. The government rations on which they were forced to depend were often scarce. Farming had to be attempted under conditions foreign to the experiences of the Pai. Old and young encountered new diseases and died in large numbers. By the spring of 1875, we are told, the decimated bands could take no more; they fled back to their ancestral homeland.

Once safely back in their former territory, the escaped western Pai suffered no illusions as to their fate. They clearly realized that they could not hope to return to their former way of life, because Anglo-American ranchers had thrown great cattle herds onto their grasslands and settled at their best springs. The old harvesting-hunting activities would—and, to the extent they were practiced, did—bring demands by the ranchers for final and irrevocable removal. The western Pai realized that to exist in their homeland they must adopt the white man's expedient of working for wages, and their wholehearted plunge into daily work at the mines gained them the mine operators' support against the antagonistic ranchers, and sealed their differentiation from the still-isolated eastern Pai.

Reservations of lands for the Pai were set aside on the plateau in the prehistoric range of the northeastern bands. The western bands known to Americans as "Walapai" received a 997,045 acre reservation in 1883 . . . and the eastern "Havasupai" group a much smaller plot of 518 acres of its once extensive range in 1882 . . . For nearly half a century neither reservation had much meaning to its theoretical occupants.

Under provisions of the Indian Reorganization Act of June 18, 1934 (48 Stat. 984), separate "tribal" governments were organized on these two jurisdictions, the "Havasupai Tribe" in 1938 and the "Havasupai Tribe" in 1939. (Kelly, Wm. H. 1953:49, 53) By such historic processes and United States administrative actions, arising from a view of the Pai which does not correspond to the native concept, have two formal, self-giverning "tribes" been created where only one ethnic group existed in pre-contact times. This process of alienation of Pai bands continues to the present in administrative actions which, for example, send "Havasupai" children to be educated at Indian Bureau boarding schools on the White River Apache reservation while "Walapai" children attend public schools in their homeland. (Dobyns and Euler 1960:55-56)

And thus is explained briefly the circumstances whereby the Yuman-speaking Pai people were divided into the groups which follow.

[It should be noted that while the author generally favors the results of field investigations and thinking of certain scholars (Dobyns and Euler 1960) (Euler 1972b) who feel that both the Hualapai and the Havasupai are directly descendent from the Cerbat branch of the Pai, at least one researcher holds that the Havasupai alone derive from the Cohonina, (Schwartz 1956) and other views are held. (*See* Whiting 1958) (*See* McGregor 1951, 1967) (Schwartz 1959:1062)]

THE HAVASUPAI (EASTERN PAI)

Location and Early History

The eastern Pai, the Havasupai (hah-vah-SOO-pie), or "people of the blue-green water," inhabit a tiny patch of ground at the bottom of Cataract Canyon, a side branch of the Grand Canyon of Arizona. This is within the area occupied by their ancestors since the 1100s at least. During the spring and summer corn, beans, and squash were irrigated with the ever-flowing clear, blue-green water. The crops were supplemented by hunting and gathering over a wide range of altitude. Food stuffs were stored in crevices or small caves above the reach of often occuring flood waters.

Social Organization

At the time of contact with the whites, the Havasupai were a peaceful, industrious, intelligent, and hospitable people. The family was the social unit, with small groups loosely bound into larger ones by blood relationships. No clan existed. Inheritance was in the male line, but wives enjoyed greater privileges and prerogatives than did most women of Arizona Indian peoples. (*See* Robinson 1954:125) No marriage or divorce laws were observed. When young people wished to marry, the man took up residence with the girl's family. They lived with her parents for a year or two, by which time they had a child or two. Then a home was built near that of the man's parents, from whence his inheritance would come. Family association was free of taboos. Women had no share in the house, land, or other property; they owned the pottery, baskets, and their personal effects.

Havasupai homes were rock shelters or houses of two types: One was circular and constructed on a framework of poles. The sidewalls and the domed roof were thatched with bundles of willow branches held in place by small, flexible poles lashed through the thatching to the framework. The other was rectangular and was constructed "by setting four posts in the ground with forks at the top in which poles were laid lengthwise and other poles crosswise, with brush on top ... and the sides thatched with reeds and willow." (Robinson 1954:127) In both instances the roof was covered with earth. No provision was made for the escape of smoke.

Six men of equal status were recognized as "chiefs," and one of them usually served as spokesman and discussion leader. They had little power, their principal duty being to give advice and to lead discussions. Chieftainship was theoretically inherited, but prestige had much to do with the selection. No office of war chief existed; rather the most competent available leader took charge of the rare defensive fighting of the Havasupai.

Religion was little developed. Prayers, in which prayer sticks were utilized, were addressed to the sun, earth, water, rocks and other natural features. The Havasupai believed in a future life and in ghosts. Shamans, or "medicine men," by means of their possession of familiar spirits, dreams, and knowledge of various magical practices, cured diseases and bone fractures, snake bites, and the like, and engaged in weather control.

At some past time the Havasupai are known to have had three dances, but the number decreased. Approximately sixty years ago, a dance of masked and painted men was performed, to bring good fortune and prosperity to the people. The largest celebration came to be a general reunion with dancing which was held annually in the early autumn. Men and women danced in a circle, to the rhythm of drum and voice. Formerly, special attire was worn, but this practice was discarded some time ago. In a measure, the dance was a prayer for rain, but social aspects predominated. Addresses by the chiefs and visitors were given at intervals.

Leisure time was spent in bathing in sweat lodges (small, domed structures about six feet in diameter and four feet high), playing games, playing with dolls, and gossiping—a very general characteristic of Indian peoples. Games included shinny, hoop-and-pole, cup-and-pin, and gambling; wrestling, foot- and horse- racing, and other pursuits were common.

Economy   The Havasupai were successful farmers, and became famous for their crops. In Cataract Canyon, where there was considerable irrigation, corn became the principal crop. Beans, squash, melons, sunflowers, and tobacco also were raised. The men did the irrigating, and the women did most of the harvesting. Plants that were gathered included mescal, cactus and yucca fruits, peaches and figs, mesquite pods, juniper berries, piñones, and the seeds and leaves of several edible vegetal items. Crops were stored in stone granaries which were sealed for protection. Wild honey was collected, and salt was obtained from the Grand Canyon.

Meat was an important part of the diet, as deer, antelope, mountain sheep, wildcat, mountain lion, raccoon, rabbit, and squirrel were hunted. Dogs were used in hunting, but were not eaten. Fish, lizards and other reptiles were not eaten. Men and boys participated in drives to kill rabbits. Other meat came from various rodents. Turkeys, quail, and doves were favorite fowls. Meat was commonly dried. Roasting and boiling were the general methods of cooking. Most of the cooking and eating took place out of doors. Three meals a day were the early practice as well as the modern.

Attire   Clothing of the Havasupai was made from animal skins until recent times—when garments of white man's manufacture came into use. The working of skins and the making of women's clothes was done by the men.

The female attire consisted of a two-part dress—an apron hung from the neck and reaching from breast to ankles in front—and a shorter piece that hung from the waist in back. Under this dress, a short apron was sometimes worn from the waist to the knees. As with the Mohave, the two parts of the dress were overlapped and held in place by tie strings. Around the waist a yucca fiber belt or a textile belt—usually obtained from the Hopi—was worn. Women's clothes had long fringes and were trimmed with metal or hoof tinklers. Later, ornamental shawls made of several colored kerchiefs sewn together also were worn. The moccasins had hard soles and a high upper which was wrapped around the calf. Sometimes the women went barefooted.

Men wore shirts, loincloths, moccasins and leggings. The shirts were similar to those worn by the Plains Indians, but influence of the whites crept in, altering the cut and sewing. The ankle-high moccasins had hard soles. Both men and women wore rabbitskin or cotton blankets for warmth; later they adopted wool blankets.

Face painting and tattooing were practiced to some extent. Adornments consisted of necklaces and ear pendants of Pueblo and Navaho shell and silver. (*See* Douglas 1931:2-3)

Native Crafts   The Havasupai women made pottery which traditionally was fired in an oxidizing atmosphere, like that of the Hopi and other Pueblo pottery makers. The vessels were brown, predominantly globular pots of coarse texture, unslipped and unpainted. They were built up by coiling and then finished by a paddle and anvil process. After being dried in the sun for some twenty-four hours, they were baked, one by one, in hot coals.

Basketry was made by the women following two techniques, coiling and twining. Training in the craft began when a girl was seven or eight years old. Shallow trays or bowls were coiled, using twigs of cottonwood or of a plant said to be known only by its Havasupai name. The sewing of the coils was on a three-rod foundation. Simple geometric and banded designs were worked in martynia black. Conical burden baskets, globular water jugs, and shallow trays or bowls were made by twining. For these, twigs of acacia were preferred, although cottonwood and willow also were used. Some of the baskets were used as cooking containers.

The burden baskets and water jugs had loops for carrying; these baskets were decorated with simple designs achieved by varieties of twining and the use of martynia, or devil's claw. Designs were generally poorly executed. The water vessels and some parching trays were coated with a yucca, or soapweed, paste colored red with hematite, over which a coating of piñon gum was applied for waterproofing. This resulted in almost completely obscuring the designs.

In weave, the old Havasupai baskets displayed some similarity to those of the Yavapai, but not those of the Walapai. Today, Havasupai baskets are extremely rare. Those made in recent times are of coil technique, and made primarily for the tourist trade.

Havasupai babies were placed on basketry cradleboards, and kept there until they were nearly old enough to walk. Care of the children was shared by both parents.

Trade   The Havasupai and their kinsmen, the Hualapai, both of whom were great traders, widely traded seashells from the Pacific and red hematite (for paint) to the Pueblo peoples.

Significantly, the historic trade routes had similar or identical prehistoric counterparts; these are indicated by a wide distribution of trade items. (*See* Colton 1941) We are told that lima beans, for which the Hopi have become well known, apparently were obtained originally from the Havasupai; and the latter received peaches from the Hopi. "Some Havasupai lived with the Hopi regularly, during the winter months, for a period of years." (Whiting 1958:58) For grinding purposes the Havasupai used a flat pounding-grinding rock and rotary mortars.

Impacts of Foreign Culture   The period of peaceful stability of the Havasupai ended near A.D. 1600, with the first impacts of foreign culture. As the whites moved onto the uplands for cattle ranching, the territory of the Indians was gradually usurped. Most of the aboriginal articles were still being made: pottery in paddle and anvil technique, clay pipes for smoking, stone knives (which among other uses, were utilized for cutting up squash), bone tools, fire drills and hearths, bows and arrows, basketry, skin clothing, and related items. Three main architectural forms persisted: a brush structure (wickiup), the rock shelter, and a talus top granary. Many old customs, such as cremation, persisted. (*See* Schwartz 1956:83; *see also* Whiting 1958:58)

The historic Havasupai were individualists in their economic pursuits, their house types, and in their lack of well organized social or religious groups. It has been stated that:

> While at times they borrowed extensively from the Hopi in economic and religious matters they remained reluctant farmers (especially after there were horses to ride or, better still, to race), indifferent craftsmen, inartistic, nonreligious and magnificently self-sustaining people. The dead, who were greatly feared, were socially ostracized and physically buried at a considerable distance from the living areas. The mode of burial varied. (Whiting 1958:56)

Upon death, the home and personal possessions were burned, and one or more horses killed on the grave. A man's saddle might be burned, or left on one of the horses. (*See* Dobyns and Euler 1971:44) His bow and arrows, war club, and personal effects were buried with him.

Modernization   Havasupai acculturation really began with the establishment of a reservation for them in 1880. Toward the end of the following decade, the federal government sent a farmer into the canyon, and then a schoolteacher. New and improved tools, modern methods, and the English language were introduced. The school forced the children to remain in the canyon. Clothing rapidly changed to the white man's garb, western style. The typical burial practice of cremation was altered to burial directly in the ground, (Whiting 1958:56) in extended position, although for another generation "there continued to be cremations, often of the medicine men. There is some hint that these men, ultra-individualistic in life, demanded to be different in death, no matter what the current pattern. Even in their treatment of new ideas this group behaved as an almost accidental amalgamation of individuals." Mourning rites of the Yuman type prevailed in the Havasupai culture.

Despite the fact that the Havasupai borrowed extensively from the Hopi at times, the rituals in imitation of the Hopi katsina dances "were strictly individually sponsored affairs. When the sponsoring individual died or when his proposed reform failed, as when prayers for rain were answered with a disastrous flood, the movement evaporated." (Whiting 1958:56)

A big flood in the Havasu canyon in 1910 washed out most of the farms and homes there and the talus top granaries, after which small wooden frame houses were erected, along with rebuilding of the brush shelters. For a time the Havasupai, like many other Indian peoples when initially confronted with non-traditional types of dwellings, used the frame houses for storage purposes while preferring to live in the old style homes.

The National Park Service established a village near the Grand Canyon Park settlement on the plateau, which came to be a center of Havasupai life. Most of the Indians work for the Park Service or for some non-Indian concerns engaged in servicing the park and visitors. Some eke out a meager living by growing garden crops and raising a few cattle.

The Havasupai   Certain lands in Arizona were reserved by an Executive Order of 8
Reservation   June 1880 for the "Suppai" Indians. That order was revoked by

another of 23 November 1880, which set aside other lands; that in turn was revoked on 31 March 1882, at which time still other lands were reserved for the "Yavai Suppai" Indians. The reservation itself consists of 518 acres, which are owned in undivided shares by the enrolled members.

The Havasupai lost their eastern fields and hunting and grazing lands on the plateau above the canyons, (*See* Dobyns and Euler 1971:21-24, 30-33) and now have use of only a few square miles. The U.S. Forest Service and the NPS issue a year-to-year permit for the Havasupai to graze their stock on land adjacent to the reservation in the Kaibab National Forest and the park.

The beauty and isolation of Cataract Canyon—now commonly called the Havasu—long have been the root resource of the Havasupai. Homes, school and other facilities could be reached only by trails on either side of the canyon, which cuts through the reservation. These are accessible by roads from the Grand Canyon and from Highway 66, just east of Peach Springs, Arizona. Horse and mule transportation and guide service are provided by the Indians, and overnight accommodations at Supai Village, a little oasis. Airlift by helicopter is available for visitors (at $120 per hour), but the Indians in need of supplies must travel to Kingman, one hundred miles from their homes. From there, it is said that merchants will ship goods back to the canyon at a 40 to 60 per cent premium. (Anonymous 1969c:21*)

The Havasupai Tribe

The Havasupai organized under a constitution and bylaws which were approved on 27 March 1939. A tribal corporate charter was ratified on 5 October 1946.

All individuals listed on tribal rolls as of 1938 are members. New members are added as follows: (1) all children born to any member after January 1, 1938, who are three-fourths or more Indian blood, and (2) by action of the Tribal Council through the passage of ordinances covering future membership and adoption of new members, subject to the approval of the Secretary of the Interior. No person is eligible for adoption into the Hualapai (*sic.*) [Havasupai ?] Tribe who has not resided upon the reservation for a probationary period of five years. (Kelly, Wm. H. 1953:55)

The Havasupai now number about 500. The population is predominantly young, with rising birth rate. (*See* Dobyns and Euler 1971:1, 61-62) As a people, the Havasupai have moved from

*Information from *Time, The Weekly Newsmagazine.*

traditional practices toward modern government in a practical manner. It was recorded that: "The governing body is a tribal council consisting of four regular councilmen, and three recognized hereditary chiefs of the tribe who are selected by the remaining subchiefs. Each of the chiefs, as a regular member of the Council, continues his duties as councilman until death or resignation, at which time a new chief is selected by the subchiefs. Any member of the Council, not a chief, may be subject to recall if he fails to fulfill his duties as a councilman . . ." (Kelly, Wm. H. 1953:55) Today all members of the council are elected.

The Havasupai Tribal Council meets once each month at the Community Building in Supai. All members of the council must be qualified voters of the reservation and thirty-five years of age or over. Elections are held every two years on 25 December. Tribal officers and tribal employees are selected by the council. The chairman and vice-chairman must be members of the council, but the secretary and treasurer may be from within or without the membership of the council. Officers also include a tribal judge and police chief. Currently, the council has seven members; men or women may serve. Special meetings are at the call of the chairman. The Havasupai have five operating committees under their chairmen who are listed as Store Manager, Assistant Manager, General Manager, Community Action Program, and Tourist Director.

Education is provided by the BIA in Supai, for those in the pre-primary through fourth or fifth grades—depending upon the need. Thereafter, students are sent to school in Fort Apache or in Phoenix. The nearest professional medical care available is at the Grand Canyon.

The Havasupai Today

By national standards, the Havasupai are considered among the most impoverished groups in the nation. They are almost totally dependent on the BIA.

It recently has been said that:

Young Havasupai who attend Government boarding schools return to the reservation confused about their place in the world. They feel inferior both to the white man [*haigu*] and to fellow Indians from larger, more advanced tribes.

Of the 142 Havasupai men able to work, only eight hold permanent jobs. While the tourist season lasts, the tribe's 300 horses are used to pack visitors to the canyon (at $16 a round trip). Some 6,000 came by foot or horseback last year, but the tribe has almost nothing in the way of handicrafted goods, restaurants or inns that might encourage visitors to leave their money behind. Moreover, the horses help to keep the tribe isolated. Efforts to put a cable car line or jeep trail into Supai have been resisted by the Indians, who fear that their only reliable source of income will be destroyed.

Havasupai are forbidden to bring alcohol onto the reservation, but it is bootlegged into the canyon and sold at exorbitant prices. Increasingly, the younger tribe members have been the best customers . . . .

The Havasupai family structure may appear to be almost nonexistent. But this is not the case. Actually, the family is extremely important; "it is the most important institution (after the BIA) in the community." (Martin 1972)

It has been noted that:

Without privacy, children imitate their elders and begin sexual activity early. Illegitimacy is rampant, birth control ignored. Havasupai men . . . practice "sequential marriages," (Martin 1972) taking one wife after another. Matches between first cousins are routine; mental retardation is common [evidence to support this statement is questioned]. (Euler 1972b) Disease, poor diet and high infant mortality combine to give the Havasupai a life expectancy of only 44 years (U.S. average 70). They also have a suicide rate 15% above the national average. (Anonymous 1969c:21*)

During the summer of 1969, a government-financed airlift set about to bring modern housing to the isolated Havasupai Indians in Havasu canyon. Helicopters, in some eighty flights, lowered five prefabricated, three-bedroom houses, section by section, to the canyon floor 5,300 feet below the rim for the Indians to erect. These structures cost about $12,000 each. They were provided at random for some of the most needy families. Later, ten more houses were put up in Supai, and thirty-five were scheduled for installation.

As in prior times, the Indians had to be talked into accepting the new houses. They knew their neighbors would be antagonistic and jealous; and the dwellings, although wired for electricity, had no source of power. The wood stoves that were supplied would be sources of trouble in an area where a firewood shortage prevails . . . and so the houses would be impossible to heat.

An official of the BIA said that the Agency planned to provide each Havasupai family with a modern house eventually, thus replacing the sub-standard shacks, many without floors. (Anonymous 1969a)

The writer of the article quoted above remarked:

---

*Reprinted by permission from *Time, The Weekly Newsmagazine;* Copyright Time, Inc.

Until now, the Bureau of Indian Affairs has invested only limited funds and manpower to ease the tribe's plight. Little in the way of imaginative social work has been attempted. Putting shingled rooftops over each Havasupai's head is a questionable response to his needs, and even this will be done only gradually. (Anonymous 1969c:21*)

Construction of houses, a community building and federal facilities, with supplemental work, and employment at the power plant provided an unusual "bonanza" for the workers. However, this will end "and the Havasupai will then be thrown back on tourism and welfare." (Martin 1972)

HAVASUPAI PRAYER

Sun, my relative
Be good coming out
Do something good for us.

Make me work,
So I can do anything in the garden
I hoe, I plant corn, I irrigate.

You, sun, be good going down at sunset
We lay down to sleep I want to feel good.

While I sleep you come up.
Go on your course many times.
Make good things for us men.

Make me always the same as I am now.

From: *Havasupai Ethnography*, by Leslie Spier (1928:226)

HUALAPAI, OR WALAPAI (WESTERN PAI)

Anciently, the western Pai, or Hualapai, appear to have occupied territory between present day Kingman, Arizona, and the Colorado River. Around A.D. 1150, the Cerbat group moved onto the plateau east of the Grand Wash Cliffs, where they displaced the Cohonina people. Their closest contacts were with the Yuman-speaking Halchidhoma, and the Southern Pai and Hopi peoples. (Euler 1972b) They had hostile encounters with the Yavapai. Before 1880

---

*Reprinted by permission from *Time, The Weekly Newsmagazine;* Copyright Time, Inc.

the Hualapai probably numbered more than 1,100, but they declined steadily to the present.

A major occupation was food gathering and hunting; vegetal products were primary, for game was limited. The main food supply consisted of fruits, berries, and nuts gathered by the women, and deer, antelope, mountain sheep, rabbits, and other game hunted by the men. Farming was practiced where moisture was sufficient to raise crops, as in many canyons tributary to the Colorado. In western Grand Canyon the Hualapai practiced agriculture as extensively as did the Havasupai in Cataract Canyon.

Dwellings commonly were small, not very substantial structures of dome-shape, made of small poles and branches covered with juniper bark or thatched and without earth covering. Sturdier winter houses were sometimes built. Rock shelters were often places of abode. Sweat houses were in common use, and a rectangular, flat-roofed shelter was built occasionally for summer shade.

Few ceremonies or dances were held, although the Pai traditionally had great faith in shamanism—usually in the hands of a medical practitioner. Some are said to believe that the spirit of the dead goes to the west for judgment and, if condemned, goes to the underworld; others have no concept of future life. In times past, the dead were cremated and their possessions burned. An annual community burning of food and clothing commemorated the dead. Cremation was replaced by the practice of burial—preferably at the place of birth.

Basketry was made exclusively by the Hualapai women. They fashioned undecorated plaques and household baskets, often covered with pitch on the interior; more or less cylindrical baskets with geometric designs in martynia, rarely painted bluish, red or white on the outside, and similarly shaped with bail-like handles; large conical carrying baskets with limited decoration; finely worked small plaques, the splints of which were dyed; baby cradles and items of fanciful shapes. The weaving technique is that of coil on three rods and splint foundation; and the products resemble those of the Apache. In time, the basketry art almost died out, but tourist demands caused its continuance to the present. The modern baskets are made of sumac twigs and in brighter colors; predominantly of bowl shape. Some beadwork is also produced for the tourist trade. Formerly, some pottery and pottery pipes were made. Tobacco grew wild in the Hualapai country; it was not cultivated. (Robinson 1954:117)

The Hualapai Indian Reservation

Rugged and varied terrain lies between Peach Springs, Arizona, on U.S. Highway 66, and the Colorado River west of Grand Canyon National Park. This relatively large reservation has only a few tillable spots near streams and springs. Small crops such as corn and beans may be raised, but the chief means of livelihood is by stockraising, while the most profitable source of income is from the sale of timber, which is treated as a capital asset with the return invested in range improvement.

The reservation in its entirety is owned in undivided shares by the enrolled Indians, and is held in trust for them by the federal government. Consolidation of the reservation was accomplished in 1947, when title to more than 500,000 acres in odd numbered sections previously held by the Santa Fe Railroad Company was quieted in the government in trust for the Hualapai. (*See* Kelly Wm. H. 1953:50) The land is used for individual homes and farms, for grazing by their cattle association, and by the Indians acting as a corporation.

The Hualapai Trading Company at Peach Springs was established in 1944 by the "tribe," for the purpose of providing a local source of groceries and other merchandise, with credit privileges. All cattle on the reservation are owned by members of the Hualapai Livestock Association, with exception of the tribal herd.

The Hualapai Tribe

This group of Indians was organized as the Hualapai Tribe, with a constitution and bylaws approved 17 December 1938; and a corporate charter was ratified on 5 June 1943. All individuals listed on the rolls as of 1938 are members, and children born to any member after 1 January 1938, who are of one-half degree or more Indian blood, are also members. Others admitted by action of the tribal council "through the passage of ordinances, subject to the approval of the Secretary of the Interior, governing future membership and adoption of new members" may be added to the rolls. The local population is now about 685.

The tribal council consists of eight members, in addition to "one hereditary chief of the tribe selected by the subchiefs of the various recognized bands and who holds office for life." Councilmen must be qualified voters of twenty-five years or more of age, members of the Hualapai tribe, and residents of the reservation. All tribal officers, committees and tribal employees are selected by the council. Council officers consist of a chairman and vice-chairman, secretary, treasurer, judge, and police chief; the first two named must be members of the council, but others may be chosen from the tribe as a whole.

As to their responsibilities:

The Hualapai Tribal Council has jurisdiction over all matters pertaining to the management of tribal property, conduct of Indians and non-Indians on the reservation, tribal business enterprises, and the welfare of tribal members. The only limits to its power are in some specific instances where the Secretary of the Interior must give approval for action, and in other instances where action must be referred to a vote of the people. (*See* Kelly, Wm. H. 1953:49)

The group has committees, each with a chairman, which give attention to Budget and Finance; Constitution and Bylaws/ Health, Education and Welfare; Law and Order, Recreation, Community Action Program and Administration Board, Northwest Planning Area; and the Tribal Herd.

The Hualapai received $2.9 million compensation for lands taken from them in northwestern Arizona in 1883. They decided to use 25 per cent of this fund for a program to better their standard of living, and 75 per cent for resources development and investment programs. (Anonymous 1970e)

The council meets the first Saturday of each month at 9:00 a.m. in the tribal office in Peach Springs. Terms of office are for three years, with elections held annually on the first Saturday in June.

Children that live on the reservation attend the Indian Service day school at Peach Springs and the public schools in Kingman, Truxton Canyon, and Seligman, or go to off-reservation boarding schools. Almost without exception, the people speak English; many retain their native tongue. The Hualapai have a PHS clinic in Peach Springs, where a medical doctor, several nurses and other personnel are assigned. Ambulance service is provided where necessary for those requiring hospitalization, as in the Kingman Hospital.

The Hualapai
at Big Sandy
Some years past, a few members of the Hualapai tribe lived at Big Sandy, southeast of Kingman. But, by 1963-1964 all that remained was "one shack, some fields, fences and the irrigation ditches .... the 'owners,' who were many, lived in Kingman. Several commuted to plant, irrigate, weed and harvest some small kitchen gardens." (Martin 1972) No tribal land exists in the Big Sandy; all tracts are held in trust allotments. Mohave county assumes responsibility for Law and Order.

THE SALT RIVER
INDIAN AGENCY

The Salt River Agency was given full status as of 1 July 1962. Prior to that time it functioned as a sub-agency of the Pima Indian Agency located at Sacaton, fifty miles distant. It now administers the affairs of Indians living in the Salt River Pima-Maricopa community and the Fort McDowell Yavapai-Apache community. The agency headquarters is located in Maricopa county, about seven miles east of Phoenix, Arizona, between Scottsdale and Mesa on McDowell Road. Its purpose is to provide facilities for the education, assistance and guidance of the Indian residents of these lands, "so that they may become more self-sufficient, may improve their social and economic status, and develop and protect their natural resources." (King 1967)

THE SALT RIVER RESERVATION This reservation was established by Act of Congress on 28 February 1859, and by subsequent executive orders. It begins approximately two miles northeast of Tempe and extends up the Salt River past the Granite Reef diversion dam and beyond the junction with the Verde River. On the west the reservation approaches Scottsdale. The reservation contains 45,627 acres of which 25,229 acres are trust allotted to individual Indians in tracts of five to 30 acres; and 21,398 acres are community land. Forage on range lands is undependable. Carrying capacity is rated at 145 head of cattle. Vegetation includes sahuaro, mesquite, palo verde, cat-claw, cacti, creosote bush, salt cedar, and arrowweed. Animal life consists primarily of jackrabbit and cottontail, mourning and whitewing dove, gopher, muskrat, desert beaver, and quail.

Virtually all of 15,000 acres of irrigated land is leased to non-Indian farmers who have developed a successful agricultural project. Valuable water rights go with the lands in this project.

The irrigated area on the west side of the reservation is the center of the Indian community, with the remainder of the reservation practically vacant of human habitation.

Flat desert land to the north and east could be subjugated for agriculture if sufficient water were available. To the east, the reservation is made up of rolling desert, some of spectacular beauty, rising into rocky prominences.

The average elevation of the cultivated lands is approximately

1300 feet; the highest point in the reservation is Mount McDowell which rises to 2828 feet. The winters are mild but killing frosts may occur from November to March. Moderate rains fall from December to April and thunder storms may appear in July, August and September; the average annual rainfall is 7.96 inches. The summers are hot, the temperature ranging from 115° to 31°, and averaging about 70.2°F. Relative humidity is generally low.

THE PIMA-MARICOPA COMMUNITY

Some 1,700 Pima-Maricopa people representing about 330 families live in the Salt River community, which was organized under the Wheeler-Howard Act, with a constitution and bylaws approved 11 June 1940. These people are descendants of Pima and Maricopa bands that migrated to the area beginning in the 1860's when the waters in the Gila River failed. A minority of Papago and Indians of other tribes have married into the community. An additional 300 tribal members live immediately adjacent to the reservation. The clothing worn is that of the regional inhabitants.

A tribal council of seven members is active, with a president and vice-president appointed from within the popularly elected council membership; other officers are a secretary, treasurer, tribal judge and police chief. Elections are held every other year, the last week in June. The community has its own Law and Order Code. Real leadership is being developed within the community, several committees operate effectively, and governmental pursuits are expanding. The council meets each Thursday at 4:30 p.m., at the Community Center.

Compared with some of the other Arizona Indians, the Pima-Maricopa are relatively well educated; almost all persons under the age of fifty years have at least a sixth grade education. Just under 15 per cent have completed high school. Virtually everyone speaks English. Despite these facts, the economic conditions on the reservation have not been good. A significant percentage of the work force is unemployed or works intermittently. Urbanization has robbed the Indians of the traditional agricultural activities in which they were experienced. Some basketry is woven; in fact a revival of the craft is underway, with younger Indian women and some non-Indians learning to weave in the traditional manner.

Because the community is in an area which is one of the largest winter tourist resort centers in the nation, future development is a certainty. Industry is getting a foothold in the area, increasing the population and economy throughout the Salt River valley. The Indians will relate to future developments. A program to upgrade the reservation's work force through vocational training is under way, and a program of social development of the Indian community is being pushed.

Among the projects being advanced are those of self-help housing, improved domestic water under the U.S. Public Health Service, establishment of a large Community Center—where an annual Indian Trade Fair has been held since the spring of 1962—and various youth programs. To aid in achieving these objectives, the agency staff has been expanded to include a resources development officer, a juvenile officer, and a graduate social worker.

An elemantary school is operated by the BIA on the reservation. And a contract with the state of Arizona provides for education of Indian children in both elementary and high school. Educational grants are sought for higher education. Indian languages are heard but little now, and in another generation it is expected they will be entirely replaced by English—unless interest in native tongues is rekindled.

THE YAVAPAI INDIANS

The Yavapai (YAH-vah-pie) are a Yuman-speaking group which the Mohave called the "People of the Sun" (*Enyaéva*—"sun"; *pai*—"The People"). They were first mentioned by Espejo in 1582.) They wandered in small independent bands or family groups over the semi-desert reaches bounded by the mountains generally north of the Gila River. Their number is said not to have exceeded 1,500. (Robinson 1954:84) These groups occupied three geographical districts, comprising the western, northeastern, and southeastern Yavapai respectively. They intermingled and intermarried. Leadership was achieved through personal merit based on wisdom, personality and ability as a warrior. (Robinson 1954:85)

Until the late 1800's, Yavapai subsistence was derived from hunting small animals, rabbits and deer (they used a recurved bow), and the gathering of native plants; occasionally corn was obtained from the Pima and Papago Indians. They were active traders and participated in expeditions to the west coast, south into Mexico, north to the Paiute country, and to the Hopi and Zuñi pueblos. They were important factors in the exchange of handiworks and in the mingling of the cultures of the diverse Indians they visited.

The Yavapai made use of caves for shelter, or built temporary pole, brush, and mud houses. Small quantities of corn were planted along stream bottomlands, but the yield was not sufficient to be counted as a staple food. A variety of fine baskets was woven for utilitarian purposes, (*See* Robinson 1954:79-84) and a few stone tools were used. Food appears to have been cooked in pottery vessels. The clothing, if worn, was made from hides; personal adornments were few. Small crosses were sometimes tied to the hair.

Their religion was like that of most other Yuman peoples. Prominent features were veneration of the sun, shamanism, and belief in dream omens. Social dances were held on occasion.

The Yavapai were long associated with the Apache, and writers have often confused them. Both being warlike, the Yavapai found it to their advantage to be associated with the Apache. They intermingled and intermarried to some extent, and were similar in attire and even physical appearance. Here the similarities ended. The Apache, of Athabascan stock, assumed an attitude of warfare against all those regarded as outsiders, while the Yavapai philosophy permitted more flexibility. They demonstrated a greater willingness to change and, in time, made the effort to learn the ways of their neighbors and to coexist with them.

General Crook was one who did not recognize the Yavapai as a people apart from the Apache—to him they were one and the same, all Apache. (*See* Robinson 1954:91) In 1872 some 750 Indians—mostly Yavapai—were living on a reservation at Camp Date Creek, southwest of present day Prescott. The surgeon there, Dr. Corbusier, was one of those more discerning than Crook and recognized the difference between the Yavapai and the Apache. However, the next year, in May, they were all transferred to the Camp Verde Reservation which had been established in 1871. Many Indians escaped from there, some of them to resume raiding the settlers of Arizona and Mexico. After an extensive campaign in April, 1873, the Yavapai, Hualapai (eastern Pai), and Tonto submitted to armed forces, or were brought in the following year. At that time the San Carlos Reservation was established, and the Yavapai, being identified as Apache, were forced to go there. It has been recorded that:

The Indians walked all the way while the soldiers rode ponies. They followed only trails, for there were no roads. Moccasins and clothes wore out, torn by rocks, cactus, and brush, and many, sick at heart, wanted to die—and did. With no time for burial, these were left lying along the way. Many streams and a large river running high were crossed. These were negotiated the best way they could, one way or another. Some of the weaker were lost at the river crossing.

Rations were meager, and were augmented by edible weeds, roots, and seeds, when they could be found. To the Yavapai Indians, this move is known as the "March of Tears." . . .

During the next several years, many of the Yavapai drifted away from the San Carlos Reservation and went to live in the area north and west of Fort Whipple and the Verde. The four branches of the Yavapai Indians and their area headquarters may be said to be divided as follows: "Weepukapa" (Camp Verde); "Tolkepaya" (Arlington); "Kewevkopaya" (Fort McDowell); and "Yavepe" (Prescott) [in the spelling "Yawape," this term is said to mean "crooked mouth people," or "sulky"]. (Bahti 1968:68) The Arlington branch has practically disappeared, the remaining members having been absorbed into the Prescott and Fort McDowell branches. (Barnett 1968:3-4)

It has been said that the older Yavapai women taught the Apache to make bowls and dishes, and also improved coiled basket making techniques while they were together at San Carlos from 1875-1900. The two peoples spent many hours working together, thus accounting for the materials, techniques, and many decorative designs that are found in the baskets of both. However, the Apache lacked legend or background for their craft. (Robinson 1954:78-84)

It is pointed out that:

Many design elements, such as the diamond for example, are claimed by the Yavapai weavers as originating with their tribe. The star (starflower) design is common in Yavapai baskets, and is a sacred symbol with the weavers. Some, but not all, of the best baskets begin with the design of the story of creation. The swastika is a mystic symbol of good luck to the Indian, and brings good fortune when used on baskets, pottery and blankets. It is believed by the Indians that this symbol was given to them by the Great Spirit.

No dye or artificial color is used in a Yavapai basket. Young shoots of cottonwood and mulberry trees, and sometimes the fine roots of the yucca or soapweed are used for the natural color. The black color is made from stripped ears of the devil's claw seed pods. Generally the first coil of a Yavapai basket is black, though some weavers do not always hold to this. (Barnett 1968:33)

To finish a basket, the last row of weaving—the rim as it were—is always done in black. Yavapai baskets are now extremely rare; only a few women can make them.

E YAVAPAI-APACHE
ID MOHAVE-APACHE
The Fort McDowell
Reservation

Originally this was established as Camp McDowell Military Reserve on 1 January 1873. It was released to the Department of the Interior on 1 February 1891 for disposal under government procedures (Acts of 5 July 1884 and 23 August 1894), reserving legal subdivisions occupied by government improvements. Some of the land subsequently was taken up by white settlers.

In November, 1901, the Federal Land Office was directed to reserve the land for Indian purposes; and an Executive Order of 15 September 1903 set aside the land of Camp McDowell that was not legally settled. Purchases and the Act of 2 April 1904 compensated the settlers for their improvements and claims, thus changing all of Camp McDowell to an Indian reservation.

Most of the present inhabitants of Fort McDowell are descendants of those Yavapai who were taken as prisoners to San Carlos in 1874-1875. They are related to and acquainted with Yavapai living in the Camp Verde vicinity and at Prescott. At the time of imprisonment the Yavapai numbered approximately 1,500; twenty-five years later only 200 remained. (Barnett 1968:4)

A limited number of Apache have intermarried with the Fort McDowell Yavapai, or "Mohave-Apache"—as they were called erroneously by the early whites—and live on the Fort McDowell Reservation.

It is located twenty-eight miles northeast of Phoenix, and adjoining the Salt River Reservation on the northeast side. It contains 24,680 acres, none of which is allotted. Total length of the reservation is ten miles, and its four-mile width is bisected lengthwise by the Verde River, beginning one and a half miles above the junction with the Salt River. The elevation of the bottomland varies from 1,350 to 1,900 feet. Some 1,300 acres of irrigable lands of the Fort McDowell Reservation were provided water by rights granted by the Kent Decree in 1910.

The climate in which the Indians reside, that of the Southwest arid region in general, is somewhat modified by proximity to the mountains. Winters although mild do experience some moderate frosts, a little snow, and limited rains from December to April. The summers are long, hot and dry, with thunderstorms in July, August, and September. Temperature during the year varies from a recorded high of 115° to a low of 13° and averages about 70°F. The annual rainfall is ten inches. Heavy clothing is seldom needed.

On 3 March 1965, the Indian Claims Commission ruled that the Fort McDowell Reservation was part of 9,238,600 acres of Yavapai tribal land confiscated by the U.S. government on 1 May 1873. This meant that the Indians owned the land all the time, and in 1904 were getting only what had been theirs all along. Following this ruling, the federal government paid the Indians $5,100,000 for the Yavapai tribal lands that had been taken—the settlement amounting to about fifty-three cents an acre!

This reservation became important to the Central Arizona Project, or CAP, because of the need for storage reservoirs. The project is supposed to help the state of Arizona, but it will put about half of the Fort McDowell Reservation lands in flood danger, and will force the Indians living there either to relocate their homes or live within the shadow of possible disaster, because practically all of the residences are located in the flood plain.

According to a report in *The Arizona Republic*:

When the CAP bill was passed, it included the construction of Orme Dam, either at the confluence of the Salt and Verde Rivers or at Granite Reef Dam a short distance to the south.

In either case, the dam will create a flood plain of 12,823 acres along the always-flowing Verde River, which runs through the middle of the reservation.

The flood plain boundary is based on the biggest flood of the last 100 years, and much of the land might not be inundated for several generations. But there will always loom the possibility that the 100 year flood might strike again tomorrow.

Land in the flood plain can be used for farming and grazing and other purposes, but construction of the permanent structures will be restricted.

Within the flood plain will be . . . 5,347 acres near the river designated as the "conservation pool," or the mud flats. Water will be backed into this area when the reservoirs are fullest during a normal year's runoff.

The federal government, meanwhile, is willing to help the Indians relocate their small village, Ft. McDowell, and to reimburse the tribe for the land in the flood plain. Also, the CAP bill provided for the gift of 2,500 acres in federal lands to the tribe. This land will probably come from nearby Forest Service lands.

But the tribe is sometimes suspicious of the way the federal government operates. For example, the tribe thought the government would set aside comparable land east of the reservation to trade for the property in the flood plain.

However, the government recently traded that land to the Page Land and Cattle Co. for land elsewhere. Now, according to a former tribal chairman the Indians have no place to get the kind of terrain they are giving up.

The chairman said that the Indians are reasonable people and that they recognize the importance of the CAP. In speaking of the federal government, however, he remarked: "They took away 9 million acres from us; then they said we'll give you this 24,000 acres and let you alone. Now they want to take half of that. My

people are starting to think that they won't stand by their word."
(Murray 1969)

The Yavapai here number approximately 57 families, totaling
about 300 persons. Most of the people live in board houses; a few
have cinder block dwellings, chiefly built under a self-help program.
They have their own government with elected council members and
working committees. Both men and women hold offices. The Fort
McDowell Council meets at 2:00 p.m., on the first Tuesday of each
month, in the Community Building in Fort McDowell. Elections are
held every year; officers are a chairman, vice-chairman, secretary,
and police chief. Law enforcement is subject to Title 25 of the U.S.
Code. Tribal policemen have jurisdiction over misdemeanors committed on the reservation by Indians.

Little farming is underway currently, and the principal source
of income is from wages paid to tribal members as employees in
pumping stations of the city water system of Phoenix. About 15
per cent commute to off-reservation employment. The sale of
permits for duck hunting, fishing, and picnicking provides a small
income for the tribe. The lands along the Verde River offer a
considerable potential for development as a recreational area,
should such be undertaken.

Presently, most recreational facilities have to be sought in
surrounding towns, such as Phoenix, Mesa, Tempe, and Scottsdale.
There, too, the shopping is done, and medical and dental services
secured. Churches of most denominations are available. Arizona
State University at Tempe is about ten miles from the agency
headquarters. A few of the younger Yavapai are college graduates.

The pressures inherent in the accelerated growth of the
surrounding cities continue to mount as those communities enlarge
on the periphery of the Salt River Reservation and the Fort
McDowell Reservation. Both tribal groups are engaged in such
studies and community redevelopment activities as may best assure
them of a meaningful place in the future of the valley. Maximum
coordination with the surrounding communities in developmental
planning is believed to have assured a mutually advantageous future.

Viable tribal housing and sanitation programs are in operation.
Modern building codes and ordinances have been adopted and all
educational and developmental opportunities offered through the
OEO and other federal sources are being utilized to the fullest by
the tribal councils.

Annual income from leases, licenses, fees and recreation

receipts approximate $76,000 for the Fort McDowell group, and $300,000 for the Salt River community.

Both of these groups have coordinated their athletic and entertainment programs with those of the surrounding communities. No special Indian-type tourist shows are held.

One criminal investigator is employed at the agency. He is charged with the responsibility of maintaining law and order on these two reservations; he drives a police car equipped with a two-way radio. Radio contact is maintained with the Pinal and Maricopa county sheriffs' offices, and messages can be relayed to police in all surrounding towns through their networks.

The Camp Verde Yavapai-Apache

An Act of 1 August 1914 appropriated $20,000 for purchase of lands for Indians under jurisdiction of the Camp Verde Indian School, said lands to be held in trust and subject to the General Allotment Act (38 Stat. 588, c 222).

The Yavapai-Apache Band was organized under a constitution and bylaws approved 12 February 1937. A tribal corporate charter was ratified on 11 March 1948. All individuals listed on tribal rolls as of 1934 and the 1936 supplement are enrolled as members; new members are added according to certain stipulations.

The governing body is an organization known as the Yavapai-Apache Tribal Council consisting of eight members elected by the qualified voters. The council

elects from its own membership by secret ballot a chairman and vice-chairman, and from within or without its membership a secretary, treasurer and such other officers and committees as may be deemed necessary. Council officers elected from without the council membership have no vote in the council. Members hold office for two years and elections are held annually on the second Saturday of July with four councilmen being elected each year. Regular meetings are held on the second Saturday of January, April, July, October, and December. (Kelly, Wm. H. 1953:57)

These meetings are held at the Middle Verde Indian Community, at 9:00 a.m.

The Camp Verde Reservation

Actually this reservation is comprised of two parts: one located on the outskirts of the town of Camp Verde, which consists of some forty acres of farmland, mostly undeveloped; and a second area about six miles to the northwest known as Middle Verde. The latter holding was established about 1916, when the U.S. government purchased 460 acres of land for use of the Indians. The paid price of $22,500 included water rights and interest in the irrigation canals which supply water to Indian and non-Indian farmers. This system is operated under a cooperative ditch association, and operation and maintenance costs are met by assessments against those using the water. A few acres are used for nonirrigated farming, 70-odd for irrigated farming, and more than 400 acres for grazing cattle.

Around two hundred of the Yavapai here share the reservation with perhaps two hundred and fifty Tonto—with whom it is said cooperation has always been difficult. The term "Tonto" has been applied to a number of distinct peoples of Apache and Yuman affiliation. "It is said to have been given to a mixture of Yavapai, Yuma, and Maricopa, with some Pinaleño Apache, placed on the Verde River Reservation, Arizona, in 1873, and transferred to the San Carlos Reservation in 1875; also to a body of Indians, descended mostly from Yavapai men and Pinaleño women." (Swanton 1952: 365; See Morris 1972:105-110)

Because of the limited resources of this reservation, only a few families could derive a living from farming. Most must earn their livelihood from off-reservation employment in and around Clark-dale and Cottonwood. They do various wagework, some engage in small scale mining, and a few lease lands for farming and grazing from the Yavapai-Apache Indian Council. More than one hundred families account for a population around 450.

Medical facilities are not provided locally for the Camp Verde Yavapai, but patients are cared for at the hospital in Cottonwood, under contract with the government.

The Yavapai Indians at Prescott

An Act of 5 June 1935 transferred seventy-five acres of land in Arizona from the Veterans' Administration to the Department of Interior, title to remain in the U.S.A. in trust for the Yavapai Indians (49 Stat. 332, c. 202). Agency headquarters is in Valentine.

This group, numbering about ninety, lives on the north edge of the city of Prescott, in an area of rolling hills on which juniper, piñon and live oak grow. Land within the reservation accommodates homesites and necessary community developments, including a cemetery. The soil is rocky and water is in short supply, so agriculture is not practiced. Adjoining acreages amounting to 500 acres are used for a small stockraising enterprise. Most of the Indians' income is derived from wagework in Prescott. This group has not adopted a constitution, but operates under an informal five-member board, which represents them in administrative matters. The board meets the second Friday of each month. Elections are held on the second Friday in July, every second year. Law and order is handled by Yavapai county and has been very effective; the expenses are met by the county and the State of Arizona.

Education for the young people of this group and for those on the Camp Verde Reservation is through the public schools. Medical facilities are provided for the Prescott Indians, under contract with the government and local physicians.

THE "PAYSON APACHE" Recently a group of people designated as Payson Apache, numbering eighty-five and dwelling in a small community within the confines of the Tonto National Forest in Arizona, sent two of their articulate representatives to Washington, D.C., to seek trust title to 85.9 acres of land upon which they live. Above all, they sought legal recognition of the Payson Apache Indian community as a tribe—a status the federal government has long denied. (*See* Brandon 1970a:35*; 1970b:27†)

Troubles stem from gold-discovery days in the 1860's. "The Rio Verde Reserve was established in 1871 for the Tonto and Yavapai Indians. But it was dissolved four years later, and the Payson Apaches claim their Tonto ancestors were forcibly removed to the San Carlos Reservation." Then, "About the turn of the century, some of the Tontos returned to Payson and took up residence in the forest just south of town. Now, about 70 years later, these Payson Apaches are considered squatters in the eyes of the law."

As the Apache representatives in Washington pointed out, because they are not considered a tribe and live on National Forest land they have not been able to bring in electricity, running water or sewage facilities. Most of their houses are made of scrap lumber from nearby mills, or of old lumber. All of the adult males are employed in the saw and planer mills; and none of the Payson Apache families are on welfare.

Despite the fact that certain Arizona legislators have introduced legislation and given other support in behalf of these Indians,

---

*" 'Indian Community' means a tribal community with a quasi-sovereignty of its own and a sense of relatedness among its people akin to that of a religious community."

†"The people of an Indian community generally will not sell out for individual opportunities no matter how alluring; will undergo any privations to remain part of their living community. The community superlife, calling for inter-personal harmony rather than inter-personal striving, is in absolute opposition to the orthodox American gods of work-as-a-virtue and amassing personal wealth as a measure of success."

their success to date has been nil. A speaker for the Department of the Interior has remarked that title can be given to the land requested by the Payson Apache, but he says they should not now recognize them tribally. In the attitude of so many bureaucrats, an assistant secretary for Public Land Management is quoted as saying: "We do not now recognize this group and believe that we should not now recognize them. If this group wishes to avail itself of Indian services, they need only remove themselves to the San Carlos Indian Reservation, which they have refused to do for a number of reasons." (Anonymous 1971a)

Since the San Carlos reservation is some one hundred miles from Payson, as the Indians point out, "to move there would require a mass uprooting of the Payson Apaches," and "establishment as a corporation would provide them no security and would force them to pay taxes." Recognition as a tribe would allow them to be recipients of the vast array of BIA services, ranging from education to health and economic development.

SMALL AND WARM

She was small and warm
her hands like cotton
her face like ropes
her hair like a waterfall
her smile like a stone
her mind like the sky
her life like a river
her death like the fever of sorrow
her memory small and warm

By Courtney Moyah, Pima-Apache

From: *Art and Indian Children.* Curriculum Bulletin No. 7, 1970. Institute of American Indian Arts, Santa Fe, N. M.

THE PIMANS

BRIEF HISTORY   The Piman peoples have a long history which reaches back into the prehistoric past. First reporting of the Pima began in 1539 by Fray Marcos de Niza, the Franciscan who introduced Christianity. Jesuit missionaries encountered Piman-speaking Indians in the state of Sonora, in northwestern Mexico, and these came to be designated as the Lower Pima when, some seventy-five years later, missions were extended into present day Arizona, *Pimería Alta*, or the territory of the Upper Pima. The Upper Pima were "a single tribe" only in that they spoke a single language. Marked cultural differences existed. Those Pima dwelling in the San Pedro valley (the Sobaipuri) and on the Gila plain, for instance, "lived in fairly concentrated rancherias sustained by agriculture," while those farther west were nomadic food-gatherers. "Moreover, there was no permanent political organization linking more than a few rancherias in any part of the Pimería. Political coordination of rancherias. for any purpose but warfare seems to have been unknown, although there were games and customs of ceremonial cooperation between the rancherias. The widest political organization probably did not link more than fifteen hundred people. (Spicer 1970:119)*

It has been recorded that when the early Spaniards encountered the valley dwellers of the Gila and Salt rivers, they asked many questions of them. The usual Indian reply was *pi-nyi-match*, or "I don't know." From this, the Spaniards took to calling them "Pima." The name by which they indicate themselves is *ah-kee-mult-o-o-tom*, meaning "River People." Thus the term *Pima*, like the word *Apache*, has no linguistic significance.

Father Eusebio Francisco Kino, an energetic Italian, who was as much an explorer as a missionary, came among the Pima in 1687, intent upon reducing the ranchería people to pueblo dwellers. His campaign lasted for twenty-five years, keeping, it is said, "at a high intensity conflicts of interest between the Indians and the Spanish settlers." The Pima were considered wild and difficult, extremely savage, inasmuch as they resisted impressment by the Spaniards for work in the developing Mexican mines and on the ranches.

Kino soon demonstrated that the majority of the Pima were friendly, industrious, and peaceful, ready to ally themselves with the Spaniards, or to live quietly under the mission system. Kino

*Quotations from Spicer reproduced by permission of the University of Arizona Press.

209

introduced livestock, wheat and other crops which the Indians readily accepted, along with metal tools. He found them carrying on some trade with other indigenous peoples, but this did not comprise an important part of their economy. By standards of the day, the Pima were better off than neighboring groups. Lacking a highly developed social organization, they did not persist in their native religious ceremonies after contact with the Spaniards and Christianity.

In the regions where the Piman peoples dwelt, little attire was necessary. Women wore a one-piece, wrap around skirt, reaching from waist to the knees. These were made of a piece of deerskin or from home-woven cotton cloth. Men wore a loincloth of the same materials, and sometimes sandals, fashioned from mountain sheep skin or of twisted fibers. The hair of all individuals was allowed to flow freely—a chief sign of beauty. Ornaments of turquois and other stones were made into ear pendants; these sometimes hung to the shoulders; they were worn by men and women alike.

Women especially painted designs on their bodies for special occasions. And they were tattooed with lines that extended from the mouth to the chin. Although a painful practice, all girls over sixteen years old had these decorations. Youngsters ran about naked most of the time.

Kino died in 1711, after which the missions soon became a thing of the past. The Pima revolted against the Spaniards in 1751, and this "constituted a shock from which the Jesuit missions had not recovered by the time of the expulsion in 1767." (Spicer 1970:132) The Franciscans who followed in missionary efforts were relatively weak, although certain individuals, such as Father Garcés, were successful in their undertakings.

On the whole, reports indicated that the Upper Pima "had returned to their 'ancient barbarism.' " And it has been said that: "An important factor in the increasing isolation was the intensification of the Apache raids after about 1810. During the late 1700's Piman-speaking people had steadily retired westward from their border position on the San Pedro River. By 1800 there were no Pimans east of a line between San Ignacio near Magdalena and San Xavier. Many had been killed, and a few had been absorbed into the central Sonoran communities of Opatas and Spaniards. The remaining Pimans, who were not at the mission sites along the Santa Cruz and Magdalena, were living in desert villages in the present area of the Papagos or the river villages along the Gila." (Spicer 1970:132-133)

In the early 1800's the Franciscans exerted themselves to bring the Pima into the Santa Cruz River missions (San Xavier and Tumacacori), and apparently were successful in getting numerous converts.

The Apache raids were intensified during the 1830's and 1840's, and the following decade saw the raiding extended throughout the southern Upper Pima domain, past the Altar valley to the coast of the Gulf of California.

Through the Gadsden Purchase in 1853, the Piman land holdings became a part of the U.S.A. This transaction brought about immediate and important changes in the lives of the Upper Pima. Foremost was the different political condition.

The new international boundary surveyed in 1858, traversed the region of the headwaters of the San Pedro and Santa Cruz rivers and ran through the middle of the desert lands to the west. This automatically placed at least three-quarters of the remaining Upper Pima as residents of the United States. As much as sixty years later there were still Pima in the desert rancherías, under the leadership of a headman named Pia Muchita, who seemed unaware of the change and still professed allegiance to Mexico. Nevertheless, the invading Anglo-Americans regarded the Upper Pima territory north of the new line as part of the United States and proceeded to act accordingly." (Spicer 1970:133-134)

THE CALENDAR The Piman year begins with the rainy season, when characteristic plants and animals appear. The year is based on the moon periods, thus a lunar calendar of twelve "moons" is followed (or was into the present day). The sahuaro, or giant cactus, which ripens at the beginning of the rainy season is highly significant in the life of the Piman peoples. It was customary for a family to establish a permanent camp in the nearest sahuaro area. The figlike fruits and seeds were gathered for food in late June and July, before the rains began. The fruit, brought down by a long, pointed staff, was fermented to yield an alcoholic beverage which was drunk ceremonially—to bring rain. (Underhill 1940:48) Sahuaro harvesting, then, marked the beginning of the new year in the native calendar.

Sahuaro ribs were used on occasion in making house walls, and calendar sticks were made from them also. Some of the recent history, dating from just before the time of the Gadsden Purchase, is recorded on notched sticks—a device like computer records to remind one of events that occurred in successive years. Perhaps six feet long, a smooth, slightly flattened inner support of the giant cactus, about an inch and a half in diameter, had mnemonic symbols representing happenings recorded on the smooth side.

In some instances, dots and circles bespeak major ceremonies for the most part, although other events may be recorded. One stick has been described as follows:

> At the beginning of each year ... a notch is cut across the stick and, at the beginning of the next year, another, an inch or two further on. Between them is placed some crude geometrical sign, such as a triangle, cross or parallel lines to indicate the outstanding event of the year. Occasionally, two events are represented. The symbols are painted with red clay, such as was used for face paint, and blue soot collected from embers of greasewood, *Covillea glutinosa*, used for tatooing [*sic.*]. (Underhill 1938a:7)

The calendar keeper invented his own symbols. The sticks appear to have been kept in various villages. They are considered as private possessions, and it was customary to break one's stick and bury it with the owner upon his death.

The Anglos, knowing little and caring less about the Piman relationships, made distinctions between the Indians who dwelt on the Gila River (whom they often called "Pimos") and those who lived in the vicinity of Tucson and westward therefrom. The Spaniards had called the desert dwellers "Papagos," and the term became general with the Anglos for all Piman-speaking peoples who lived south of the Gila residents, whom they called the "Pima."

THE PIMA (THE RIVER PEOPLE)

Living at the very northern edge of the Spanish frontier, the Pima of the Gila River valley—where they had dwelt since prehistoric times—had the least contact with the Spaniards. With permanent water from the Gila, the Pima had irrigated their agricultural lands by means of an elaborate canal system. Kino had come among them in 1694, and other missionaries followed. Spanish officials had presented canes to the Pima, as they did to the Pueblo peoples. Accepting these, or at least official designations, the Pima "had acquiesced in a nominal obedience to the King of Spain."

Friendly relations existed between the Indians and the Anglos. During the 1820's fur trappers passed through the Pima territory, following the Gila trail. On these occasions the trappers were furnished food by the Pima. Reports of these contacts and those of General Kearny and the Mormon Battalion stated that the Gila Pima were the "most civilized Indians in the United States." Thousands of Anglos traversed the Pima holdings during the gold rush to California, beginning in 1849. They, too, found the Indians friendly, peaceful, and the source of plentiful food. The Pima were anxious to trade for metal and other goods.

It was not until 1855 that Pima leaders learned that their territory had come under the control of the U.S.A. as result of the Mexican War and the Gadsden Purchase. One of them consulted with the U.S. Boundary Commission, and was "assured that the United States had friendly intentions, that the land right under the Spaniards would be fully recognized, and also that the United States government had in mind giving the Pimas agricultural implements to assist them in the valuable service they were rendering providing food for parties of travelers." (Spicer 1970:147)

In characteristically tardy manner, it took the government four years to get the implements delivered, but the promise was fulfilled and this consolidated friendly relations between the Pima and the whites. At that time, however, the federal policy began to be applied to the Pima.

The Pima Reservation   An act of 28 February 1859 "required the President to have the boundaries of the lands then occupied by the confederated bands of Pima and Maricopa Indians near Gila River, Arizona, surveyed and to have it set apart as a reservation, not exceeding 100 square miles and $10,000 was to be presented to said Indians (11 Stat. 401, c. 66 sec. 305)." (Kelly Wm. H. 1953:61) The reservation was established south of Phoenix, on the Gila and Santa Cruz rivers; and the Pima agency was located in Sacaton about forty-two miles southeast of Phoenix, in 1871. (Robinson 1954:15) The appropriation of ten thousand dollars was used in part to buy tools for the Indians' use, but the remainder had to cover "the expense of a survey of the land on the Gila River for the purpose of setting aside not more than sixty-four thousand acres as a reservation." (Spicer 1970:149) The Pima who had lived on the Gila for centuries, having descended, it is believed, from Hohokam ancestors, claimed a much larger area; and the issue remained in dispute for a decade. In 1869, the survey was increased by 81,000 acres, giving a total of 145,000 acres—still far less than the Pima claimed.

Drought and the encroachment of settlers from the east caused the Pima to appeal to the federal government for consideration of their mounting problems. Leaders went to Washington in 1873 to present their case—and learned of the power of the white officials. "It was proposed that the Pima problems could be solved by removal to Indian territory." One of the leaders, Antonio Azul, went to Oklahoma and looked over the land to which they might be assigned. He was favorably impressed, but all the other Pima were opposed to any removal from their homeland. As result of the failing water supply some twelve hundred, or more than a quarter of the Pima group, moved north on the Salt River, where they farmed among the white settlers; the remaining Pima spread along the Gila in three major areas of water seepage, where marginal farming was carried on.

As one authority has stated:

> The period ... from about 1870 to about 1900 was one of increasingly intensive contact with Anglos and of numerous changes in Pima life. The surrounding of their land by Anglo settlers became an established fact. The Southern Pacific Railraod traversed their territory in 1878. Florence on their eastern margin became an important territorial town with an increasing population. By 1887 the irrigation canal constructed to take water out of the Gila River for the white settlers utilized the whole flow. No water reached any of the Pima fields downstream. Settlers were pressing to the edge of the reservation from the south in the Casa Grande area. Protests and representations had no effect except to increase by small parcels the size of the reservation. The real need, however, was for water, not land, as most government reports recognized; yet no effort whatever was made to protect the Indian water rights. The government ignored the problem, although agents in rapid succession continued to push for the Indian rights. (Spicer 1970:149)

During all this period from 1876 to 1915 no less than a dozen US executive orders increased or reduced their land or modified the boundaries. (*See* Kelly, Wm. H. 1953:61)

New Ways for the Pima   In 1881, the BIA established a boarding school in Sacaton—long after the Presbyterian Church, which was active among the Pima, had started a day school there (in 1868). A force of Indian police was initiated, and a Court of Indian Offenses set up. "An Indian Bureau farmer was brought to the reservation to give agricultural advice. At the same time that the Indian Bureau made these efforts to give some services to the Indians, activities of the Presbyterian Church were intensified." (Spicer 1970:149)

This authority tells of the work of a particular missionary-schoolteacher (Charles H. Cook) who, following a pitched battle between two Pima villages, began a vigorous missionary campaign, not only to baptize Pima people, but in an effort to reorganize their deteriorating communities. "Poverty through lack of water with which to farm and replacement of functions formerly performed by village headmen through the government agency had resulted in some degree of demoralization of the Indians." Three distinct factions had developed from water problems.

Before 1899, the missionary had baptized half of the Pima and established churches throughout the reservation.

In each community he appointed an elder, assisted by deacons, whom he held responsible for law and order and general moral standards. The elders were usually former village headmen. Gradually a transformation in village life took place, centering around the new religious organization. Annual revival meetings took the place of old ceremonies. Christian mythology and theology replaced older beliefs and the strict morality of the Presbyterians tended to reintegrate the disintegrating villages. The church affairs were almost entirely in the hands of the local Pimas, and ministers were trained to do the preaching. The Presbyterian missionary, Cook,* became the most influential force from Anglo society among the Pimas, although at the same time the Sacaton Boarding School and other boarding schools set up elsewhere by the Indian bureau were well attended by Pimas and worked together with the missionary in the transformation of Pima society. (Spicer 1970:149-150)

Worsening Economy   Economically, conditions on the reservation continued to worsen. In 1895 food rations had to be issued by the government. Individual Pima efforts did little toward solving the overall problem. And, "The Indian Bureau attempted nothing that would involve it in the matter of water rights on the Gila. It did however begin a program for solution of the water problem—the digging of wells to be served by electric pumps—in the eastern and central part of the reservation. Some fifteen wells were put into operation between 1903 and 1910." (Spicer 1970:150)

In 1914 the BIA put an allotment plan into effect, with the result that some of the Pima began coming back to the reservation to take up ten-acre plots. The consequence was wide scattering of the Indians over the reservation, "again disrupting community life."

*NOTE: Inasmuch as the influence of one particular man on the Pima people was so great, surely he should have more than passing mention. Mr. Cook, living in Chicago in 1870, heard of the spiritual need of the Pima and recognized this as his call. No church or denomination was back of him, but he left for the Southwest, taking a small organ which cost him thirty dollars. The train, then, went only to Dodge City, Kansas. From that point Cook continued on by coach and by walking; his funds were reduced to twenty-five cents by the time he reached Cow Springs, New Mexico.

Preaching along the way resulted in an unexpected but gratifying small sum of money. Cook continued on his weary route, reaching his destination, the Sacaton agency, on 23 December. In January 1871 he was hired as a teacher to the Pima Indians, at six hundred dollars per annum. On 15 January he started a little school with thirty-five youngsters whom he found well behaved and apt for learning.

During his years of service, Cook was awarded a medal by President U. S. Grant. In his old age he retired to Iowa where he died and was buried. To the last, he loved the Pima people.

The Cook Christian Training School, at Tempe, Arizona, was established in Dr. Cook's honor, and a centennial celebration was observed on 6 February 1971—with Indian dances and singing, art exhibit and a drama of Cook's life, and an open pit barbecue. In March a formal banquet was held. (*See* Walker 1970)

Climatic   Although the Gila River Indian Reservation of today encompasses
Influences   371,932 acres—good farming land, if irrigated, and nonirrigable
stretches—the physical conditions influence the lives of the approximately 5,300 souls who are enrolled there. Pima comprise the
majority, with a few Maricopa and Papago included in the census.
At Sacaton, which may be reached by Arizona Highways 87 and 93,
the highest rainfall occurs in July and August, and summer
temperatures have been as high as 117°F. The lowest rainfall is in
April, May and June. The temperature rarely goes below 20°. Mean
daily range of temperature between day and night is 35°. The
frost-free period is about 263 days.

Largely through efforts of representatives of the Presbyterian
Church, the San Carlos Project Bill was passed in 1924, and
construction of a dam near the old San Carlos Apache agency was
initiated. This promising action was welcomed by the Pima and
many began returning to their reservation to make land ready for
the water. Two years later, an advisory council of Pima men was
formed by the BIA, primarily to have some tribal body with which
to deal on legal matters pertaining to the entire Pima group.

In 1930, after completion of Coolidge Dam and the San Carlos
reservoir, preparation for the new supply of irrigation water began.
"At the same time extensive road-building programs were instituted, there was a shift to day schools from boarding school, and
agricultural extension service was put into operation. In 1934 under
the Indian Reorganization Act the Pima prepared a constitution
and formed a tribal council. In 1937 District Farmers Associations
were formed over the reservation, and in 1938 a high school was
established at Sacaton." (Spicer 1970:151)

The farm program resulted in misunderstandings and disputes,
and loss of prestige of the tribal council. Family income declined
and the Pima farmers lost interest. In 1951 the council initiated a
tribal farm which became a paying venture; but individual farming
declined in importance.

Assimilation   At the time, 94 per cent of all the Pima were literate, and 98 per
cent spoke English. It has been said that, "The Gila Pimas probably
were the most nearly culturally assimilated of all Indians in New
Mexico or Arizona. The Pima Tribal Council continued in operation
but it did not function as a political institution for Pimas as a
whole. The tribe as a unit of social organization or culture had
ceased to exist in the Arizona milieu. The tribal organization

existed as a rather specialized mechanism for managing some economic matters for Pima settlements nearest the agency." (Spicer 1970:151)

Modern Government The Gila River Pima-Maricopa Community was organized under a constitution and bylaws approved 14 May 1936, and a tribal corporate charter was ratified on 28 February 1938.

In establishing tribal status:

> All individuals listed on the official allotment roll of the Gila River Reservation are members. New members are added as follows: (1) all descendants are entitled to membership if they are of at least one-quarter degree of Indian blood—those having a lesser degree may be admitted to membership by a majority vote of the council of the community; (2) members who have remained away from the reservation continuously for a period of 20 years and automatically forfeited their membership may be reinstated by a majority vote of the council with the consent of the district in which he or she proposes to take up residence; and (3) persons of Indian blood marrying members of the Gila River Pima-Maricopa Indian Community may be adopted into the community by a three-fourths vote of the council. (Kelly, Wm. H. 1953:61)

A community council made up of seventeen members is the governing body; these must be twenty-five years of age or over, and a resident for at least one year immediately preceding the election of the district from which he or she is elected. Councilmen hold office for three years, with one-third of the membership being elected each year. The council meets on the first Wednesday of each month at 9.00 a.m., in Sacaton, Arizona. Meetings on the third Wednesday of each month are held in the districts. All tribal officers, committees, and extra law enforcement officers are selected by the council. Tribal officers are selected from within or without council membership; if selected from without the membership they do not have a vote in the council. The presiding officer, however, has the right to vote in case of a tie. (Kelly, Wm. H. 1953:62)

Affairs of the community are in the hands of fifteen committees, each with its chairman. The committees are concerned with: Arts and Crafts, Education, Farm Board, Government and Management, Health, Homesite, Housing Authority, Irrigation, Land Board, Model Cities Program, Planning and Zoning, Police Commissioners, Skill Center, Social Development, and Youth Home Board. In addition, chairmen are named for the Gila River Development, Gila River Indian Enterprises, Gila River Products Corporation, Pima-Chandler and Pima-Coolidge districts, Pima Education and Agricultural Development Corporation, and the SanTan Industrial Development Corporation.

Officers of the community are a governor, lieutenant governor, secretary, treasurer, tribal judge, and police chief. The council has jurisdiction over all matters pertaining to the management of tribal property, conduct of Indians and non-Indians on the reservation, tribal business enterprises,and the welfare of tribal members.

The tribal court at Sacaton handles

all cases within the Pima Agency jurisdiction which includes, besides the Gila River Pima-Maricopa Community, the Salt River Pima-Maricopa Community, the Fort McDowell Community, and the Maricopa (Ak-Chin) Community. The judge and associate judge are appointed by the Indian Service and their salaries are paid by the government. The clerk of the court is appointed by the Governor with the approval of the Community Council and receives his salary from court funds. The chief of police, also appointed and paid by the Indian Service, serves the Pima Agency jurisdiction. (Kelly, Wm. H. 1953:62)

Present-Day Economy   Principal income for years has come from leases of lands to white farmers. Other revenue is derived from traders' licenses, apiary rents and sand and gravel sales. Since 1 July 1966 the Gila River Indian Community has been in the midst of what is almost "a non-native revival movement, a home-grown and BIA and OEO supported economic, social, and political development program they call *Vh-thaw-hup-ea-ju*, 'It Must Happen'." (Fontana 1967) This was set up as an eighteen-month accelerated program with some fifty-one projects. By the end of the first year significant progress had been made, and has continued under the direction of the Indians but utilizing resources and assistance available from the BIA, federal and state agencies, and those of neighboring communities.

The Gila River Indian Community has attacked the problem of unemployment by luring industry to the reservation and preparing the available work force for jobs in industry. The industrial development is centered primarily in three industrial parks, the site improvement of which is being funded by the Economic Development Administration. This development was geared to be supplemented by service facilities, commercial enterprises and residential construction. Systematic development of the interchange areas on Interstate Highway 10 was also part of the program. It was anticipated that by the end of 1968 a significant number of new jobs would be created on the reservation. Other aspects of economic development centered around increasing income from agriculture and development of the reservation mineral potential. (Cumming 1967)

Social Development   The Ecomonic Opportunity Act of 1964 provided stimulus to social development on the reservation. The Community Action Program has a number of components: Headstart, Day Care Center for children, guidance, adult education, alcoholism prevention and treatment, health aides, and community improvement. Other OEO activities include a NYC program, a state-administered Title 5 work experience program, VISTA program, and agricultural loans under Title 3.

    The BIA branch of Social Service, HEW (division of Indian health) social workers personnel of Title 5, and the Gila River Indian Community Action Program cooperate in social service programs aimed at helping those families with social problems to make satisfactory adjustments.

    During 1967 the public school was consolidated with the BIA school at Sacaton. The facilities are used jointly, and the first grade was transferred from the BIA to the public school. Thenceforth, each year, a successively higher grade has been transferred, with the end that the BIA school will be phased out.

    Since 1966 an increasing number of new, mutual self-help houses have been built. In the Casa Blanca area, many new bathrooms were added to existing structures. Several modern homes have been constructed through FHA insured loans, and a number have been renovated. Water and sanitation systems have been improved at Casa Blanca and Upper SanTan.

    One of the major objectives of the Vh-thaw-hup-ea-ju plan was to improve management and government by the Gila River Indian Community. Projects included a review of the Community constitution, development of a tribal roll, codification of tribal ordinances, development of a law and order code, and a management review of the community organization structure.

    As in many of the other Indian communities, the primary function of the BIA agency is coming to be one of providing services to the Gila River Indian Community and individual Indians, so that they may better attain their goals.

Pima Arts   Pima women have long been noted for their beautifully woven and artistically decorated basketry. These have enjoyed many useful purposes. Three native materials are employed: willow, devil's claw (*Martynia*), and cattail, or tule (*Typha angustifolia*). The weavers harvest these at the proper seasons, prepare them for future use, and store them away until the time comes.

In the old days it was estimated that six out of ten Pima women were basket weavers. Today the number has dwindled to a few. This art entails time-consuming labors. The late Bert Robinson has described the making of basketry by the Pima and other Indian peoples of Arizona in an extensively illustrated volume that is recommended to interested readers. (Robinson 1954)

Three types of designs are used by the Pima: geometric, symbolic, and original. The fret design is the most commonly employed. None of the designs are drawn, but are carried in the mind of the weaver, just as the designs of pottery makers. A squash blossom design is next in popularity, and is executed in numerous variations. Another attractive design is known as butterfly wings; and among the favored ones is the whirlwind—an oft occurring phenomenon of the Southwestern desert areas. Star designs are infrequently used. In some instances, design motifs may be used in combination with other features, such as swastikas and coyote tracks. Original designs are not very common.

The most universal form of Pima basketry is that of relatively shallow bowls. Formerly made in quantities, storage baskets woven of wheat straw and the bark of young mesquite trees have become increasingly rare. Basketry jars are made in various sizes, and they are almost exclusively for the tourist trade, as are miniature specimens. A few of the Pima weavers make baskets of horse-hair—again for the tourists; they are fine little items. The old type of burden basket, or *giho* (*kiaho*), has not been made for many years.

Much of their traditional ceremonialism has been lost to the Pima, yet native social urges are present. Annual fairs are favorite celebrations. On a Saturday and Sunday in March, one may witness the *Mul-chu-tha*, or fair, at Sacaton, south of Phoenix. They have a rodeo; parade and exhibits; and Indians from several of the Pima villages, such as Bapchule, assemble to present rain and basket dances, and to engage in a *taka* game and various contests. It is now customary to select a Miss Mul-chu-tha Queen annually.

THE PAPAGO (THE DESERT PEOPLE)   The native name for these Piman-speaking people, *Tóno* (TOH-ono) *oóhtam*, signifies "people of the desert." They have, among other designations, been called *papáh óotam*, or "bean people." (Swanton

1952:357) They occupy the southwest portion of the Southwest—the foothills and valley floors of northern Sonora (Mexico) and southern Arizona.

It appears that Father Kino was the first white man to visit their territory, in 1694. He found them living essentially as they did until very recent times. Other than not having so much contact with the whites as did the Pima, the history of the two groups has been similar. Cultural differences are minor. They recognize themselves as one people. The location of the Papago has made them less agricultural than the Pima; in early times some of the former completely lacked farming opportunities.

CELEBRATION

I shall dance tonight.
When the dusk comes crawling.
There will be dancing and feasting.
I shall dance with the others
  in circles,
    in leaps,
      in stomps.

Laughter and talk
  will weave into the night,
Among the fires of my people.
Games will be played
and I shall be
  a part of it.

By Alonzo Lopez, Papago
From: *The Writer's Reader*, 1962–1966, The Institute of American Indian Arts, Santa Fe, N. M.

The Papagueria The lands of the Papago—*Papagueria*—are hot and arid. Elevation runs from 1,400 to 3,000 feet, encompassing extensive flat plains from which short mountain ranges or peaks rise rather abruptly. Rainfall varies in different parts of the area, amounting to from four to twelve inches during the year. Typically desert vegetation grows there: "creosote predominates the low dry plains, mesquite and paloverde line the usually dry stream beds, and the hill slopes are variably covered with cacti." (Gabel 1949:12)

Two periods of rain occur, one in winter and one in summer;

the latter permits limited, undependable farming. Understandably, the Papago long engaged in hunting—chiefly of rabbits, some deer, antelope, and other animals—and gathering wild foods; and they traveled considerable distances to get drinking water. Basically, and largely for these reasons, they were somewhat less sedentary than the Pima. During the summer they moved from their more permanent villages in the foothills, where the water supply was constant, to lower areas where they could take advantage of increased opportunities for farming and food gathering afforded by the rains. They were good farmers who worked their small plots intensively. Their aboriginal crops were maize, beans, pumpkins, gourds and cotton. The wild foods consisted of yucca and cactus buds and fruits, mesquite beans, seeds of ironwood and paloverde, certain greens (such as amaranth, lamb's quarter, saltbush, and *cañaigre*), and sand root—sometimes called wild potato.

No permanent streams or lakes are in the Papago territory, and springs are widely scattered, The usually dry, sandy washes, or arroyos, carry flood waters for short distances and then spread out on the flood plains. Such a place is known as *Ak Chin*, "mouth of the arroyo." Several locations were so called by the Papago. This confused the government people, with result that the designation was conferred on a single village south of the Maricopa station on the Southern Pacific Railroad, on Vecol Wash.

The generally inhospitable nature of the Papago habitat helped spare the Indians from white aggressions to a degree. Yet, following the Gadsden Purchase, when the land of Papaguería was considered available for non-Indian settlement, "many springs, wells and grazing areas were soon claimed by ranchers moving into the area. Little was done to secure land for the exclusive use of the Papagos. . . ." (Papago Indian Agency 1970:12) The nature of the region, to some extent, "made the Americanization of the Papago a relatively peaceful and unhurried process. It was not until the twentieth century that miners and cattlemen began encroaching in sufficient numbers to create the need for a reservation." (Gabel 1949:15)

Reservations Anglo Style On 1 July 1874 an executive order established a reservation adjoining the city of Tucson, San Xavier del Bac. Next, an executive order of 12 December 1882 set apart lands just north of Gila Bend for the Papago living there; and an executive order of 16 June 1911 established small reserves of 80 acres each at Indian

Oasis (now Sells) and San Miguel. Four executive orders of 28 May 1912 set up the Maricopa, Cockleburr, *Chui Chuisch,* and *Tat-murl-ma-kutt* reservations.

Then it followed that:

An Executive Order of December 5, 1912, added another reservation at the foot of Boboquivari Peak—Santiergos. An Exeuctive Order of January 14, 1916, established the "Sells," Nomadic Papago, or Papago Villages, Reservation which included the area formerly within the Cockleburr, Chui Chuische, Tat-Murl-Ma-Kutt, land (the Maricopa Reservation became a part of the Piman Indian Reservation). Congressional Acts in 1926, 1931, 1937, and 1940 authorized the purchase of patented land to be added to the Papago Reservations in addition to inclusion of public domain land." (Papago Indian Agency 1970:12)

All of the orders and acts brought about a total of 2,855,984 acres of reserved lands for use of the Papago Indians. Within the present Sells reservation are 2,774,370 acres; 71,201 acres within the San Xavier reservation; and 10,409 within the Gila Bend reservation. The main reservation stretches ninety miles across Pima county, and from the Mexican border north to within about ten miles of the town of Casa Grande, Arizona. Of the Papago holdings only some 7,000 acres are irrigated; about 1200 acres are at San Xavier. It is said that "Little change of any importance in Papago land holdings has been made since 1940's, but a very important change in the nature of Indian title came about in 1955 when, by Act of Congress, the Papagos were given all mineral, as well as surface rights to the reservations." (Papago Indian Agency 1970:12)

Early in 1971 a grant of $82,398 was made by the BIA for a pilot project on the Papago reservation at San Xavier. Given to the environmental research laboratory of the University of Arizona, the money was to be used for "designing and studying the feasibility of establishing controlled greenhouses on Indian reservations (using a technique which utilizes a farming-under-plastic idea—the plants being grown under huge sheets of plastic)." (Anonymous 1971g) If feasibility is proven for the raising and marketing of small vegetables, it was expected that construction could begin and actual marketing of products could start within the following year.

Late in the same year, an 800-acre farm, to be known as the San Xavier Indian Cooperative, was established through federal grants and loans of $115,000 to more than 175 landowners on the Papago Indian Reservation. For more than ninety years the Papago land has been divided among descendants from generation to generation "until no one landowner can make a living from the small, desert plots." (Anonymous 1971C) Products grown on the cooperative farm are to be "channeled into the commercial market, with emphasis on selling the products to other Papago Indians."

Currently, seventy-four settlements on the main reservation are inhabited, forty-three of them permanently. Nine of the communities are considered as major villages. Of these, Sells on Arizona Highway 86 is the largest, and it is the Papago headquarters; its population is approximately 1,000. The other major villages include *Ali Chukson, Topawa, Quijotoa, Gu Achi, Gu Vo, Pisinimo, Gu Oidak,* and *Chuichu.*

Administration   For purposes of administration the main reservation is divided into nine districts: Baboquivari, Chukut kuk, Gu Achi, Gu Vo, Hickiwan, Pisinimo, Schuk Toak, Sif Oidak, and Sells. The Gila Bend and San Xavier reservations make up two more districts, bringing the total to eleven. Each district has its own elected council and also elects two delegates to the Tribal Council. The latter meets on the first Friday of each month at 9:00 a.m., in Sells. Elections are held annually, the first Friday in February, in a building adjacent to the rodeo grounds. The tribal government has offices and an assembly hall there.

The basic political document of the Papago is the constitution and bylaws ratified by the tribal members on 12 December 1936, and approved by the Secretary of the Interior on 6 January 1937. The council has twenty-two members, men and women who are elected for two-year periods. Each district is self-governing in local matters under its elected District Council, made up of not less than five members. Should vacancies occur in the Tribal Council they are filled by the district councils. All individuals listed on the official census roll of 1936 are tribal members. Additional members include all children of resident members; and children born off the reservation may be adopted by the council if they are offspring of members and have at least one-half Indian parentage.

All tribal officers, committees, and tribal employees are selected by the council and serve for one year. The officers are: chairman, vice-chairman, secretary, treasurer, judge, and chief of police. Committees include: education, health, a housing authority, legal, mining board, an office of economic opportunity (OEO), and a rodeo board.

Law enforcement is a combined tribal-federal activity. Personnel includes a non-Indian investigator, a Papago captain of

THE PAPAGO INDIAN RESERVATION, SOUTHERN ARIZONA

police, and seven tribal policemen. A radio system keeps the police department in touch with county and state police, with whom close cooperation is maintained. The first woman to hold an elective office among the Papago was selected as tribal judge. Office of the police department, jail, tribal court, and living quarters for the police captain are in the Municipal Center, a building constructed in 1962.

Economy   The Papago number about 10,000, but most of these do not live in their reservation homes all of the time; ties, however, take them back. Slightly less than 6,750 reside on the main reservation. Gila Bend residents number about 250, and San Xavier has a population of some 680. Income of the Papago has long been one of the smallest of any Indians in Arizona, but is now improving. For years, cattle raising and some subsistence farming yielded most of the livelihood. The land is overstocked and crop failures occur about one out of five years. Because of the very limited economic resources many have been forced to leave the reservation yearly to seek work of various types. A number engage in agricultural labor.

The total of Papago people employed in 1970 was 3,107. Federal employment brought in 62 per cent of all wage income. Per capita income for the Papago was then estimated to average about $700 annually.

Permanent colonies of Papago have grown up in Tucson, Casa Grande, and Ajo—south of Gila Bend on Arizona Highway 85—and in a number of other southern Arizona communities. An entirely new village has been built at Gila Bend. About forty Papago families live in the Sonoran Desert of Mexico; although they are Mexican citizens they maintain close ties with the Arizona Papago.

Dwellings   Among the changes to be observed today in Papaguería are the types of dwellings. The old Papago homes were constructed with strong, tough ocotillo (*Fouquieria splendens*) stalks or sahuaro ribs placed upright and with occasional horizontal stalks laced together and covered with adobe plaster, or wattled; sometimes, if available, rocks were used in the walls. Roofs were of ocotillo withes covered with brush.

Today, almost 65 per cent of the 980 houses enumerated on the reservation are considered to be below minimum standards. The Papago Tribal Housing Authority and the BIA are working in close cooperation with HUD to obtain modern, durable housing for the

Papago people. Present construction planning calls for five hundred new housing units by 1975.

Family Rights   In commenting on the family responsibilities of the Papago in maintenance of the household, the late Mr. Robinson said:

> If a woman needs a new dress or some article for the house, it is her responsibility to provide the money for its purchase. Likewise, the man must purchase his overalls or his harness or farm implements with *his* earnings. This attitude toward a division of communal earnings and property extends even down through inheritance rights. The parents or the brother of the husband feel that, upon his death, their right to his farm implements or livestock supersedes that of his wife, and it is only through the application of the white man's inheritance laws that justice is achieved in such cases. In the case of death of the wife, her mother or sister may make claim to personal or household articles which she had made or purchased. (Robinson 1954:42–43)

Papago Arts   Encouragement is given to the traditional art of basketry. It has been said that, despite the attention given to the making of baskets, no records have been found to indicate that they have had a part in the religious ceremonies and rituals of the Papago. They have long been highly prized, and may be kept in a family for generations. They have had extensive use as gifts; often such gifts have been buried with a recipient upon death.

No dyes are used in Papago basketry. The materials are much like those of the Pima; they are prepared and woven in natural colors. On a white (natural) background, designs are worked in green or black, or both, and occasionally in red. Thin, flexible leaves of narrowleafed yucca (*Yucca elata*) are used for white, yellow and green, and devil's claw for the black; the red is derived from yucca root or root of the desert willow (*Salix nigra*). Yucca grows only on a small portion of the Papago country. The leaves, therefore, constitute an economic item, being used by the gatherer, traded, or sold.

Papago baskets are made by the coil method with foundation bundles of beargrass (*Nolina erumpems*) or yucca, sometimes of cattail, sewn with willow splints or sotol—usually the latter if the baskets are made to be sold. Two types of stitching are used. Designs are chiefly geometric, though life forms are produced also. More devil's claw appears in the decoration of Papago baskets than in those made by the Pima. Forms include bowls—some with high curving walls, others shallow trays—jars with or without lids, tall containers with straight or outward sloping walls, miniatures, and figurines in the likeness of animals, reptiles, birds, cacti, humans, and composites of these.

The Papago produce more basketry today than any of the other Indian peoples. Nearly three thousand baskets are marketed annually through the Papago Self-help Program alone. Outstanding items are sold at many state and county fairs and rodeos, as well as in museum shops and various stores and trading posts. Outlets for basket sales have been opened in Los Angeles and Toronto, Canada; and annual sales are held in Massachusetts and New Jersey.

The use of pottery has been found to reflect "the daily life of the members of the cultures which produce it," according to a recent anthropological study. The writers of that work say:

> In the case of the Papagos, canteen water jars, vessels with a small mouth and a long, constricted neck, ceased to be made when wells were drilled and when aluminum canteens were introduced. A reduction in the number of saguaro-wine vessels suggests a similar reduction in the frequency of certain Papago ceremonies. Items such as pottery ashtrays, toothpick holders, and piggy banks being made today tell us that Papago life has changed sharply in the last sixty or seventy years; these items even offer some suggestion as to the nature of this change. (Fontana et al 1962)*

The work mentions that pottery is the keystone of much archaeological analysis, and it points out that the study of pottery of a living culture has a great deal to offer the archaeologist, "suggesting to him the culturally significant limits of pottery analysis. There is a point in the study of pottery remains which arrives at technological sherd-splitting, going beyond limits that have any meaning for the understanding of a culture. The study of Papago pottery shows at what point this is true and why it is so."

It was found in the study conducted that numerous problems relate specifically to the Papago Indians, their culture and their history, which could be clarified by examination of their pottery, modern and archaeological. "One of the most intriguing of these problems," the writers found, "is the relation between the Papago Indians and the prehistoric Hohokam culture of the same area." (Both made their ceramics by the paddle and anvil technique.)

Pottery forms and decorations, when considered as a whole, have meaning. "Both are tradition-bound, just as is the technique of making pottery. The clay body, inasmuch as the component clay and temper derive from the same environment, has meaning. So does slip. But the difficulty in always being able to distinguish Pima from Papago pottery, even at this contemporary date, should tell the student of prehistory to beware." (Fontana et al 1962:136)

Today, the only vessels made for Indian use are bean pots, water-cooling jars, and an occasional small syrup jar. The others are made for the tourist trade—but that market is collapsing; the Papago black-on-red pottery is in little demand. It is predicted that within another generation no more Papago pottery will be manufactured. (Fontana et al. 1962:137)

Industries   The Papago tribe maintains a small herd of registered cattle under professional management; and it has the only all-Indian Credit Union in the U.S.A.

Due to an unusually severe drought which began in 1969, and continued for several years wells ran dry and the water holes (*charcos*), upon which the Papago cattlemen depended for water for their stock, dried up completely. Hundreds of their cattle died, reducing the already destitute people almost to total devastation. Entirely on their own, a Livestock Relief Operation was formed by the Papago. It was headed by the late Tom Segundo, a Papago graduated from the University of Chicago Law School.* The Operation determined the specific needs of the stockmen, itemized them carefully and applied to the BIA for a grant of $500,000. Reporting on this a syndicated writer stated:

A bureaucratic powwow in Washington decided to grant the Papago $200,000 of which $40,000 was to be used for overtime payments to Indian Affairs Bureaucrats. Not a single Indian was invited to the meeting.

The Washington sages also solemnly forbade the Papago to use the money for cattle feed, despite the fact this was the most urgent need. Cattle feed, it was decided in Washington, was the responsibility of tribal families. (Anderson 1969)

The same writer commented that the Papago are a proud and intelligent people; and he mentioned their domestic water supply:

Most villages have one well for a water supply. The residents have to haul water to their homes in large metal oil drums. In some cases, it has to be carried over long distances, which requires a truck. For this, the family has to pay $1 a barrel. The Indian Affairs Bureau long ago decided that plumbing was too expensive to install. (Anderson; 1969)

---

*Most unfortunately, Mr. Segundo, then tribal chairman, was killed at the age of fifty-one years in an air crash at Casa Grande on 6 May 1971.

With $145,000 of the BIA grant, the salaries were paid, and the Papago were enabled to buy hay and pay for water hauling, and other items. Disaster was averted. Domestic water is being supplied by the PHS.

In 1971 the Papago received more emergency funds, which provided for technical advice, mechanical equipment, and about $92,000 for buying hay and getting water relief—including cleaning of the charcos. Some of the wells are still pumping; water is hauled in critical areas. As a result, death losses have been lessened, though hot weather heightens the risk. The relations between the Papago and the BIA have been greatly improved. (Whitfield 1971)

The Past vs. the Present Taxes on cattle sales, income from land and mineral leases, license fees paid by traders and hunters, and court fines have been the chief sources of tribal income. At the present, the Tribal Council is actively working to bring about the optimum economic development of the reservations. As a result, a new day is dawning in Papaguería, as shown by the following developments:

Two large mining companies, Hecla and Newmont, have each discovered significant deposits of high grade copper ore in the northern part of the Reservation and are now preparing for full mining operations there. Training of Papagos for this kind of employment has begun and several hundred individuals will eventually be hired as regular full-time workers receiving full-scale wages. A third mining company—American Smelting & Refining—will soon begin copper mining operations at San Xavier near Tucson.

More jobs and land lease income have been generated by the opening of the San Xavier Industrial Park in 1970; this project is coming along well. Funded by a loan-grant from the Economic Development Administration, the 40-acre park is expected to quickly attract several light industries to the San Xavier Reservation. Additional industrial acreage will be developed at San Xavier to match demand.

A planned earth dam and reservoir, to be built by the Corps of Engineers, has been approved. The project will provide run-off control and a means to irrigate many thousands of acres in the north section of the main reservation. Campgrounds, fishing, and a recreational park are being planned in conjunction with this water project. (Papago Indian Agency 1970:5)

The Papago derive between $250,000 and $300,000 per year from fire-fighting engagements. This provides employment for some 365 men.

Educational Facilities Public educational facilities are provided on the Papago reservation by the Sells Consolidated School (Indian Oasis School District

Number 40), a Pima county grade school. Elementary schooling is provided by the federal government for those students who live an excessive distance from Sells; this is at day schools in three isolated villages and a boarding-day school at *Achi*, or Santa Rosa village. Three reservation parochial schools are maintained by the Franciscan Order.

High School education is available at federally operated Indian schools, and the Phoenix Indian School is the primary choice of the Papago students. Some attend public high schools in Tucson or go to Catholic Indian high schools, such as Saint John's at Laveen, Arizona. A few students have gone on for training at the Institute of American Indian Arts in Santa Fe, New Mexico; others are attending college. Adult education classes are conducted in several of the Papago villages through the cooperative efforts of the tribal government, the OEO, and the BIA. The Papago are diligently working toward providing adequate scholarship funds for their young people.

When Kitt Peak on the Papago reservation was selected as site for a new astronomical observatory, which was built by the National Science Foundation, the Indians were very pleased. Steller telescopes of 16, 36 and 80 inches were installed, and a giant solarscope—the largest in the world—is the only one of its particular type of construction. A wide, paved highway leads to the summit of the peak, where a large picnic area has been provided near the top. Kitt Peak is open to the public every day, from 10:00 a.m. to 4:00 p.m. The observatory is one of the most important in the country.

Other Community Facilities   The BIA and PHS offices are in Sells. For the latter, a hospital facility with a 50-bed installation, costing $2,260,000 was opened in 1961; it is entirely modern and well equipped and staffed. A Post Office building was dedicated in 1964.

Religious Groups   Religious activities are available through Catholic and Protestant groups. More than three-fourths of the Papago are of Catholic faith and have churches in every sizable village. Among the Protestants, the Presbyterian, Baptist, Assembly of God, and Nazarene denominations likewise have churches.

Festive Occasions   Today, the Papago sponsor a rodeo and fair at Sells, which is one of the most exciting shows of its kind in Arizona; it is held on the last Saturday and Sunday in October. Hardriding, working Indian cowboys display their skills in daring events. Also featured are dances and ceremonials. The Papago have erected comfortable and adequate grandstands for spectators, and they treat their guests to a barbecue.

YONDER STANDS A YOUTH

Yonder stands a youth beyond
  the fires of the sunset.
In his eyes a misty cloud floats,
  telling that he weeps.
His crystal-white tears add to
  the sea of negligence
Which stretches endlessly before him,
Barring his crossing into the
  land of happiness.
Within the palms of his hands,
He cradles the jewel of his life,
Waiting hopefully for one to
  cast it to.
But, walking the sands
  of their own contentment,
Those who have reached the shore
  refuse to look toward him.

Look yonder!
There stands a helpless youth,
  crying as a child;
Toward you,
  outstretched, his hand.

By Alonzo Lopez, Papago

From: *The Writers' Reader,* Fall, 1966. Institute of American Indian Arts, Santa Fe, N. M.

THE MARICOPA
.... MOVERS BY CHOICE

From prehistoric times, various Yuma-speaking Indians moved up the Gila River and settled.

About the beginning of the nineteenth century a group of Yuma-speaking Indians who called themselves *Pipatsje*, or "The People," occupied an area along the Colorado River, south of present day Parker, Arizona. The Anglos called these people "Maricopas." Apparently these disagreed with the other Yuma Indians with regard to selection of their leaders. As a consequence, they withdrew from the Colorado and moved eastward up the Gila River, where they made friends with the Pima Indians. There they were given land and protection from their hostile kinsmen. The Pima and Maricopa fought as allies in the battle of 1857 against Yuma and Mohave forces, whom they defeated severely. Although the Pima and Maricopa could not understand each other's mother tongue, this proved no barrier to a lasting relationship.

The retreat of the Maricopa from the Colorado left a large area of river bottom land vacant, and it was into this territory that the Mohave expanded from the north, and the Ute-related Chemehuevi also ... to become residents of what came to be named the Colorado River Reservation.

Descendants of the Maricopa are found today among the Pima on the Gila River Reservation and on the Salt River Reservation, as previously discussed. Today, two Maricopa Indian settlements are recognized: one on the northwest corner of the Gila River Reservation and the other in the Lehi district of the Salt River Reservation. From their long association with the Pima, the Maricopa seem to have lost all knowledge of their ancestors having lived elsewhere. However, until recently they followed certain practices of the past, and it was said:

MARICOPA ARTS
Their lives are dream directed as are the Mohaves; they cremate their dead; they have a clan-name system; and they speak the Yuman tongue .... In 1858, the U.S. Army census listed 518 Maricopas. Today, through intermarriage with Pimas they have lost most of their Yuman identity. They have adopted much of the Piman culture and are now almost one with them. (Johnston 1970:58)*

*Reproduced by permission of the University of Arizona Press.

233

MARICOPA ARTS

The Maricopa women produced pottery of utilitarian type, with vessels for many uses, and chiefly without design—made much like that of the Pima and Papago Indians. An outstanding ceramist of the Maricopa was Ida Redbird, whose mother, *Kwehadk*, taught her the art. Like so many of the Indian people, Mrs. Redbird had a wide command of the English language as well as her mother tongue. She served as informant and interpreter for several well known scientists. Although her eyes dimmed with advancing age, she continued to make fine pottery and contributed to the advancement of her people until the time of her tragic death. During a thunder-storm on 10 August 1971, a tree fell on her while she was resting and she was crushed to death. Her age was said to be seventy-nine. (Anonymous 1971e:21; Anonymous 1971f:1) Several other Maricopa women produce good vessels.

Their effigy pottery is traditional and is still made. But the majority of pieces decorated with black-on-red or black-on-buff are largely non-Indian in original concept; they are made for the tourist trade, and are highly popular. A variety of jars and bowls of glossy red or buff, or a combination of the two, with simple designs are attractive. The long-necked jars are adapted from an old form used for syrup, or for safe-keeping of the scalps of enemies. The Maricopa have not been producers of basketry.

Old ceremonies, the great emphasis on dreams, and distinctive native social customs now are nonexistent.

FARMING

The economy today rests mainly on subsistence farming, cotton raising, and wage work. Most of the individual Maricopa land allotments are too small to be farmed profitably; for this reason most lands are leased to non-Indians for agricultural development.

It has been noted that the Maricopa dwell on the Gila and the Salt reservations. They do not, as one might expect, live on the Maricopa Indian Reservation (Ak Chin) just south of Maricopa, Arizona. This is another good example of the confusion concerning Indian groups that has come to obtain—particularly in Arizona—since the coming of the white man. It is the Papago Indians who occupy the Maricopa Indian Reservation lands.

········ THE CAHITANS

THE YAQUI INDIANS

Of the Indians speaking Cahitan, those known as the Yaqui (YAH-key) are the southernmost of the Indians discussed, to the South of the Papago. The Cahitan-speaking people of the UTO-AZTECAN stock lived in southern Sonora, Mexico. (*See* Kurath and Spicer 1947:11) They dwelt at the mouths of large rivers, and along the entire length of the Río Yaqui. With abundant water, they tended to have somewhat concentrated settlements, or rancherias, and practiced dry farming. The density of their population led to development of genuine tribal organization with permanent ceremonial groups. In addition to shamanism, at least rudimentary forms of priesthood came into being. Emphasis on war fare led to integratio of all the Yaqui rancherias.

Brief History

The armed intrusion of the Spaniards into the Yaqui territory was resisted from the beginning. The first contact occurred in 1533, and the Yaqui were eminently successful in the encounters. They were strong enough to set their own terms for the entrance of the Jesuit missionaries. In time, the relationship became both hostile and friendly. After a major affray in 1609, in which the Yaqui were victorious, it is said that:

Suddenly, to the surprise of the Spaniards, the Yaquis asked for peace. This was an event which the Spanish in their chronicles spoke of as unprecedented in military history. The reasons for the Yaqui action remain uncertain; there were two versions current. One held that Hurdaide [Spanish captain head-quartered on the site of modern Sinaloa] circulated stories about the arrival of the reinforcements by sea. Another version was that the Yaquis were so impressed by the Spanish military ability and Hurdaide's miraculous escape [from the conflict] that they thought it would be safest to ally themselves with the Spaniards rather than keep on fighting. (Spicer 1970:47)

Yaqui acceptance of the Jesuit missions was rapid. For several score years unusual tranquility prevailed, with economic and religious development. Government of the towns, except for the Spanish captain-general, was in the hands of the Indians.

With the discovery of rich silver mines at Alamos in 1684, things began to change, but the Yaqui initially were not much affected. In less than a half-century, however, the antagonism of

235

one of the Spanish governors against the missionary program led to increasing discontent. In 1740, the Yaqui and their kindred, the Mayo, revolted. Just what precipitated the revolt and what actually occurred is not known, but it was costly to the Indians and Spaniards alike. Over one thousand Spaniards were killed and more than five thousand Indians.

Practically all of the mines were abandoned; all missionaries were forced to leave; livestock was killed or driven away; and an atmosphere of suspicion and distrust had been created. (*See* Spicer 1970:52) A new governor was named and he began to rule "with an iron hand."

The Jesuits returned to the missions when things quieted down, and the governor instituted "a series of restrictive measures, requiring that no Indian be permitted to leave any pueblo without the permission of missionaries, impressing Indians for forced labor on mines and haciendas, and requiring that there be daily recitation of prayers by all Indians in the mission communities. . . . After 120 years the typical Spanish frontier situation had finally developed in the Yaqui-Mayo country. . . ." (Spicer 1970:52–53)

With the return of the missionaries to their missions—which had not been destroyed—an attempt was made to reestablish things as they had been before. But the attitude of the Indians was changed, and their old level of prosperity was not regained. The Yaqui population, like that of the Mayo, declined; it was estimated that some 23,000 Yaqui remained. This was partly due to the migrations that were taking place. It was reported in 1760 that thousands of Yaqui were living away from the lower Yaqui River settlements; the people were widely dispersed. "This emigration dismayed the missionaries and gave the civil authorities the feeling that an era of decline had set in in the formerly thriving Sonoran missions." (Spicer 1970:53) They intensified their efforts among the Indians that remained, and the civil authorities concerned themselves with ways and means of increasing economic activity.

By the early 1800's, it is said, "The blending of Spanish-Catholic theocracy and Indian democracy resulted in very stable and tightly organized communities. These communities were not, however, conceived by the Indians as units in a European nation. Rather the Yaquis and Mayos, for example, still conceived themselves as independent tribal units holding their land from immemorial times and not by fiat of the Spaniards. It was growing clear that the Spaniards were fearful of challenging that view." (Spicer 1970:59–60) It was not until the Mexican government attempted to integrate the Mayo and the Yaqui into the dominant cultural pattern that hostilities really came to a head.

After the War of Independence (1821), the Mexicans considered the Indians to be citizens of Mexico and therefore taxable. The Yaqui, who had never been taxed, consistently resisted efforts to divide their land for individual ownership; they endeavored to maintain their own local government as distinct as possible from provincial or state governments, and refused to pay taxes. Conflicts ensued. Laws were enacted to integrate the Indians. These the Yaqui could not comprehend.

Through the years administrations changed; sometimes the Indians were deeply involved, again they were left practically alone for years. Perhaps one Yaqui group would take a certain action, while another had no part in the transactions or encounters. Military conflicts were many; sometimes the Yaqui winning, and at other times their opponents. Many of the defeated Yaqui were in desperate circumstances, without food and clothing, and decimated by smallpox and other illnesses. Prisoners were sent out of the Yaqui country to work, or sold as slaves.

Beginning in the 1880's, some of the Yaqui left their homeland and moved northward into southern Arizona and settled in rancherias. They were accepted there as refugees. Of the stronger groups, some Yaqui retaliated by raiding the ever encroaching farms and ranches of the Mexicans and settlers from the U.S.A. By 1900 their numbers equaled those of the Yaqui in the old Yaqui territory. In 1919 only three of the original Yaqui towns remained. After 1900 a conspicuously large influx of Yaqui into Arizona occurred.

A visit of President Obregón to the Yaqui country in 1926 precipitated a battle between the Mexican troops and the Yaqui. As a result, more of the Indians fled to the U.S.A. to live in a half-dozen communities that had grown up in southern Arizona.

The history of the main Yaqui groups in their encounters with and reactions to the foreigners who invaded their country makes fascinating reading. The publications of Spicer, who has studied the Yaqui in great detail, and the references to other authorities which he has cited, are recommended (*see* bibliography).

The Arizona Yaqui   Our interest lies with those Yaqui who have come to dwell in Arizona. Their migrations, incidentally, have continued slowly to the present time. Here, in several recognized settlements and lesser clusters, Yaqui ceremonial organizations have persisted, minus the accompanying political organizations that affect the Sonoran Yaqui. Cultural ties are maintained between the Arizona and the Mexican groups.

Probably the best known of the Yaqui villages was Pascua, once on the outskirts of Tucson, then engulfed by the spreading metropolis, and finally demolished by an Urban Renewal project. Dwellings in Pascua were fashioned of adobe bricks and corrugated sheet iron. Each house had a yard enclosed by a wire fence, with a few trees, small plots of green and colorful flowers. Almost every family had an open ramada in which much of the living took place, and which served as a gathering center at fiestatime. At one end of the village plaza was a small church, brilliantly white; at the opposite end, the fiesta ramada which was under the direction of the ceremonial societies. A wooden cross stood in front of each of these structures. At the side was a community kitchen in which the Yaqui women prepared foods over open fires—tortillas, stew, and coffee, primarily—during the fiestas. Many ceremonies took place in the plaza. Similar scenes may be witnessed in other Yaqui villages.

Just north of the San Xavier Indian Reservation of the Papago, the Yaqui have built a whole new village, on a section of land provided by the government. At first, as they became able to do so, those who wished to leave the old village and build homes in the new community might do so. Then, with the razing of Pascua, those who had remained there moved to the new village or elsewhere. Another Yaqui settlement, Barrio Libre, has been established in South Tucson.

Other Yaqui villages are Guadalupe near Tempe, and another in the Phoenix area—Water Users Village at Scottsdale; about 1,800 Yaqui dwell in the two communities. Marana and Eloy each have Yaqui villages. All together, the Yaqui in Arizona now number in excess of 3,000. The village organization is entirely in terms of the ceremonial groups in each instance. In each of their locations the Yaqui merge with the neighboring populations, Indian and Anglo.

Having no reservation, the men have made a place for themselves in the cotton fields, on ranches and farms, in the construction trades, and in other jobs. Because the Yaqui speak a tongue foreign to the other Indians living in Arizona and the Anglos alike, and since many of them have lacked educational opportunities, the Yaqui have found these factors something of a barrier to significant economic advancement.

Yaqui
Ceremonials Being of Old Mexican origin and long influenced by the Catholic religion, the ceremonial pattern of the Yaqui is a rich blend of aboriginal and introduced traditions. The ceremonies—based on Miracle Plays of the Jesuits, in which the life of Jesus was dramatized, and to which the Yaqui added their own beliefs and rituals—are enacted with a devoted consecration. The Yaqui remember no native supernatural beings, "but legend and memory remind them of the belief, similar to that of other Indians in the Southwest, that special power was obtainable from the natural world of forests, mountains, caves, and from dreams." (Painter and Sayles 1962:5)*

The symbolism that the blood of Jesus "as it fell from the cross was by a miracle of heaven transformed into flowers," is found throughout the Yaqui ceremonies. Flowers are offered as tribute to the holy ones. Especially during Holy Week and climaxing with Easter, crowds gather in the Yaqui villages, particularly in the Tucson locations and at Guadalupe, where religious rituals, processions, dancing and pantomime continue through the night—deer dances, *matachines, pascolas, fariscos*, and related activites. At dawn special prayers greet the morning. Members of the ceremonial societies serve in "fulfillment of vows made to Jesus or to Mary in return for help in time of crisis. The work of carrying out these sacred duties is known as 'flower.' It must be done faithfully and 'with good heart' to merit heavenly reward of 'flower.' Some of the regalia is also called 'flower'." (Painter and Sayles 1962:5; *see* Spicer et al. 1971)

One who has viewed many of the colorful Yaqui cermonies and written of them, tells us that:

Melodious bells and the rustle of cocoon ankle rattles herald the arrival of the Pascolas. When a Pascola dances to the high notes of the flute and the pervasive rhythm of a drum played by one man he wears his painted wooden mask over his face and beats on his palm with a small instrument [*matraca*] that jangles like a tambourine. For the alternate music of violin and harp he pushes his mask to one side. The string that ties his hair in a top knot is called 'flower.' In addition to dancing, the Pascolas delight the people with nonsense, double talk, jokes, and stories, some of age-old tradition. (Painter and Sayles 1962)

As to a deer dance, it is said that:

With a brisk shake of his gourds and his belt of deer-hoof rattles, the Deer

*Quotations from Painter and Sayles reproduced by permission of the University of Arizona Press.

dancer makes his entrance. His headdress is a stuffed deer head tipped with red ribbons which symbolize flowers. A red ribbon between the antlers is tied in the form of a cross. The deer songs to which he dances are treasured poetry from the past, reminiscent of the forest home of the deer, of flowers, clouds, rain, and wild creatures. The three Deer singers play native instruments of water drum and swift-moving raspers. The songs and dances were originally hunting rituals. (Painter and Sayles 1962:6; *see* Spicer et al. 1971)

Visitors to the Yaqui ceremonies will better understand what they are observing if the work cited, or other sources, are read in advance. Painter and Sayles include a calendar of annual events.

It should be remarked that not only do the Yaqui of Arizona attend the ceremonies given there, but they go by the hundreds to Magdalena, Sonora, which is fifty-five miles south of Nogales, to attend the fiesta of Saint Francis of Assisi on 4 October of each year. There they mingle with the Sonoran Yaqui and Mayo, as well as with Papago and Pima peoples.

STAR, STAR, MY LITTLE ONE

Star, Star, my little one
Star, I love you.
The name Star was taken
Out of the sky
And given to you, my little one.
Let me water you with
Shining praise, listen to
Your grandmother. She shall
Give you part of her knowledge
And me, I only have love
For you.
        You will learn lots.
You will be of beauty
With the knowledge, love, courage
Following you, taking every
Step with you.
Star shine bright for
Everyone to respect
You and your name.

By Sharlene Enos, Pima

From: *Art and Indian Children.* Curriculum Bulletin No. 7, 1970. Institute of American Indian Arts, Santa Fe, N. M.

7 arts and crafts

The crafts of the Indian had their practical and esthetic origin in needs of the people. In these days of easy access to manufactured goods, they might disappear entirely if it were not for sales to non-Indians. Even so, they are diminishing or vanishing year by year, or are being altered considerably. The Indians are practical as well as artistic and, in some instances, they are modifying traditional forms to suit other tastes and uses. For example, the burden basket has become a waste basket; pottery is made in special forms for lamps, ash trays, cigarette boxes, candlesticks, and other ornamental features; and embroidery and jewelry are produced in pieces that will find a variety of uses.

BASKETRY AND WEAVING Basketry and weaving were among the earliest of handicrafts in the Southwest. (It is probable that they developed simultaneously at a

241

time when the Pueblos lived in pit houses, or much earlier.) The distinction between the two crafts is often an arbitrary one, based upon form and use rather than upon method of construction. One authority has said that basketry has two fundamental classes: coiled, which leads to the needle, and woven, which leads to the loom.

Coiled basketry was preceded by twined types and wickerwork, which date back to about 7000 B.C. Sandals woven of fibers were made in ancient times. Coiled baskets have been made in the Southwest for more than two thousand years.

Relatively little basketry is produced today by the Indians in New Mexico and Colorado. A few of the Pueblo Indians still weave wickerwork baskets of willow and basket bowls of beargrass or yucca. Jemez produces the latter in some quantity; and the Hopi make attractive ones in contrasting colors. So extensive are the taboos pertaining to the making of Navaho basketry that the Navaho make but a small number of the baskets which they use. They find it much simpler to purchase those made by the Ute or Paiute, who accommodate them by weaving baskets with typical Navaho designs.

When the program of Navaho Community College was being arranged, it was found that of all the residents on the reservation only two Navaho women still were weaving ceremonial wedding baskets. They were taken to the college to teach this skill to others; the tour of duty was one year at a time for each. As students developed proficiency under this intense tutelage, they took over the teaching of basketry making.

Similarly, other artisans skilled in weaving textiles, producing leather work, pottery making, and silversmithing had to be located and brought to the college. Kenneth Begay, for instance, famous the world over for his silver working, left a lucrative practice in Scottsdale, Arizona, to return to the reservation and teach his people this art. (*See* Berry 1971)

The beautiful coiled bowls of split yucca, characteristic of the Mescalero Apache, are now rarely, if ever, produced. Attempts to stimulate basketry weaving among the Mascalero women have been made, but these were short-lived. The Jicarille Apache continue to make a few of their coiled baskets, some of fine workmanship, others of inferior quality. The western Apache continue the art to a certain degree.

Among the Hopi, fine wicker plaques are made on Third Mesa, and beautiful coiled baskets on Second Mesa. The Papago and some of the Pima-Maricopa still make fine basketry. The former are enjoying a revival of interest in this art, with the youngest basket maker reported to be a girl of five years old, and the oldest a matriarch of many years. Some women make as many as 100 baskets in a year. A very few women know how to fashion the watertight baskets used in Papago ceremonies. Yavapai and Hava-supai baskets are now very rare; the Hualapai make some bright colored baskets for the tourist trade. Good modern baskets are expensive and old ones are still higher—running to hundreds of dollars, even thousands.

The weaving of cotton textiles has existed among the Pueblos since about A.D. 750. The oldest known piece of cotton fabric is thought to have been made in A.D. 858. During the 14th century, the Pueblos reached their highest development in this art. Fine openwork, delicate gauzes, and elaborately patterned damask fabrics were all produced, along with the simpler techniques still practiced.

Weaving in wool began some time around 1600, after the introduction of sheep into the Southwest by the Spaniards. The Pueblo and Navaho looms are practically identical, and they show no European influence to this day.

By 1706, Navaho weaving was well enough established to attract the attention of a Spanish chronicler. In the following years rapid progress was made in beauty and quality. The oldest known examples of Navaho weaving have come from Massacre Cave, Canyon del Muerto, in Arizona, where a group of Navaho women and children were killed in 1805. The golden age of Navaho weaving came after that date, and by 1850 Navaho women had brought their weaving to its peak of perfection. From 1863–1868, the Navaho were confined at Fort Sumner. After their return to their home country, changes in weaving took place (1875–1890), with the introduction of commercial dyes, commercial yarns, and new ideas of design.

After 1890, rugs began to take the place of blankets. Until about 1910 there was a "dark age" in Navaho weaving; quality fell off, and the native designs almost ceased; bordered specimens predominated. Then came a change for the better, due largely to efforts of the traders to raise the standard of Navaho weaving. Art lovers and scientists did their part, too. Again, relatively thin blankets began to appear, with stripes, terraces, and colors of an earlier day. With government help, new soft colors were developed from native plants. Fineness of weaving and quality increased. At the present time, a very limited amount of fine Navaho weaving is being produced, but for the most part, the work seems to reflect the final expressions of a nearly extinct art—many of the designs are bizarre, the colors gaudy, and the workmanship careless.

All of the family helps with shearing the sheep, but the woman washes, cards, dyes, and spins the wool. She still uses the primitive spindle—a smooth, slender hardwood stick about two feet in length, which is pushed through a thin wooden disc from four to five inches in diameter. The loom consists of two upright poles and two cross bars supporting the warp frame. The weaver works from the bottom up, and manipulates her batten, comb, and yarns with dextrous fingers.

Practically no textile weaving is done now by the Pueblo Indians, with exception of belts, head bands, and garters, which are made by men or women, and by girls in the schools. It was the ancient custom for men to weave the shoulder robes and black dresses (*mantas*), sashes, and belts. In most of the pueblos the ordinary clothing worn by the women is purchased from a store or trading post. Ceremonial weaving is largely obtained from the Hopi Indians who still produce traditional garments and accessories. Embroidery, formerly a man's craft, may now be taught to girls in school.

The Navaho women weave some of the red belts that they wear, and these are almost indistinguishable from those woven by the Hopi. The Apache do no weaving other than what the girls may do in school.

POTTERY Pottery making was probably introduced into the Southwest from Mexico. The earliest evidences, found in southern New Mexico and Arizona, date from a few centuries before the Christian era—e.g., 350 B.C. at Snaketown. (*See* Dittert 1972) After considerable time this art spread to the Pueblo Indians.

The making of pottery is woman's work. Throughout the centuries household vessels were created, broken, and thrown out on the refuse heaps. With this simple procedure, history was written—history which the archaeologists can read almost as easily as a book. To reveal the records of the past, the archaeologist cuts a trench through one of the abandoned middens, thus exposing layer upon layer of accumulated debris. In these strata, fragments of pottery—the well known potsherds—withstand the passing of time and tell their story. Thanks to the fact that the pot makers were conformists, they have provided (and are still supplying) an invaluable archive of their activities. In the various regions, certain forms, types, manufacturing techniques, and styles of decoration, were developed; and from time to time changes in color, shape, quality of paste (clay mixed with water), occurred. Thus these bits of broken pottery show sequences and modification, and trade from one area to another. They contribute much toward reconstruction of the ancient cultures. If the visitor in the Southwest can learn only a little of what these potsherds mean, if he can place but a few of them in their proper historical position, it will add much to the enjoyment of his travels through the land.

With astonishingly little effort, one can learn to distinguish the pottery styles of the modern pueblos. Design patterns are traditional and, in the main, each pueblo holds to its own. A Fiesta day spent under the portal of the Palace of the Governors or a few hours at the Museum of New Mexico in Santa Fe, the Arizona State Museum in Tucson, the Museum of Northern Arizona at Flagstaff, the Heard Museum and Pueblo Grande in Phoenix, or museums in other Southwestern cities, will send the observant traveler away rich in new lore. The sky band, bird, and cloud motifs of Zía; the floral designs and realistic fauna of Cochiti; the strong geometric arrangements of Santo Domingo; the precision and beauty of the Acoma workmanship; and the mask and conventionalized bird symbols of the Hopi, are but a few of the characteristics that will cling in his memory.

By the early part of this century, pottery making in the Río Grande pueblos had in some instances died out entirely, while other villages were producing mainly utility wares. A few pueblos were making polished red and/or polished black, black-on-cream, or polychrome wares. It is known that polychrome ware was being made at San Ildefonso by 1875; it was the dominant type in the 1890's, and continued until about 1920. The plain black ware, similar to that long produced at Santa Clara, also may have been made at San Ildefonso as early as 1875.

In 1908, while excavating in a cave in the Rito de los Frijoles, archaeologists of the School of American Research uncovered some prepared pottery clay which had never been fashioned into vessels by the prehistoric artisans. The material was given to Marie, or María, and Julian Martínez of San Ildefonso, who made several pieces of pottery from it, decorating the specimens and firing them according to the procedure of that period. The results were very satisfactory. This, and encouragement given María (*Po-ve-ka*) by members of the School of American Research staff, appears to have stimulated her and other Tewa artisans to produce wares of increasing quality and quantity.

During the early 1900's the black-on-red style of the San Ildefonso potters, which appears to have been made as early as the first half of the nineteenth century, gained some popularity and improved in quality, but the public never responded to it very well. About 1919, experiments were begun at San Ildefonso which resulted in the now popular black burnished and matte ware. Santa Clara began to produce a similar ware about 1930. The first pieces made at both pueblos had the mass dull and the design burnished. Then, with exception of the *Awanyu*, or serpent, element of San Ildefonso—which is always polished—this combination was sometimes reversed. Today the standardized ware has the mass burnished and the design in matte.

The incised pottery of San Juan represents a revival of an old form of decoration. About 1931, the late Mrs. Regina Cata began copying the technique employed on an archaeologic ware known as *Potsuwi'i Incised*, which occurs commonly at ruins on the Pajarito plateau. The deeply carved wares in red and black are of recent origin in the Tewa pueblos. Tesuque did not adopt this form of embellishment until 1942.

In 1954, the French government presented the much coveted *Palmes Académiques* to two Pueblo pottery-makers, María Martinez, San Ildefonso, and Severa Tafoya, Santa Clara.

It is to be hoped that the visitor in the Southwest, as well as those who dwell here, will be selective in making their purchases of Indian products. In the markets, trading posts, and pueblo homes, both good works and bad will be found. If one selects good pieces, he himself will be the gainer. And he will also assist the Southwestern Association on Indian Affairs, and others, in their efforts to maintain high standards for Indian-made goods. It will add interest if he informs himself as to the more usual of the classic designs. The conventionalized serpent, the triangular rain bird, the different water symbols—rain at a distance, rain nearby, etc.; when he can recognize some of these he will have taken a step back into time, a time when myth was reality.

Commercialization has brought about changes in some of the pueblos. It has resulted in new and smaller forms, often lowered quality and careless execution, and flamboyant use of color in decoration. At Tesuque, for instance, several good potters can produce fine pottery (and they will do so if good ware is appreciated), but most of the present output consists of the cheap, gaudily painted (with show card colors), novelty items that are made expressly for the tourist trade. They cannot even be classed as true Indian ceramics, inasmuch as the decoration is applied *after* the pottery is fired. Jémez, Isleta, and Santo Domingo, lamentably, are also producing similar pseudo-Indian ceramics. In defense of the Indian, however, it should be explained that the idea for this type of product seems to have originated with a white man. The designs are often well done.

A variation in decoration of Maricopa pottery may be noted, and that of some other Indians of southern Arizona, who sometimes repaint their designs and fire vessels a second time. The firing must be in the tradition of the makers, utilizing a simple outdoor kiln and fuels of immemorial usage. Manufacturing techniques, shapes, designs, and colors must be representative of the pueblo or cultural group in which the pottery originates. (*See* Dutton 1966:5) The Papago still make a few bean pots, water cooling jars, and syrup jars.

Visitors who wish to know more than can be suggested here, will find exhibits on display at most of the Southwestern museums.

In examining the collections of Southwestern pottery, it may be of interest to remember that the method of manufacture is as traditional as the form and design. The smoothing stone used by the potter may be centuries old, handed down from mother to daughter, or picked up from an ancient ruin. An Indian woman does not sit down to make a vessel at random. Much preparation is necessary. Clays must be brought in from the hills and made ready. For strengthening the clay, tempering materials must be at hand. Paints are to be collected, such as the mineral earths to be obtained for the colored washes and designs, and perhaps *guaco*, or Rocky Mountain bee plant, or Tansy mustard, to be gathered and boiled to produce a black pigment. Paint brushes are the leaves of the spiked yucca or soap weed, chewed until only the stiff fibers remain.

No potter's wheel is used. All aboriginal American pottery is strictly hand made. A pancake of paste is patted into shape for the base of the bowl, and the walls are built up by successive coils of rolled clay, which are afterward smoothed to uniformity. After a vessel is made it is dried for a while in the air, then the slip is applied and after further drying it is decorated. Finally the pottery is fired. A convenient dry spot is selected near the home of the potter, and a fire is made on the ground. When a bed of coals is formed, a rude grate is constructed from any items at hand—bits of iron, stones, old bricks, tin cans. Then the pottery is arranged over the grate, usually upside down. Cakes of dried dung are placed around and over the vessels. The fire is renewed with shredded juniper bark or other suitable material. Small pieces of dung are tucked into the crevices, but space is left for air to circulate.

The black pottery is a highly polished red before it goes into the fire. If it is to remain red, it is fired with an oxidizing flame. If black is desired, the fire is smothered with fine, loose manure, permitting the smudge or carbon to penetrate the porous clay.

Hopi pottery has shown much degeneration, but good pieces are still produced on First Mesa. In southern Arizona, as among the Papago and Maricopa, a paddle-and-anvil method was used, rather than coiling and scraping of the Pueblo and other Indians.

The Apache Indians have not made pottery for a number of years. The Navaho continue to make their traditional vessels in some quantity, cylindrical pots with pointed bottoms, which may be arranged easily in the coals of a campfire. From the Pueblos they have learned to make certain Pueblo-like pieces, which are primarily decorated with red on a buff colored background. Tin cans and commercially manufactured utensils are too readily available to make pottery production worth the effort to most of the Navaho of today.

JEWELRY   Often we speak of turquois and silver in the same breath. But turquois has been cherished by the Southwestern Indians for centuries, while the use of silver came to them through white men. The cult of the turquois goes into legendary backgrounds. The stone was said to have benign powers; even a bead of it tied in the hair would ward off calamity, and the wearer would be immune to many of life's hazards. The Indians have traveled great distances to obtain turquois. The hard, deep blue stones have always been the most prized.

Metal work among the Navaho dates from about the middle of the nineteenth century. The first work was done in iron. A few learned metal working from the Spanish-Americans, but it was mainly while detained at Fort Sumner that some of the Navaho men learned the craft. There they were given coils of brass and copper which they fashioned into bracelets and ornaments for ring bits. No silver work was done until after the Navaho returned home from Fort Sumner. From then on the production of silver increased gradually. Their equipment was incredibly crude. One of the early metal workers used a discarded shovel as a melting pot, and his tools were scissors, a hammer, and a file. Bells were hammered from quarters, and American dollars were melted and made into tobacco canteens, bridles, bow guards, etc. Then the American coins were discarded for the Mexican *peso*, which was richer in silver content and more malleable. The Indians now use slug, sheet, and wire silver.

A wide range of silver articles, in many patterns and for many uses, is now made by the Navaho, but the objects they make primarily for their own gratification as well as that of the tourist are largely items of personal adornment: conchas for belts, buttons, bracelets, finger rings, earrings, necklaces, hat bands, and so on. The common type of Navaho necklace is made of large, hollow, silver beads separated by flower-shaped pendants, with a crescent-shaped ornament in front. These are generally called "squash blossom" necklaces, from the pendant features. Actually, this is a misnomer, for the blossom element is derived from the Mexican trouser and jacket ornaments fashioned to represent the young fruit of the pomegranate. The pomegranate pattern has been a favorite Spanish design for centuries. The terminal crescent, or *najah*, which may also be used as a bridle decoration, is likewise traceable to a Moorish origin; on the other hand, a similar form was known to the ancient Pueblos, for shell ornaments of this shape are found in ruin sites.

Silver bow guards were formerly made for use by the Navaho, and they may still be worn as ornaments. The practical need for the *ketoh* was to protect the wrist when using the bow and arrow. They may well serve in that capacity today, with the archery enthusiast, or as an unusual wrist ornament for dress occasions—particularly with evening wear—or with sport attire. As to the conchas (*concha* is the Spanish word for shell), the silver discs secured on leather belts, some authorities feel that it has been conclusively demonstrated that the Navaho derived them from the Plains Indians, their traditional enemies, such as the Kiowa and Comanche. On the contrary, since conchas identical with those found on old Navaho belts are made as bridle ornaments throughout Mexico, and by the Arabs on the southern edge of the Sahara desert, others think that their Old World derivation is certain.

Until about 1880, no settings of any kind were made. Then bits of glass, beads, buttons, and native garnets and jet began to be used. Turquois was not set in quantity much before 1900. No symbols are represented by the designs stamped and engraved on

Navaho jewelry; most of them are the same as those used for centuries by the Spanish and Mexican leather workers. Of course, innovations occur.

The French *Palmes Académiques* was awarded to Ambrose Roanhorse, in 1954, for outstanding production of Navaho silverwork.

The Pueblo Indians, as well as the Navaho, are masters in jewelry making. They have known the art of carving turquois, shell, and other substances, for centuries. Of the Pueblos, the people of Zuñi rank foremost in the production of jewelry. Their work in metals also started with the use of iron. They hold that they learned metal craft from the Spaniards, but this is questionable. About 1830–1840, they began to fashion jewelry from brass and copper. Old pots and pans, melted and hammered into shape, became buttons, rings, bracelets, and bow guard mountings. Later, copper and brass wire were used. Around 1870, the Zuñi learned from the Navaho how to work silver and make dies. When silver was introduced, working in brass and copper gradually died out for the most part.

During the 1870's and 1880's, Zuñi silver was simple and massive, like that of the Navaho. After the Zuñi learned to set turquois, about 1890, their craft became increasingly complex in design. Until about 1920, the silver output of the Zuñi smiths was sold or traded entirely to Indians of that or other pueblos or to the Navaho. Then the traders began buying their jewelry for the tourist trade. At that time not over eight silversmiths were practicing at Zuñi. Today there are hundreds; practically every man, woman, and child learned the art during the days of World War II, and the amount of production was astounding. Popular modern designs found in Zuñi jewelry include Knife Wing and Dragon Fly figures; men and women dressed in Zuñi attire; deer, butterflies, and other realistic figures in flat relief work. Some carving in the round, as of fetishes, occurs.

Speaking generally, it is easy to distinguish Zuñi style from that of Navaho silversmiths—though it may be impossible to correctly identify individual pieces. With Zuñi jewelry, emphasis is on the *turquois*; almost every piece shows many small, individually set stones, or channel or mosaic work in larger stones. Zuñi silver pieces are of lighter weight than those of the Navaho. With the Navaho, it is the *silver* that counts most, and the turquois settings are secondary. Almost every piece of Navaho workmanship shows stamped designs, but the Zuñi smith uses dies most sparingly, if at all. There are other minor differences which may aid one in telling Zuñi jewelry from the Navaho. Now, many Navaho wear jewelry made by the Zuñi Indians.

It has long been a practice of many traders who have engaged Indian jewelry makers to have Navaho craftsmen fashion the basic pieces in silver, and then have Zuñi artisans set the stones, shell, jet, or other decorative elements. More recently, other dealers have taught Pueblo peoples to make silver pieces ornamented with the traditional materials. From Mexico, the use of tortoise shell, or *carey*, was introduced, especially to the Zuñi smiths. This is easily worked and harmonizes well with the traditional substances, but the Mexican source has been stopped.

Some Hopi silverwork has been done since the latter part of the nineteenth century, having received its inspiration from Zuñi and Navaho smiths. In 1938 the Museum of Northern Arizona made silver manufacture among the Hopi one of its major projects. Hopi designs were utilized and distinctive pieces produced. Today, Hopi silverwork stands on its own merits; overlay is especially popular.

Several of the other pueblos have a history of silverworking which dates back roughly to 1890. Acoma and Isleta had a few silversmiths in the early days. Some of the younger people have learned this craft in school or in shops in the cities. The Laguna Indians have known silversmithing since 1870 or earlier. Among the Río Grande villages, the Santo Domingo people make more jewelry than the other Indians. The silver craft has been known there since 1893. Santo Domingo silver jewelry is essentially an imitation of the Navaho. But the traditional jewelry of this pueblo consisted of necklaces made of small disc beads of shell or turquois; of shell beads and chunk turquois; of jet—plain or inlaid with turquois—and turquois; and jet, shell, and turquois mosaic. These necklaces often had a crescent pendant of jet or shell inlaid with turquois. In later years, though the necklace form had changed little, jet gave way to the similar appearing materials afforded by old phonograph records or battery cases; shell largely was superseded by cylindrical beads made of gypsum; and shell and turquois mosaic work was frequently replaced by red-dyed gypsum and teeth from colored plastic combs. (Please see page 263.)

Modern necklaces, together with rings, bracelets, and various types of Indian jewelry, may often be purchased from itinerant Pueblo traders on the streets of Santa Fe and Albuquerque, and sometimes in more distant cities.

The Santo Domingo Indian men carry two or three blankets

over the left shoulder, and hold their wares, invitingly, in either hand. Dressed more or less in Pueblo attire, with a colorful kerchief about the head or the hair done up in traditional *chongo* (French, *chignon*), these traders add a colorful note to the cities' throng. The vendors may be women, dressed in the clothing of the home pueblo.

Santa Ana and Jémez took up silversmithing about 1890, when they learned the craft from the Navaho. Santa Clara had taken up this style of jewelry making a few years earlier. Several Pueblo silversmiths work in Santa Fe, Albuquerque, and Taos. Probably a few silversmiths reside in each of the pueblos.

The Apache and Ute Indians engage in the making of beadwork to some degree. Their clothing of yore was beautifully beaded, as were their moccasins and other accoutrement. Currently, most of the beadwork is in the form of necklaces, small bags, and miscellaneous items attractive to the tourist trade.

The Mohave Indians make beadwork in the form of yokes, necklaces, and other craft items. Other Yuman peoples, such as the Hualapai, produce a few beaded specimens.

The Genuine vs.   The buyer of native Indian arts and crafts items needs to exercise
the Imitation   caution, and particularly with regard to jewelry. Unfortunately, things are not always what they seem. Most dealers are honest and conscientious, but a large quantity of so-called Indian arts and crafts is commercially manufactured and sold as of genuine Indian make in many parts of the country, particularly in the Southwest. Even some Indians may include commercially manufactured silverwork or treated or imitation turquois or coral settings with their native handicrafts. Frequently they are duped by some disreputable trader.

If you want a truly *handmade* Indian article, be sure to inquire about its authenticity. Some Indians are employed by commercial establishments in the manufacture of jewelry, and some do make such items in part, but the term *genuine Indian handmade* means jewelry that an Indian silversmith fashions with his own hands with tools of his own, and using real silver—not stainless steel or nickel-plated copper.

In order to distinquish the genuine from the imitation, it is suggested that you take these three simple precautionary measures: find out about the reliability of the firm or the individual with whom you are dealing. In buying a piece of jewelry, be especially wary of perfection! In a handmade piece, neither the silver work nor the setting is perfect. Examine the materials carefully; even an untrained eye can usually tell the difference between a semi-precious turquois and a reconstructed or imitation stone.

To be classified as authentic, an article must have a high sterling silver content, (today, nearly all handmade silver pieces are sterling), and the stone, if turquois, must be genuine and unaltered. In most imitation pieces, the mounting is copper plated with nickel, and the stone is plastic or altered turquois.

In a genuine Zuñi channel inlay piece, the materials (turquois, shell, coral, jet, etc.) are cut and laid into silver partitions, leaving a slight metal break between the setting and the partition. In imitation articles, materials resembling settings are poured in, leaving no break. And in the imitation pieces, the blue is too blue for turquois, the red is too red for coral or shell, and the white is too white.

The sawtooth bezel (housing for a setting) on an imitation piece does not really grasp the setting, as it does it a Zuñi piece of cluster work. The spurious article is cast in a mold, after which the setting or stone is glued in.

A Navaho imitation setting has a vinyl tile effect, and the metal in a fake Navaho bracelet has no ring to it when struck with a hard object. Moreover, the design around the stone is obviously pressed out, rather than soldered to horizontal bands as it would be on a genuine Indian-made bracelet. A machine-made bracelet never has the design stamped as deep as a handmade article.

A sure test for determining the validity of the silver in a piece of jewelry is with a drop of nitric acid. Sterling silver turns white when the acid is applied; coin silver will be a little darker than sterling; Mexican silver may vary from a high silver content to very low, and the coloring from the acid reaction will vary from white for high silver content to dark for lower content. Nickel-plated copper in imitation jewelry will turn green.

New Mexico and Colorado have laws that require imitation Indian jewelry to be so labeled, but no means for enforcing them. Thus, one has to rely on reputable traders and merchants or his own good judgment.

An Indian craftsman turns out a piece of authentic jewelry slowly and laboriously. Assembly-line jewelry can be manufactured and turned out by the hundreds in the time it takes an Indian craftsman to make one piece. The Indians cannot begin to compete with the manufacturer of Indian jewelry, but the uninformed buyer often pays as much for the imitation as for the genuine. Silversmithing and other Indian crafts provide a livelihood for many Indians; they are important sources of income for the Indians.

With a little care you can know what you are buying, and demand the genuine. It is essential to the preservation of the traditional in Indian arts and crafts. You are justified in feeling proud of genuine Indian jewelry. It is truly beautiful, and many honest Indians, through many years, have been proud to make it so you may wear it.

[This section was contributed by Al Packard.]

PAINTINGS   Countless artistic records of the Indians of the Southwest are pecked, incised, or painted on the rocks—petroglyphs and pictographs. Pottery, from prehistoric times to the present, shows an extensive array of art forms. Occasionally, kiva paintings from ruin sites are uncovered. Fine examples of these wall paintings were found at Kuaua, an ancient pueblo near Bernalillo, New Mexico, now the Coronado State Monument. The kiva walls were found to have been covered with at least eighty-five layers of thin plaster, seventeen of which were decorated in true fresco painting. (*See* Dutton 1963) The kiva was restored, and the walls painted with replicas of the original frescoes. Other examples of these ancient works of art are shown in the Kuaua museum.

Archaeologists of the University of New Mexico unearthed beautiful kiva paintings at Pottery Mound, a prehistoric pueblo on the Río Puerco, southwest of Los Lunas. Some of these are similar to the Kuaua murals, others are very much like those excavated by Peabody Museum of Harvard University at Awatovi, in northeastern Arizona. The Museum of Northern Arizona at Flagstaff has built a replica of a Hopi kiva and has reproduced kiva paintings on its walls. At the Tiwa pueblo of Picurís in the northern Rio Grande drainage, ancient ceremonial rooms were excavated and found to display paintings on the walls. A chamber of this nature has been built in cross section in a new multiple purpose building, which contains a museum, and some of the paintings are reproduced on the walls.

When the Indians decorate their pottery or weave rugs of intricate patterns, they do not first draw the design and measure the space as would a white artist, yet the pattern of a good artist never fails to come out even and well balanced. Another example of sure eye and steady hand is illustrated by the Navaho sandpaintings. The "painters," depending upon the size and complexity of a painting, usually start near the center and work outward. The only marking of space is made by a string snapped on the background sand for the tall yé' ii figures; the rest is freehand. According to most authorities, the Navaho learned the art of sandpainting from the Pueblos, who still make drypaintings during certain ceremonies. The Jicarilla Apache and Pima use drypaintings in some rituals.

In Santa Fe, the Museum of Navaho Ceremonial Art makes a special exhibition of Navaho sandpaintings. It has a collection of more than six hundred copies in color of sandpainting designs. As mentioned above, visitors do not often have an opportunity to witness the making of sandpaintings inside a ceremonial hogan, but this art may be observed at the museum mentioned, on occasion, and at the Museum of Northern Arizona, Flagstaff, during certain special exhibitions.

Early in this century, a few of the Indian School teachers and other individuals began to take an interest in the drawings that certain young Indians produced when given colored crayons or water colors and paper. Pupils in the San Ildefonso day school were encouraged to draw the dance figures and to make cut-out patterns in colored papers, using Indian designs. Among these young artists showing promise were *Wen Tsireh* and *Awa Tsireh* (Alfredo Montoya and Alfonso Roybal respectively). In 1910 the paintings of Alfredo were furthered by providing him with suitable materials. Soon he was painting pictures which his white friends were glad to purchase. Unfortunately the young artist died in 1913. But he had influenced others at San Ildefonso.

A cousin of Alfredo's, Cresencio Martínez, according to the custom of that pueblo, was painting designs on the pottery made by the womenfolk of his family. Then he began making water color paintings. In 1917, he announced that he could paint all of the costumed figures in their ceremonial dances. He was given supplies, and promptly made good his claim. His work attracted the favorable attention of eminent artists. But he, too, was destined for an early death, in 1918.

Within a short time after Cresencio began painting ceremonial figures, other Indian boys made it known that they also could paint pictures. One of these was Awa Tsireh. Another was a Hopi boy, Fred Kabotie. There was Otis Polelonema, also a Hopi; and the late *Ma-pe-wi,* or Velino Shije Herrera, of Zía. These young men, inspired by Cresencio's example and by the appreciation accorded his work, showed the same singular talent which he possessed.

Never were any experiments made with their colors or patterns. Each picture was mentally completed, then with elaborate precision in drawing and color it was skillfully executed.

In 1919, an exhibit of Indian water colors was held in the Arts Club of Chicago. Three years later, the School of American Research in Santa Fe employed Awa Tsireh, Velino, and Kabotie to paint a few hours each day; no one instructed or influenced them, but their work during the period has never been excelled for color and composition. Velino appears to have been the first to introduce the element of pure design into Pueblo water color painting. At the same time, he was painting beautiful, action-filled horses in a masterly way. He continued to produce excellent works throughout the years, until an auto wreck on Christmas eve, 1956, incapacitated him extensively. Kabotie has painted less, but has taught arts and crafts among his people to this day. Polelonema was inactive for many years, while raising and educating a family, but now has resumed his art. Awa Tsireh painted hundreds of pictures until his death, in March, 1955. The day before he died, he was in Santa Fe to get paper for more paintings. One of the first young women to attract attention by her artistic production was the late Tonita Peña, a San Ildefonso girl married to a Cochiti man. Many dealers have the works of these artists for sale, and museums all over the country exhibit their pictures.

Indian art is as distinct from European or American art as is Chinese or Japanese, to which Indian art is more nearly related. It is decorative and imaginative, usually two-dimensional, although the Hopi and other individuals have painted in the round. Seldom is a background shown, but a few recent painters have indicated backgrounds in a simple, thoroughly original, but satisfying manner. Sacred subjects such as rain, the rainbow, and clouds are represented symbolically. Indians do not paint from models; because of their powers of observation and memory they have no need for them. Traditionally, more important objects may be made larger or more prominent. In some ways, it may be said that Indian art is four-dimensional; they actually paint the rhythm and steps of the dance, the action of the horse, the speed of the antelope, the heat of the desert.

As late as 1928, it was the general practice to forbid the painting of Indian subjects in the government Indian schools. But, in 1932, the Bureau of Indian Affairs established a painting department in the Santa Fe Indian School, and placed it under the direction of Miss Dorothy Dunn (now Mrs. Max Kramer). Some good paintings were also produced in the Albuquerque Indian

School at that time. One of the outstanding artists to come from that institution was José Rey Toledo of Jémez.

Each year, exhibitions of Indian paintings from the Santa Fe Indian School were held in museums all over the United States and in many foreign countries, including galleries in London and Paris. The department was not only self-supporting through the sales of student work (paying 50 per cent to the artists), but it also contributed to other school activities. In 1940, one of the students, Ben Quintana of Cochiti pueblo, won the Youth Administration prize of $1,000, over more than fifty thousand contestants from all parts of the United States. In 1951, Vidal Casiquito, Jr., Jémez, was one of twelve winners in a poster contest sponsored by the National Cartoonist Society and the U.S. Treasury. Indian artists have won many honors and awards.

After about a decade of outstanding artistic productions by students in the art department, the war's demands on the young people, changes in policy at the Santa Fe School, and a variety of factors resulted in an appalling degeneracy of Indian art. Fortunately, a few of the prewar artists still produce fine works, such as Gilbert Atencio of San Ildefonso; Theodore Suina and Joe H. Herrera of Cochiti; Pablita Velarde Hardin, Santa Clara; Geronima Cruz, San Juan (now Mrs. Juan Montoya); and Harrison Begay, Narciso Abeyta (Ha-So-De), and Jimmie Toddy (Beatien Yazz), Navaho. Among the Apache artists are Allan Houser, Rudolph Treas, Emmet Botella, and Frank Vigil now living at Jémez. Houser's sculpturing also commands worldwide attention. He and Fred Kabotie have both been honored by the Guggenheim Foundation, each receiving fellowships to continue their art work. When the *Palmes Académiques* were presented to Indian artists in 1954, those recognized for their paintings were: Fred Kabotie, Joe H. Herrera, Pablita Velarde, Harrison Begay, Allan Houser, Awa Tsireh, Velino Herrera, and Andrew Tsihnahjinnie, a Navaho painter from Arizona.

The initial days of promoting painting and allied arts at the Sante Fe and Albuquerque Indian schools were followed by similar programs at the Phoenix Indian School and other schools which Southwestern Indian students attended. At the same time, some of the reservation schools gave attention to Indian art, as at Zuñi, the Hopi villages, and elsewhere. A number of artists came to the fore and their works found buyers from the world over. Some have continued painting while others have given up their art, at least for the most part.

New ideas of education for the Indians were developed, and as a result the Santa Fe Indian School was discontinued. In its stead a new establishment came into being and, as the Institute of American Indian Arts, was opened in October, 1962. Since then new structures have been added at the old site.

A stated purpose of the Institute is to "open new doors of opportunity for self-expression (of young Indians from Federally recognized groups, with at least one-quarter Indian blood) in the whole rainbow of the arts." A comprehensive academic program of studies for selected art-interested students is offered in grades eleven through twelve. That is, the high school program is intended to "meet the needs of art students preparing for fine arts work in college, art students preparing for technical schools, art students completing their formal education upon graduation from high school."

For students desiring work in advance of the twelfth grade, a two-year program of specialized studies is offered. The arts courses encompass fine arts and crafts (painting, sculpturing, ceramics, textile arts), and dramatic arts (including creative writing, dramatics, dancing, and music). Related courses are also offered, including business training and mathematics, English, literature, folklore, history, applied science, typing, Indian history and identification, ethnic studies, etc.

The Institute started with a small student body. The second year saw enrollment increased to 140, and in 1970-71 it was 288, embracing ninety-three tribes. Many of the administrative officers and staff members are Indians. They are sensitive, creative, and alert; they are attuned to the youth of today. Students come from Alaska to Florida, coast to coast, and points between. The director of IAIA has said:

Thus far in our job, we have found that by stressing cultural roots as a basis for creative expression and by offering a wide range of media in which to work, Indian students can be inspired to new personal strengths in dimensions heretofore unrealized. As a result of the Institute's heritage-centered approach, a gratifying number of its students do discover who they are and what it is they have to say to the world; and they develop the self-respect and confidence to express themselves accordingly. They are helped to function constructively, in tune with the demands of their contemporary environment but without having to sacrifice their cultural being on the altar of either withdrawal or assimilation. (*See* New 1968:12)

KATSINA FIGURES   Mention has been made of the importance of the katsina cult in Pueblo social organization (*see* p. 44ff.).

The small wooden representations of katsinas are commonly

called "dolls." They are not dolls as non-Indians think of them, as toys. They are likenesses of a whole array of supernaturals who, through various manifestations, interact between man and his deity; thus they are messengers. As such, they may appear in numerous forms, with specific identifying characteristics. This class of katsina representations has a separate designation within the Indian groups. For instance, the Hopi call them *tihü* or *katsintihü*. While they are not play things, it is not considered wrong if an Indian child carries one of them about, as a non-Indian youngster might carry a doll.

Primarily, the katsinas are benevolent beings who reside in the mountains, clouds, springs and lakes, and who are purveyors of many blessings, especially rain, good crops, and general well being. However, as all good has its contrary agency, some katsinas are ogres or demons with disciplinary functions. Ogres have a reputation for eating children if they are not good, and if the katsinas are not obeyed. Indian lore and social mores are transmitted from generation to generation by means of the katsinas. In many ways, the supernatural ones and the katsina organizations reflect the ordinary life of the Pueblo peoples; the family relationship is the same: father, mother, children, grandparents, uncles, and so on.

In further explanation of the little wooden figures, it has been noted that, faithfully portrayed they provide a means of education; they also serve as gifts at ceremonials, and as decorative articles in the home; but, transcendently, they act as a constant reminder to the Indians of the "real" katsinas.

Not all of the figurines represent katsinas. How, then, does one distinguish them? Although it is sometimes difficult to determine, the essential feature is the mask. Unmasked figures are *not* katsinas. Examples of these are buffalo, deer, eagle, and snake dancers, and the like.

Another expression of Indian art, consequently, is to be seen in the carved wooden figures of katsinas or ceremonial personages. Here, the Hopi Indians lead, for religious restrictions in the Río Grande valley do not allow production of ceremonial figures in the manner that is permitted the Hopi. The late James Kewanwytewa, a Hopi well known at the Museum of Northern Arizona, in Flagstaff, won the *Palmes Académiques* in 1954 for his katsina productions. Although many katsinas, or dolls, are offered for sale, one has to be careful that he is securing authentic specimens, for non-Indians are making many imitations.

If made in traditional Hopi manner, katsina figures are carved from a solid piece of root wood from a dead cottonwood tree; for this reason, they are of a very light weight. They should be so well balanced as to stand alone. Protruding eyes, ears, and nose, horns, and headdress ornaments may be attached with tiny pegs. Clothing and costume articles are indicated by painting. First, a coat of very fine white clay, called kaolin, is applied over all of the figure. Then colored pigments are laid on. Formerly these were native earth or mineral colors. Today, opaque water color paints are used commonly.

The Zuñi style, and that of some of the Río Grande Pueblos, calls for the use of pine wood for katsina figures. These are then painted, and are dressed in costumes of deerskin, fur, feathers, and cloth—miniature replicas of the human size beings. Zuñi "dolls" are generally taller, more slender, and heavier in weight than the Hopi figures, and they usually have movable arms. They do not stand without support, as a rule. The Zuñi also make some bead dolls.

INDIAN MARKETS AND EXHIBITS

Visitors who are fortunate enough to be in Santa Fe during the summer months will find that the Indians and their products under the portales surrounding the plaza make a picturesque spectacle. There purchases may be made directly from the Indians.

In 1974, the Southwestern Association on Indian Affairs observed the fifty-third Indian Market that it has sponsored. In front of the Palace of the Governors and down the east and west sides of the plaza, rows of colorful, canvas-covered booths are erected for the two-day event. The Market is held annually two weeks *before* the Santa Fe Fiesta, which always occurs on Labor Day weekend.

Early in the morning on market days, the Indians, carrying their wares wrapped in pieces of calico or packed into paper cartons, come into town and arrange themselves for the day. They sit on rugs or on low stools; some have counters or show cases.

Each exhibitor has an assigned space for which a small fee has been paid. This fee helps defray the expenses of holding the Market. Here, the Indians spread their pottery, drums—both fullsize and toy—dressed dolls, jewelry, baskets, moccasins, tanned goat skins, paintings, beaded trinkets, textiles, and unpredictable articles. Indians are imaginative and inventive, and each year they come forth with new examples of their productive minds.

Usually the price is fixed for items sold in the Indian markets, though sometimes the Indians enjoy a little bargaining. But be assured that the Indians are quite as shrewd as you are. They will not sell for less than an article is worth.

Before the opening, Association judges view the displays and award prizes for outstanding achievements. The exhibitors include artisans from the Rio Grande pueblos and from Hopiland, Navaho, Apache, Ute, and some of the Plains Indians. Together with their displays they afford an unforgettable sight.

Twice daily on Saturday and Sunday, complementing the Market, the Association arranges Indian dances in the patio back of the Palace of the Governors. (*See* Chaban 1971:19)

Annually, the Museum of Northern Arizona centers a Hopi Arts and Crafts show around July 4, when thousands of the Hopi and western Navaho, as well as their Indian neighbors, gather at Flagstaff. Another set event is their annual *Navajo Craftsman Exhibit*; these are interspersed with other special showings of Indian arts and crafts. On these occasions fine productions may be purchased.

In 1971 the fiftieth anniversary of the Inter-tribal Indian Ceremonial in Gallup, New Mexico was observed. During half a century the Ceremonial has had as its purpose the making known of American Indian culture through their arts and crafts, dances, and related expressions. Indians of the Southwest, of many other states, and from Old Mexico came year by year; and thousands of visitors came from the world over to view them and their attainments. The 1971 occasion was especially significant for it coincided with facts of change. Highway developments threatened the location used since the original Ceremonial. Future of the Inter-tribal Indian Ceremonial Association thus became uncertain. However altered its program, backers of the Ceremonial are determined that it will continue in a new homesite.

Colorful fairs are held in the Navaho country during the autumn season at Shiprock, New Mexico, and Window Rock, Arizona. Visitors will do well to attend either or both of these events. The New Mexico State Fair at Albuquerque in late September, and the Arizona State Fair in Phoenix in early November, have exhibits of fine Indian arts and crafts which are for sale.

On the Salt River reservation, near Scottsdale, Arizona, an annual Indian Trade Fair was initiated in 1967. Not only do the local Pima-Maricopa and Yavapai-Apache peoples display their productions, but they are joined by the Navaho, some of the Apaches, Havasupai, Mohave, several from the Plains Indian groups, and many others. As at the celebrations on the Navaho reservation, at the Museum of Northern Arizona, and elsewhere, artisans demonstrate their skills: weaving baskets or rugs, making jewelry, perhaps carving and painting katsinas, doing beadwork; and on occasion making certain of their native foodstuffs.

In 1971, the Zuñi initiated a mid-May Arts and Crafts Fair with the local artists showing their paintings, jewelry, pottery, katsinas, and other wares—these for display and sale. A panel of judges awarded prizes in student and non-student classes.

Since 1959, the Santa Clara Indians have brought their ancient homesite, Puyé, an important ruin with mesatop and cliff dwellings, to life again with a spectacular festival during a weekend late in July. The Santa Clara Indians and those from other pueblos assemble there, displaying and selling artistic products and performing dances.

On or off of the highways are trading posts which handle Indian products. Throughout the Navaho country, certain trading posts, or booths, exhibit Navaho rugs and other items to attract the traveler. With the Navaho goods one may also find Chimayó textiles for sale. These are fine in their own way, but they definitely are *not* Indian. They are made by the Spanish-American weavers in their small villages in the upper Río Grande drainage. Trading posts in Arizona and Colorado handle more Hopi and Papago items, and wares of other groups. Traveling through the various Indian lands, especially in Papaguería or among the Pueblos, one may find places where wares may be purchased directly from the maker. And among the set events that afford opportunities to see exhibitions and buy art and crafts articles are the yearly Scottsdale National Indian Arts Exhibition and the Annual Indian Fair at the Heard Museum in Phoenix.

For the traveler who has limited knowledge of Indian arts and crafts, it is recommended that he do his buying from established dealers or exhibitors throughout the Four Corners region. Their trained buyers make frequent trips to the reservations or pueblos and select the best. They often have arrangements with craftsmen of particular skill to take their entire output, or they have expert Indian workmen in their own shops.

Early in this decade imitation Navaho rugs suddenly appeared for sale in many places. Most of them were of Mexican origin. Many are beautiful and well woven, but they are *not* Navaho. Beware of deceptions!

Inspired by the popularity and current value of carved katsina figures, some Navaho have taken up the carving of Yé'ii and dance personators. Also other expressions of Navaho life, such as craftsmen at work and nativity assemblages, have been carved. Looms in miniature are made, sometimes with weavers dressed in typical Navaho clothing. Similar portrayals of corn grinders are produced. The demand for such items far exceeds the supply.

In late years certain Santo Domingo jewelry makers have used turquois, coral, and silver, as well as shell, for beads of exceedingly small diameter in stunning necklaces. Some of the craftsmen have adopted new styles for silver ornaments. Many *non*-Indian artisans have copied the works of the Indians so well that they may be indistinguishable. Improved techniques for creating imitation or altered turquois have made it increasingly difficult to differentiate the true from the false. Do be sure of your dealer's reliability.

Ever-increasing thefts of Indian jewelry, rugs, and other valuable articles have given birth to the Indian Arts & Crafts Association, P.O. Box 1358, Gallup, New Mexico. It was created to provide an organization capable of coping with the problems and situations confronting American Indian arts and crafts today. It is structured to benefit all concerned: craftsmen, traders, jobbers, dealers, collectors, museums, and other interested parties; the chief concerns are security, ethics, and public image. (For information, write to the Association.)

CALENDAR OF ANNUAL
.... INDIAN EVENTS

NOTE: Do NOT take pictures, make sketches or recordings, or
       take notes without obtaining permission. This is
       VERY IMPORTANT!

In the pueblos are plazas, and the ranchería peoples and other
Indian groups have their dance places, where ceremonial events are
presented. Many observances occur over a period of several days,
but of these the major portions are held in the kivas or in places
where only the initiated ones may witness them. Parts that may be
seen by the public are customarily attended by adults and children,
Indian and non-Indian.

Remember that these are sacred and commemorative rituals. It
is expected that visitors will be *quiet and respectful.*

Ceremonies are held in Hopiland throughout the year. The

dates of these are determined according to Hopi customs and traditions, without reference to the BIA personnel. Exact dates are made known a few days in advance only, even to the Hopi. During the summertime, one or more ceremonies or dances are held usually each weekend.

Indian dances and ceremonies are based on Indian needs and Indian time. To translate these to the white man's calendar is not always practicable. It is advisable to check locally whenever possible.

JAN 1 Taos turtle dance usually (*See* Dutton 1972a: 3-12); dances in many of the pueblos on New Year's and/or three succeeding days, e.g. cloud dance at San Juan.

JAN 3 Isleta corn, turtle, and various dances

JAN 6 King's Day: installation of secular officers; dances in most of the pueblos during afternoon; buffalo or deer dance at Taos, eagle dance at San Ildefonso. Dancing in the Keres pueblos. Dancers go to the houses of people named *Reyes* (kings), where dwellers are waiting on the roofs. After the dancers perform for a while, the house owner and family members throw gifts to the dancers below and the gathered crowd. Everybody scrambles for presents, but most are aimed directly to the dancers. The gifts include bread, canned and boxed foods, fruit, tobacco, soft drinks, and household items. Many pueblos have dances on the three succeeding days.

JAN 23 San Ildefonso feast day—animal dances in one plaza, Comanche dance in the other

JAN (Late January) Acoma and Laguna governor's fiesta

FEB 2 San Felipe buffalo dance; also dances in several other pueblos

FEB 4–5 *Llano* dances, *Los Comanches*, at Taos (Spanish-American interpretation of Plains Indian dances)

FEB 15 Dances at San Juan; perhaps turtle dance at Taos, eagle dance at Santo Domingo

FEB (Usually in February) Hopi *Powamû* (bean dance)—first rites of the katsina cult

FEB (Late February) Isleta evergreen dance

MAR (Palm Sunday) Most pueblos, green corn dances, ceremonial foot races

MAR-APR (Easter Sunday and succeeding two or three days) Dances in most pueblos; ceremonial foot races. Several pueblos observe ditch-opening, or *acequia*, ceremonies with dances; some play ceremonial shinny.

MAR-APR (During Holy Week, with the climax on Easter) Yaqui Indians have elaborate celebrations at Barrio Libra (south Tucson) and at Guadalupe near Phoenix. Deer dancers, *matachines, pascolas, fariseos*, et al., take part. (*See* Painter and

Sayles 1962:24) On the first Friday after Easter, the Tucson Festival Society sponsors an annual pageant that commemorates the founding of Mission San Xavier del Bac. Papago and Yaqui dancers participate.

MAR Phoenix Plains Indian Club sponsors Scottsdale All-Indian Day

MAR Gila River Pima *Mul-chu-tha* at Sacaton, Arizona

MAR 27 Dances generally at the Keres pueblos and Jémez

MAR (Late March) Indian Trade Fair, Pima-Maricopa and Yavapai-Apache communities, near Scottsdale, Arizona

SPRINGTIME Colorado River tribes hold motor boat races and Northern Yuma County Fair at Parker, Arizona

APR (Last Saturday) *Nizhoni* dances at Johnson Gymnasium, University of New Mexico, Albuquerque; numerous Indian groups in beautiful costumes (benefit)

APR or MAY Ute Mountain Ute bear dances

MAY 1 San Felipe feast day, green corn dance (two large groups)

MAY 3 Taos ceremonial races (about 8:00-10:00 a.m.); Cochiti corn dance (Coming of the Rivermen)

MAY 14 Taos San Ysidro fiesta (blessing of fields); candle light procession May 15

MAY (About 29 May through June 4) Tesuque corn or flag dance (blessing of fields)

MAY (Late May) Salt River Pima Industrial Fair

MAY (Last week of May or first week of June) Southern Ute bear dance

JUNE 6 Zuñi rain dance

JUNE 13 Sandía feast day, corn dance; observance of San Antonio's Day dances at Taos (corn dance), San Juan, Santa Clara, San Ildefonso, Cochiti, and Paguate

JUNE 20 Isleta governor's dance

JUNE 24 San Juan feast day, dancing there; observance of San Juan's Day dances at Taos (afternoon), Isleta,* Cochiti, Santa Ana, Laguna; Acoma and Jémez rooster pulls

JUNE 29 San Pedro's Day at Laguna, Acoma, Santa Ana, San Felipe, Santo Domingo, Cochiti, and Isleta—generally rooster pulls

JUNE (Late June, or during July) Hopi *Nimán* ("going home")—last rites of the katsina cult; katsinas are believed to go to their traditional home on San Francisco Peak. One of the ceremonial officers from Shungopavi announced that the Nimán rites and snake dances are closed because "rules against recording, picture taking and hand-drawing have been disregarded again by both Hopis and non-Indians . . . and sacred prayer feathers have been taken away." (Action Line, *Albuquerque Journal,* 15 August 1972)

*Since Isleta adopted its constitution, the ceremonial calendar has undergone various changes. One may see dances performed by either the Laguna group which dwells in the pueblo, or by the Isleta group. Dates should be checked annually.

JULY 1-4   Mescalero Apache *Gáhan* ceremonial at Mescalero, New Mexico

JULY 4   Jicarilla Apache feast (no ceremonies); Nambé celebration at Nambé Falls—special events and dances

JULY 4   Flagstaff Pow-Wow (Check annually)

JULY 14   Cochiti, feast day of San Buenaventura—corn dance

JULY   (Mid-July or August) Ute sun dance, Ignacio, Colorado

JULY 24   Acoma rooster pull

JULY 25   Santiago's feast day at Acoma, Laguna, Cochiti, and Taos—dances, rabbit hunt

JULY 26   Feast day of Santa Ana, corn dances; also at Taos

JULY   (Late July) Santa Clara festival at Puyé cliff ruins; arts and crafts exhibits, dances (entrance fee entitles one to take photographs)

AUG 2   Jémez, old Pecos bull dance

AUG 4   Santo Domingo feast day, corn dance—large and fine; two groups

AUG 10   San Lorenzo's feast day; corn dances at Picurís, Laguna, and Acomita

AUG 12   Santa Clara feast day; corn dances

AUG 15   Zía feast day of Nuestra Señora de la Ascensión; dances

AUG   (Two weeks before Labor Day) Dances in patio of Palace of the Governors in Santa Fe, in conjunction with annual Indian Market sponsored by the Southwestern Association on Indian Affairs

AUG 28   San Agustín fiesta at Isleta

AUG   (Late August) Hopi snake dance—a solar observance; in even years at Shipaulovi, Shungopavi, and Hotevila; in odd years at Mishongnovi and Walpi. Usually takes place about 4:00 p.m. Alternately, when snake dances are not held in a village, flute ceremonials are given. The dances are announced sixteen days before they are due to happen.

See note under June (late) or during July.

SEPT 1   Southern Ute fair

SEPT 2   Acoma feast day of San Estéban—corn dance atop mesa

SEPT 4   Isleta feast day, harvest dance

SEPT 8   Encinal (Laguna) harvest and social dances

SEPT 8   San Ildefonso, harvest dance*

SEPT 14-15   Jicarilla Apache celebration at Horse or Stone Lake

SEPT   (Mid-September, or earlier) Navajo Tribal Fair, Window Rock, Arizona—exhibits, horse races, rodeo, dances

*Because so many San Ildefonso Indians work at Los Alamos, the ceremonies traditionally held at this time of the year have been shifted to the weekend closest to the old dates. The same situation prevails at San Juan, Santa Clara, and Tesuque with regard to dances. Check dates annually.

SEPT 19 Laguna, feast day of San José; harvest dance and others; trading

SEPT 29 Taos, sundown dance—begins at sunset

SEPT 30 Taos, feast day of San Gerónimo—relay races (early) and pole climbing; dancing

SEPT (Usually in September) Hopi *Maraüm*, women's social function

FALL (Some time in fall) Fall Southern Ute Fair; rodeo; Northern Ute sundance

OCT (1st week) Annual Navajo Fair at Shiprock, New Mexico

OCT 4 Nambé, feast day of San Francisco (Saint Francis); dancing

At Magdalena, Sonora, Mexico, the Fiesta of Saint Francis of Assisi; hundreds of Papago, Pima, Yaqui, and Mayo Indians (who are affiliated with the Yaqui) converge there each year.

OCT (Last Saturday and Sunday) Papago rodeo and fair at Sells, Arizona

OCT 31-NOV 2 On one of these days, ceremonies in most of the pueblos; gifts to the padres, and gifts to the dead placed on graves

OCT (Usually in October) Hopi *Oáqol,* women's social function

NOV 1-2 In the San Xavier cemetery, near Tucson, hundreds of candles are lighted around the graves at night; this is true in all Papago cemeteries

NOV 12 Jémez and Tesuque, feast day of San Diego; dances

NOV (Usually in November) Hope *Wüwüchim*—tribal initiation ritual for all boys about 10-12 years

NOV Colorado River tribes two-day rodeo at Parker, Arizona

NOV-DEC (Some time in November or December) The *Shalako* at Zuñi; dancing in new houses and in house of the Koyemshi

Navaho reservation Nightway and Mountain Topway ceremonies

DEC 3 Ceremony at San Xavier in honor of Saint Francis Xavier

DEC 10-12 Fiesta of Tortuga Indians in honor of Our Lady of Guadalupe, near Las Cruces, New Mexico: processions and dancing

DEC 12 Guadalupe day at Isleta and Santo Domingo—gift throwing

DEC 12 Jémez *matachines;* Tesuque flag, deer, or buffalo dances

DEC 25 Taos deer or matachines dance (afternoon)

Christmas Day and two or three days following, dances at most of the pueblos

DEC 31 *New Year's Eve*, before midnight mass and dancing in church at Laguna, Sandía, San Felipe, Santo Domingo, and other pueblos

DEC In the various Hopi villages, *Soyala*—winter solstice rites; opening of the katsina season, the purpose of which is to induce the sun to start on the first half of its journey. After this ceremony, other katsinas may appear at any time during the next six months.

HOPI *(6,019)*

First Mesa	*1,371*		
Polacca	755		
Walpi	81		
Sitchumovi	335		
Hano (Tewa)	200		

Shungopavi   742
Sun Light Mission   65

Third Mesa   *1,938*
  New Oraibi   720
  Old Oraibi   180
  Bacabi   238
  Hotevila   800

Second Mesa   *1,435*
  Shipaulovi   202
  Mishongnovi   426

Moencopi   *1,019*
Keams Canyon   *256*

THE ATHABASCANS
(ca. 140,100)

NAVAHO (126,267)

Chinle Agency   21,150

Eastern Navaho Agency   28,210
  Cañoncito   ca. 1,125
  Checkerboard   ca. 24, 785
  Puertocito (Alamo)   920
  Ramah   1,380

Fort Defiance Agency   28,485

Shiprock Agency   25,379
Tuba City Agency   23,043

APACHE *(13,837)*

Jicarilla   *1,742*

Mescalero   *ca. 1,740*

Western Apache*
Ft. Apache, San Carlos ca. 10,355

THE UTE INDIANS
(3,506)

UTE MOUNTAIN UTE

(Towaoc, Colo.)
(est. 1,146 enrolled)

SOUTHERN UTE

(Ignacio, Colo.) (760 enrolled)

NORTHERN UTE

(Ft. Duchesne, Utah) (1,600)

THE SOUTHERN
PAIUTE
(CA. 1,200)

KAIBAB PAIUTE

(over 100)

SHIVWITS PAIUTE

(150-200 enrolled)

CHEMEHUEVI

(now enrolled with Colo. River
tribes) (ca. 600)

RANCHERIA
PEOPLES
(22,700)

COLORADO RIVER
INDIAN TRIBES (4,451)

Chemehuevi, Mohave, Navaho,
and Hopi together number
1,120 on reservation and 500
off reservation   1,620

Mohave at Fort Mohave
(Parker, Ariz.)   511

Yuma (Quechan)—Ft. Yuma
Reservation (1,007, plus
618 off reservation)   1,625

Cocopah (95 enrolled; includes
ca. 300 in Mexico)   ca. 695

THE PAI (970)

Havasupai (eastern Pai)   ca. 270

Hualapai, or Walapai
(western Pai)   ca. 685

Hualapai at Big Sandy,
Ariz.   ca. 15

*Arizona census figures *do not* include
off-reservation Indians.

POPULATION FIGURES
.... (1 January 1970)

PUEBLO INDIANS	*TANOAN (10,017)*	*Towa*	*1,765*
(35,351)	*Tewa* *3,658*	Jémez	1,765
	Nambé 328		
	Pojoaque 107	*KERESAN (13,675)*	
	San Ildefonso 358		
	San Juan 1,487	*Keres, eastern* *5,728*	
	Santa Clara 1,119	Cóchiti 779	
	Tesuque 259	San Felipe 1,632	
		Santa Ana 472	
	Tiwa, northern *1,806*	Santo Domingo 2,311	
	Picurís 163	Zía 534	
	Taos 1,623		
		Keres, western *7,947*	
	Tiwa, southern *2,788*	Acoma 2,861	
	Isleta 2,527	Laguna 5,086	
	Sandía 261		
	Guadalupe Indian Village *	*ZUÑIAN (5,640)*	
		Zuñi *5,640*	

271   *Unknown

*INDIANS OF THE SALT RIVER
AGENCY (3,375)*

Pima-Maricopa Community (1,700, plus 300 on nearby reservation)	*2,000*
Yavapai (Ft. McDowell Reservation)	*ca. 300*
Mohave-Apache (Ft. McDowell Reservation)	*ca. 450*
Yavapai Community	*625*
Yavapai-Apache (Camp Verde, Ariz.)	ca. 200
Tonto-Apache (Camp Verde, Ariz.)	ca. 250

Yavapai at Prescott	ca. 90
"Payson Apache"	85

THE PIMANS (ca. 11,100)

Pima (river people)—Gila River Community; a few Maricopa and Papago included enrolled:	*ca. 5,300*
Papago (desert people)— main reservation	*ca. 5,800*
Maricopa—enumerated with Pima	

THE CAHITANS (over 3,000)

Yaqui in Arizona	*over 3,000*

.........BIBLIOGRAPHY

Agogino, George A., and Michael L. Kunz (1971). "The Paleo Indian: Fact and Theory of Early Migrations to the New World," *The Indian Historian*, vol. 4, no. 1, Spring, pp. 21-26. The American Indian Historical Society. San Francisco.

Anderson, Jack (1969). "Papagos Living in Severe Poverty," Washington Merry-Go-Round, *Albuquerque Journal*, 15 November, pp. 3, 5.

_____ (1971). "Paiutes Nation's Most Deprived Tribe," *Albuquerque Journal*, 11 August.

Anonymous (1967). "Archeologists find Apache 'pueblos' near Las Vegas," *The New Mexican*, 23 April. Santa Fe.

_____ (1969a). "On Grand Canyon Floor. Havasupai Tribe to Get Houses," *Albuquerque Journal*, 15 June.

275

____(1969b). (On Navajo industries). *Arizona Republic*, 12 December. Phoenix.

____(1969c). "Indians: Squalor Amid Splendor," *Time*, 11 July. Chicago.

____(1969d). "White Mountain Apache Cattlemen," *New Mexico Stockman*, March, p. 49. Albuquerque.

____(1970a). "The Peyote Story," *Diné Baa Hane*, vol. 1, no. 11, August, pp. 12-13. Fort Defiance, Ariz.

____(1970b). "Ute Mountain Utes Ask Industrial Visits," *Albuquerque Journal*, 16 April.

____(1970c). "U.S. Government Honors Apache Tribes," *Albuquerque Journal*, 26 April: E-8.

____(1970d). "Indian Tribes Buy Part of Heritage," *The New Mexican*, 1 May. Santa Fe.

____(1970e). (On Hualapai Indians) *Albuquerque Journal*, 10 July.

____(1970f). "Zuni War Chief Dies," *The New Mexican*, 30 January. Santa Fe.

____(1970g). *Albuquerque Journal*, Action Line, 15 February.

____(1971a). "Arizona's 85 Payson Apaches Stump for Title to Tonto Land," *Albuquerque Journal*, 22 August: A-6 (Washington UPI)

____(1971b). "Luxury Complex Planned. Southern Ute Tribe Will Enter Tourist Business," *Albuquerque Journal*, 26 November.

____(1971c). "Papago Indians Get Farm Grant," *Albuquerque Journal*, 25 December.

____(1971d). "Indians Build $2 Million Resort," *The New Mexican*, 16 May. Santa Fe.

____(1971e). "Master Potter of Maricopas Crushed to Death under Tree," *Arizona Republic*, 11 August, p. 21. Phoenix.

____(1971f). "Ida Redbird Dies," *Newsletter*, The Heard Museum, September-October, Phoenix.

____(1971g). "Fannin Asks Indian Aid," *The New Mexican*, 14 February. Santa Fe.

____(1972). News Release, Window Rock, Ariz. 18 February.

____(1973). *The New Mexican*, 5 August, p. B9. Santa Fe.

Arizona Commission of Indian Affairs (1971). *Tribal Directory.* 71 pp. Phoenix.

Arizona Writers' Project, WPA (1941). "The Apache," *Arizona Highways,* vol. xvii, no. 11, November, pp. 32-35, 42. Phoenix.

Bahti, Tom (1968). *Southwestern Indian Tribes.* KC Publications. Flagstaff.

Baldwin, Gordon C. (1965). *The Warrior Apaches.* Dale Stuart King. Tucson.

Ball, Eve (1970). *In The Days of Victorio.* Univ. of Arizona Press. Tucson.

Barnett, Franklin (1968). *Viola Jimulla: The Indian Chieftess.* Southwest Printers. Yuma, Ariz.

Bartel, Jon (1970). "First Indian High School Starts Classes at Ramah," *The Gallup Independent,* 12 August, p. 2B. Gallup, N.M.

Barton, Robert S. (1953). "The Lincoln Canes of the Pueblo Governors," *Lincoln Herald,* Winter, pp. 24-29.

Basehart, Harry W. (1967). "The Resource Holding Corp. Among the Mescalero Apache," *S. W. Journ. Anthro.,* vol. xxiii, pp. 277-291. Univ. of New Mexico Press. Albuquerque.

_____(1970). "Mescalero Apache Band Organization and Leadership," *S.W. Journ. Anthro.,* vol. xxvi, no. 1, pp. 87-104. Univ. of New Mexico Press. Albuquerque.

Barry, Norm (1971). "Light in the Desert," *Mountain Bell,* vol. ii, no. 2, Summer. Denver.

Bloom, Lansing B. (1940). "Who Discovered New Mexico?" *New Mexico Historical Review,* vol. xv, no. 2, April, pp. 101-132. Albuquerque.

Bolton, Herbert E. (1950). "Pageant in the Wilderness," *Utah Historical Quarterly,* vol. 18. Salt Lake City.

Brandon, William (1969). "American Indians: the Alien Americans," *The Progressive,* vol. xxxiii, no. 12, pp. 13-17. Madison, Wis.

_____(1970a). "The American Indians: the Un-Americans," *The Progressive,* January, pp. 35-39. Madison, Wis.

_____(1970b). "American Indians: the Real American Revolution," *The Progressive,* February, pp. 26-30. Madison, Wis.

Brennan, Bill (1966). "This is River Country," part one, The Colorado River Indian Reservation, pp. 9-11, 30-32; part two, Parker, Arizona—the Heart of the River Country, pp. 32-39 in *Arizona Highways,* vol. xlii, no. 2, February. Phoenix.

_____(1967). "Parker—Power Boat Racing Capital of the Southwest," *The Parker-Lake Harasu Story,* pp. 16-17. Phoenix.

Breuninger, Evelyn P. (1970). "Debut of Mescalero Maidens," *Apache Scout,* vol. xvi, no. 5, June, pp. 1-5. Mescalero Reservation. Mescalero, N. M.

Brugge, David M. (1969).   "A Navajo History," unpublished manuscript. 22 pp.

Bunzel, Ruth L. (1932a). "Introduction to Zuñi Ceremonialism," 47th Ann. Rep., *Bureau of American Ethnology,* pp. 471-544. Govt. Printing Office, Washington, D.C.

_____(1932b). Zuñi Katcinas: An Analytical Study," 47th Ann. Rep., *Bureau of American Ethnology,* pp. 843-903. Govt. Printing Office, Washington, D. C.

Carta Contenante le Royanne du Mexique et al Floride (n.d.) Old French map of early 1700s, in New Mexico State Record Center and Archives. Santa Fe.

Chaban, Ruth (1971). "The 1971 Annual Indian Market," *The Quarterly of the Southwestern Association on Indian Affairs, Inc.,* vol. vii, no. 2, Summer. Santa Fe.

Colton, Harold S. (1941). "Prehistoric Trade in the Southwest," *Scientific Monthly,* vol. 52, pp. 309-319. Amer. Assn. for the Advancement of Science. Washington, D. C.

Coues, Elliott (1900). *On the Trail of a Spanish Pioneer:* (the Diary and Itinerary of Francisco Garcés in his Travels Through Sonora, Arizona and California). 2 vols. Francis P. Harper. New York.

Coze, Paul (1952). "Of Clowns and Mudheads," *Arizona Highways,* vol. xxviii, no. 8, August, pp. 18-29. Phoenix.

_____(1971). "Living Spirits of Kachinam," *Arizona Highways,* Vol. xlvii, no. 6, June. Phoenix.

Cumming, Kendall (1967). Personal Letter, 21 April.

Davis, Irvine (1959). "Linguistic Clues to Northern Rio Grande Prehistory," *El Palacio,* vol. 66, no. 3, June, pp. 73-83. Museum of N.M. Santa Fe.

Dittert, A.E., Jr. (1958). "Preliminary archaeological investigations in the Navajo project area of northwestern New Mexico," *Papers in Anthro.,* no. 1, May, 25 pp., Museum of N.M. Press. Santa Fe.

_____(1959). "Culture Change in the Cebolleta Mesa Region, Central Western New Mexico," Doctoral dissertation, Univ. of Arizona (unpublished). Tucson.

_____(1967). Personal Information.

_____(1972). They came from the South," *Arizona Highways,* vol. xlviii, no. 1, January, pp. 34-39. Phoenix.

Dobyns, Henry F. and Robert C. Euler (1960). "A Brief History of the Northeastern Pai," *Plateau,* vol. 32, no. 3, January, pp. 49-56. Museum of No. Ariz. Flagstaff.

_____(1971). *The Havasupai People*. Indian Tribal Series. Phoenix.

Dobyns, Henry F., Paul H. Ezell, Alden W. Jones and Greta Ezell (1957). "Thematic Changes in Yuman Warfare: cultural stability and cultural change," *Proceedings,* Amer. Ethnol. Soc., pp. 46-71, annual spring meeting. Amer. Ethnol. Soc. Seattle.

Dockstader, Frederick J. (1954). *The Kachina and the White Man: A Study of the Influences of the White Culture on the Hopi Kachina Cult,* Bulletin no. 35. Cranbrook Institute of Science. Bloomfield Hills, Mich.

Douglas, F. H. (1931). "The Havasupai Indians," *Leaflet No. 33,* Denver Art Museum. 4 pp. Denver, Colo.

Drucker, Philip (1937). "Cultural Element Distributions:V" *Southern Calif. Anthropological Records,* vol. i, no. 1, Univ. of Calif. Press, Berkeley.

Dutton, Bertha P. (1963). *Sun Father's Way: The Kiva Murals of Kuana.* Univ. of N. M. Press. Albuquerque.

_____(1966). "Pots Pose Problems," *El Palacio,* vol. 73, no. 1, Spring, pp. 5-15. Museum of N. M. Press. Santa Fe.

_____(1972a) "The New Year of the Pueblo Indians of New Mexico," *El Palacio,* vol. 78, no. 1. Museum of N. M. Press.

_____(1972b). *Let's Explore: Indian Villages Past and Present.* Museum of N.M. press. 65 pp. Santa Fe.

Eddy, Frank W. (1965). "The Desert Culture of the Southwestern United States," Lecture at St. Michael's College (College of Santa Fe), 9 February (unpublished). Santa Fe.

_____(1966). "Prehistory in the Navajo Reservoir District, Northwestern New Mexico," *Papers in Anthro.,* no. 15, pt. I. Museum of N.M. Press. Santa Fe.

_____(1974). "Population dislocation in the Navaho reservoir district, New Mexico and Colorado," *Amer. Antiquity,* vol. 39, no. 1:75-84.

Eggan, Fred (1950). *Social Organization of the Western Pueblos.* Univ. of Chicago Press. Chicago.

Eklund, D. E. (1969). "Pendleton Blankets," *Arizona Highways,* vol. xlv, no. 8, August, p. 40. Phoenix.

Ellis, Florence (Hawley) (1964). "Archaeological History of Nambé Pueblo, 14th Century to Present," *American Antiquity,* vol. 30, no. 1, July, pp. 34-42. Soc. for Amer. Archaeology. Salt Lake City.

Emmitt, Robert (1954). *The Last War Trail — The Utes and the Settlement of Colorado.* Univ. of Oklahoma Press. Norman.

Euler, Robert C. (1961). "Aspects of Political Organization Among the Puertocito Navajo," *El Palacio,* vol. 68, no. 2, Summer, pp. 118-120. Museum of N.M. Santa Fe.

_____(1966). "Southern Paiute Ethnohistory," *Anthro. Papers.* no. 78, April. Univ. of Utah Press. Salt Lake City.

_____(1972a). *The Paiute People.* Indian Tribal Series. Phoenix.

_____(1972b). Personal Letter, 7 July.

Ezell, Greta S. and Paul H. Ezell (1970). "Background to Battle: Circumstances Relating to Death on the Gila, 1857," in *Troopers West: Military and Indian Affairs on the American Frontier,* pp. 169-186. Frontier Heritage Press. San Diego.

Faris, Chester E. (n.d.). "Pueblo Governors' Canes," Mimeographed report. 7 pp.

Fontana, B. L. (1967). Personal Letter, 6 January.

Fontana, B. L., Wm. J. Robinson, C. W. Cormack and E. E. Leavitt, Jr. (1962). *Papago Indian Pottery.* Univ. of Wash. Press. Seattle.

Forrest, Earle R. (1961). *The Snake Dance of the Hopi Indians.* Westernlore Press. Los Angeles.

Forrestal, Peter P. (transl.) and Cyprian J. Lynch (historical intro. and notes) (1954). *Benavides' Memorial of 1630.* Academy of Amer. Franciscan Hist. Washington, D. C.

Fort Mohave Tribal Council (California-Arizona-Nevada) (1970). *Letter and Resolution,* 27 October, 6 pp. Needles, Calif.

Fowler, Catherine S. (1971). Personal Letter, 14 June.

Fowler, Don D. and Catherine S. Fowler (Eds.) (1971). "Anthropology of the Numa: John Wesley Powell's manuscripts on the Numic Peoples of Western North America, 1868-1880," *Smithsonian Contributions to Anthro.,* No. 14, Smithsonian Institution. Washington, D. C.

Gabel, Norman E. (1949). *A Comparative Racial Study of the Papago,* Univ. of New Mexico Publications in Anthro., no. 4, Univ. of N. M. Press. Albuquerque.

Galvin, John (Transl. and Ed.) (1967). *A Record of Travels in Arizona and California, 1775-1776, Father Francisco Garcés.* John Howell Books. San Francisco.

Gerald, Rex E. (1958) "Two Wickiups on the San Carlos Indian Reservation, Arizona," *The Kiva*, vol. 23, no. 3, February, pp. 5-11. Ariz. Arch. and Hist. Society. Tucson.

Gilliland, H. M. (1972). Personal letter and data sheets. *Hopi Indian Agency*, 16 March. Keams Canyon, Ariz.

Gonzales, Clara (1969). *The Shalakos Are Coming.* Museum of N. M. Press. 13 pp. Santa Fe.

Goodwin, Grenville (1942). *The Social Organization of the Western Apache.* Univ. of Chicago Press. Chicago.

Graves, Howard (1970). "Jobs, Tradition, Urbanization Key Navajo Race Factors," *Albuquerque Journal,* 24 August.

Gunnerson, James H. (1960). "An Introduction to Plains Apache Archaeology—the Dismal River Aspect," *B. A. E. Anthro. Paper No. 58.* Washington, D. C.

_____(1969a). "Apache Archaeology in Northeastern New Mexico," *American Antiquity,* vol. 34, pp. 23-39. Soc. for Amer. Archaeology. Salt Lake City.

_____(1969b). "Archaeological Survey on and near Pecos National Monument—Preliminary Report," mimeographed report, pp. 1-9.

Gunnerson, James H. and Dolores A. (1970). "Evidence of Apaches at Pecos," *El Palacio*, vol. 76, no. 3, pp. 1-6, Museum of N.M. Santa Fe.

_____(1971a). "Apachean Culture: A Study in Unity and Diversity," reprinted from *Apachean Culture History and Ethnology, Anthro. Papers, No. 21,* pp. 7-22. Univ. of Ariz, Tucson.

_____(1971b). "Apachean Culture History and Ethnology," *Anthro. Papers, No. 21,* 22 pp., Univ. of Ariz. Tucson.

Hackett, Charles Wilson (1937). *Historical Documents Relating to New Mexico, Nueva Vizcaya, and Approaches thereto, to 1773.* 3 vols. Carnegie Institution. Washington, D. C.

Hanlon, C. J. (O. F. M.) (1972). "Papago Funeral Customs," *The Kiva*, vol. 37, no. 2, Winter, pp. 104-112. Ariz. Arch. and Hist. Society. Tucson.

Harrington, John P. (1940). "Southern Peripheral Athapaskawan Origins, Divisions, and Migrations," *Essays in Historical Anthropology of North America, Smithsonian Misc. Colls.,* vol. 100, pp. 503-532. Smithsonian Institution, Washington, D. C.

Hawley, Florence (1950). "Big Kivas, Little Kivas, and Moiety Houses in Historical Reconstruction," *S. W. Journal of Anthro.,* vol. 6, no. 3, Autumn, pp. 286-300. Univ. of N.M. Press. Albuquerque.

Hawley, Florence and Donovan Senter (1946). "Group-designed Behavior Patterns in Two Acculturating Groups," *S. W. Journal of Anthro.*, vol. 2, no. 2, pp. 133-151. Univ. of N. M. Press. Albuquerque.

Hayes, George (1971). Personal Information. Pojoaque, New Mexico, 18 November.

Hester, James J. (1962). "Early Navajo Migrations and Acculturation in the Southwest," *Papers in Anthro.* no. 6, 131 pp. Museum of N.M. Press. Santa Fe.

Hewett, E. L. and B. P. Dutton (1945). *The Pueblo Indian World.* Univ. of N. M. Press. Albuquerque.

Hill, W. W. (1940). "Some Aspects of Navajo Political Structure," *Plateau*, vol. 13, no. 2. Reprint, 6 pp. Museum of No. Ariz. Flagstaff.

Hodge, Frederick W. (Ed.) (1910). "Handbook of American Indians North of Mexico," *B. A. E. Bull. 30*, part two: p. 186. Smithsonian Institution. Washington, D. C.

Hoebel, E. Adamson (1958). *Man in the Primitive World.* McGraw-Hill Book Co. New York, London and Toronto.

Hoijer, Harry (1938). *Chiricahua and Mescalero Apache Texts.* Univ. of Chicago Press. Chicago.

_____(1956) "The Chronology of the Athapaskan Languages," *International Journal of American Linguistics*, vol. 22, no. 4, October, pp. 219-232. Baltimore.

Hoijer, Harry et al. (1963). "Studies in the Athapaskan Languages," *Publications in Linguistics,* University of California.

Hopi Reservation. (a mimeographed leaflet of information) issued by the Hopi Tribe. 13 pp. Keams Canyon, Ariz.

Houser, Nicholas P. (1972). "The Camp"—An Apache Community of Payson, Arizona," *The Kiva*, vol. 37, no. 2, Winter, pp. 65-71. Ariz. Arch. and Hist. Society. Tucson.

Hume, Bill (1970a). "Sandia Pueblo Adopts Best of Two Cultures," *Albuquerque Journal*, 9 August, p. D-1.

_____(1970b). "Prehistoric Site, Scenic Canyon Boost Santa Clara's Finances," *Albuquerque Journal*, 4 October, p. G-1.

_____(1974). "The Havasupai Prisoners of Grand Canyon," *Indian Affairs*, No. 86 (Newsletter). March-April, pp. 1-2, 7. New York.

Huscher, B. H. and H. A. (1942). "Athapascan Migration via the Intermontane Region," *American Antiquity,* vol. 8, no. 1, pp. 80-88. Soc. for Amer. Archaeology. Menasha, Wis.

_____(1943). "The Hogan Builders of Colorado," *Colorado Archaeological Society*. Gunnison, Colo.

James, Harry C. (1956). *The Hopi Indians.* The Caxton Press. Caldwell, Idaho.

Johnston, Bernice (1970). *Speaking of Indians.* Univ. of Arizona Press. Tucson.

Kaut, Charles R. (1957). "The Western Apache Clan System: Its Origins and Development," *Publications in Anthro.,* no. 9, 85 pp. Univ. of New Mexico. Albuquerque.

Kelly, Dorothea S. (1950). "A Brief History of the Cocopa Indians of the Colorado River Delta," in *For the Dean,* pp. 159-169. Hohokam Museums Association and the Southwestern Monuments Association. Tucson, Arizona and Santa Fe, N. M.

Kelly, Isabel (1964). "Southern Paiute Ethnography," *Anthro. Papers,* No. 69. May. Univ. of Utah Press. Salt Lake City.

Kelly, William H. (1953). *Indians of the Southwest: A Survey of Indian Tribes and Indian Administration in Arizona.* 1st Ann. Rep. Bureau of Ethnic Research, Dept. Anthro., 129 pp. Tucson.

King, William S. (1967). Information from Salt River Indian Agency, Scottsdale, Arizona, 11 April, 3 pp.

Kluckhohn, Clyde and Dorothea Leighton (1962). *The Navajo.* Doubleday & Co., Inc. Garden City, N. Y.

Kluckhohn, Clyde and Leland C. Wyman (1940). "An Introduction to Navaho Chant Practice," *Memoirs,* no. 53, Amer. Anthro. Assn. Menasha, Wis.

Kurath, William and Edward H. Spicer (1947). "A Brief Introduction to Yaqui, a Native Language of Sonora," *Bulletin* (Social Science Bull. no. 15) Univ. of Ariz. Tucson.

Levy, Jerrold E. (1965). "Navajo Suicide," *Human Organization,* vol. 24. no. 4, pp. 308-318. Soc. for Applied Anthro. Ithaca, N. Y.

Levy, Jerrold E., Stephen J. Kunitz, and Michael Everett (1969). "Navajo Criminal Homicide," *S.W. Jrnl. of Anthro.,* vol. 25, no. 2, Summer, pp. 124-149. Univ. of N. M. Albuquerque.

Link, Martin A. (1968). (Introduction to) *Treaty between the United States of America and the Navajo Tribe of Indians,* KC Publications. Flagstaff, Ariz.

Lister, Robert H. (1958). "Archaeological Excavations in the Northern Sierra Madre Occidental, Chihuahua and Sonora, Mexico," *Univ. of Colorado Studies,* Series in Anthropology, no. 7. Boulder.

Lumholtz, Carl (1902). *Unknown Mexico,* 2 vols. Charles Scribner's Sons. New York.

McGregor, John C. (1951). *The Cohonina Culture of Northwestern Arizona.* Univ. of Illinois Press. Urbana, Illinois.

———(1967). *The Cohonina Culture of Mount Floyd, Arizona.* Univ. of Kentucky Press. Lexington, Ky.

McNitt, Frank (1970). "Fort Sumner: a Study in Origins," *New Mexico Historical Review,* April, pp. 101-115. Albuquerque.

Mangel, Charles (1970). "Sometimes We Feel We're Already Dead," *Look,* vol. 34, no. 11, 2 June, pp. 38-43. New York.

Martin, John (1972). Personal Letter. 3 April.

Matthews, Washington (1887). "The Mountain Chant: A Navajo Ceremony," Bureau American Ethnology, pp. 385-467. Washington, D.C.

———(1897). *Navaho Legends.* American Folklore Society. New York.

———(1902) "The Night Chant, a Navaho Ceremony," *Memoirs,* vol. vi, May. American Museum of Nat. Hist. New York.

Miller, Wick R. and C. G. Booth (1972). "The Place of Shoshoni among American Languages," *Introduction to Shoshoni Language Course Materials.* Aug. 9 pp. Owyhee, Nevada.

Montgomery, Ross Gordon, Watson Smith and J. O. Brew (1949). "Franciscan Awatovi, the Excavation and Conjectural Reconstruction of a 17th Century Spanish Mission Establishment at a Hopi Indian Town in Northeastern Arizona," *Papers, Peabody Mus. of Amer. Arch. and Ethnol.,* vol. xxxvi. Harvard Univ., Cambridge.

Montgomery, William (1970a). "Fruitland Mine, Plant Liked," *Albuquerque Journal,* 18 August, pp. A-1 and A-5.

———(1970b). "Black Mesa Coal Provides Indians Jobs," *Albuquerque Journal*, 19 August, pp. A-1 and A-5.

———(1970c). "Navajo Generating Plant Now Building," *Albuquerque Journal,* 22 August, pp. A-1 and A-5.

———(1970d). "Water Key to Southwest's Growth," *Albuquerque Journal,* 26 August, pp. A-1 and A-5.

Moon, Sheila (1970). *A Magic Dwells.* Wesleyan Univ. Press. Middletown, Conn.

Morris, Clyde P. (1972). "Yavapai-Apache Family Organization in a Reservation Context," *Plateau,* vol. 44, no. 3, Winter, pp. 105-110. Museum of No. Ariz. Flagstaff.

Murray, Clyde A. (1969). "Homes in Flood Plain: CAP to Displace Indians," *The Arizona Republic*, 9 November, p. 24-B. Phoenix.

Nabokov, Peter (1969). "The Peyote Road," *The New York Times Magazine*, Sec. 6, 9 March, pp. 30-31, 129-132, 134.

Navajo Census Office (1970). Window Rock, Arizona.

Navajo Community College (n.d.). *Introducing the Navajo Community College,* 25 pp. brochure.

Navajo Tribal Museum (1968). *Historical Calendar of the Navajo People.* 15 July. Window Rock, Arizona.

New, Lloyd (1968). "Institute of American Indian Arts, Cultural Difference as the Basis for Creative Education," *Native American Arts,* no. 1. U. S. Dept. of the Interior, San Francisco. Washington, D.C.

Opler, Morris E. (1935). "The Concept of Supernatural Power Among the Chiricahua and Mescalero Apaches," *American Anthro.,* vol. 37, pp. 65-70. Menasha, Wis.

_____(1938a). Ethnological Notes in *Chiricahua and Mescalero Apache Texts,* by Harry Hoijer. Univ. of Chicago Press. Chicago.

_____(1938b). "Myths and Tales of the Jicarilla Apache Indians," *Memoirs* of the Amer. Folklore Society, vol. 31, 393 pp. New York.

_____(1941). *An Apache Life-Way; The Economic, Social, and Religious Institutions of the Chiricahua Indians.* Univ. of Chicago Press. Chicago.

_____(1942). "Myths and Tales of the Chiricahua Apache Indians," *Memoirs* of the Amer. Folklore Society, vol. xxxvii, 101 pp. New York.

_____(1943). "Navaho Shamanistic Practice Among the Jicarilla Apache," *New Mexico Anthropologist,* vols. vi, vii, no. 1. Jan.-Mar., pp. 13-18. Univ. of Chicago Press.

Ortiz, Alfonso (1969). *The Tewa World.* Univ. of Chicago Press. Chicago and London.

Painter, Muriel Thayer and E. B. Sayles (1962). *Faith, Flowers and Fiestas.* Univ. of Arizona Press. Tucson.

Papago Indian Agency (1970). *Facts about the Papago Indian Reservation and the Papago People.* (Mimeographed.) 12 pp. Sells, Ariz.

Parsons, Elsie Clews (1925). *The Pueblo of Jemez.* Phillips Academy. Andover, Mass.

_____(1939). *Pueblo Indian Religion.* 2 vols. Univ. of Chicago Press. Chicago.

Powell, John W. (1891). "Indian Linguistic Families of America

North of Mexico." Bureau American Ethnology, *7th Ann. Rep.* Washington, D. C.

Reed, Verner Z. (1896). "The Ute Bear Dance," *American Anthro.,* vol. ix, July, pp. 237-244. Menasha, Wis.

Reichard, Gladys A. (1963). *Navaho Religion,* Bollingen Series 18, Pantheon Books. New York

Richards, David (1970). "America's Silent Minority," *TWA Ambassador,* vol. 3, no. 5, pp. 7-12. St. Paul, Minn.

Robinson, A. E. (Bert) (1954). *The Basket Weavers of Arizona.* Univ. of N. M. Press. Albuquerque.

Sandoval, H. (1971). "Views on 'A Gunfight,' " *The Jicarilla Chieftain,* 1 November. Dulce, New Mexico. (editorial)

Sapir, Edward (1929). "Central and North American Languages," in *The Encyclopaedia Britannica* (14th Ed.), vol. 5, pp. 139-141.

Schaafsma, Polly (1966). *Early Navaho Rock Paintings and Carvings.* Museum of Navaho Ceremonial Art, Inc. Santa Fe.

Schevill, Margaret Erwin (1947). *Beautiful on the Earth.* Hazel Dreis Editions. Santa Fe.

Schoenwetter, James and A. E. Dittert, Jr. (1968). "An Ecological Interpretation of Anasazi Settlement Patterns," in *Anthropological Archaeology in the Americas.* The Anthro. Society of Washington. pp. 41-61. Washington, D. C.

Schroeder, Albert H. (1963). "Navajo and Apache Relationships West of the Rio Grande," *El Palacio,* vol. 70, no. 3, Autumn, pp. 5-20. Museum of New Mexico. Santa Fe.

Schwartz, Douglas W. (1956). "The Havasupai 600 A.D.–1955 A.D.: A Short Culture History," *Plateau,* vol. 28, no. 4, April, pp. 77-84. Museum of No. Ariz. Flagstaff.

_____(1959). "Culture Area and Time Depth: the Four Worlds of the Havasupai," *American Anthro.,* vol. 61, no. 6, December, pp. 1060-1069. Menasha, Wis.

Shepardson, Mary (1963). "Navajo Ways in Government (a Study in Political Process)," *Memoir 96,* Amer. Anthro. Assn. vol. 65, no. 3, pt. 2, June. Menasha, Wis.

Smith, Anne (1965). *New Mexico Indians Today.* A report prepared as part of the N. M. State Resources Development Plan. Museum of N. M. June, 279 pp. Santa Fe.

_____(1966). *New Mexico Indians:* Economic, educational, and social problems. Museum of N. M., Research Records no. 1. 58 pp. Santa Fe.

_____(1968). *Indian Education in New Mexico.* Div. of Govt. Research, Institute for Social Research and Dev. Univ. of N. M., July, 49 pp. Albuquerque.

_____(1974). *Ethnography of the Northern Ute.* Museum of N. M. Press. Papers in Anthropology no. 17. 285 pp. Santa Fe.

Smith, Watson (1952). "Kiva Mural Decorations at Awatovi and Kawaika-a, with a Survey of Other Wall Paintings in the Pueblo Southwest," *Papers*, Peabody Mus. of Amer. Arch. and Ethnol., Harvard Univ., vol. xxxvii. Reports of the Awatovi Exped. Report no. 5. Cambridge.

_____(1971). "Painted Ceramics of the Western Mound at Awatovi," *Papers,* Peabody Mus. of Amer. Arch. and Ethnol., Harvard Univ., no. 38. Cambridge.

Sonnichsen, C. L. (1958). *The Mescalero Apaches.* Univ. of Oklahoma Press. Norman, Okla.

Southwestern Monuments Monthly Report, Supplement for November (1937). U. S. Dept. of Interior, Natl. Park Service. p. 396. Coolidge, Ariz.

Spencer, Katherine (1947). *Reflection of Social Life in the Navaho Origin Myth.* Univ. of N. M. Press. Albuquerque.

Spencer, Robert (1940). "A Preliminary Sketch of Keresan Grammar," Master's Thesis, Univ. of New Mexico (unpublished).

Spicer, Edward H. (1970). *Cycles of Conquest* (the impact of Spain, Mexico, and the United States on the Indians of the Southwest 1533-1960). Univ. of Ariz. Press. Tucson.

Spicer, Edward H., Phyllis Balastrero, and Ted DeGrazia (1971). "Yaqui Easter Ceremonial," *Arizona Highways,* vol. xlvii, no. 3, March, pp. 2-10, 11, 34, 45-47. Phoenix.

Spier, Leslie (1928). "Havasupai Ethnography," *Anthro. Papers,* Amer. Museum of Natural History, vol. 29, pt. 3:286. New York.

_____(1955). "Mohave Culture Items," *Bulletin 28,* Museum of Northern Arizona, Northern Arizona Society of Science and Art, Inc. Flagstaff.

Spinden, Herbert J. (Transl.)(1933). *Songs of the Tewa.* New York.

Stephen, Alexander M. (E. C. Parsons, Ed.) (1936). *Hopi Journal,* 2 vols., Columbia Univ. Contribs. to Anthro., vol. 23. New York.

Steward, Julian H. (1955). *Theory of Culture Change.* Univ. of Illinois Press. Urbana, Illinois.

Stewart, Kenneth M. (1967). "Chemehuevi Culture Changes."

Plateau, vol. 40, no. 1, Summer, pp. 14-20. Museum of Northern Arizona. Flagstaff.

Strong, William Duncan (1927). "An Analysis of Southwestern Society," *American Anthropologist,* vol. 29, no. 1, Jan.-Mar. 1927. Menasha, Wis.

Swadish, Morris (1967). "Linguistic Classification in the Southwest," in *Studies in Southwestern Ethnolinguistics,* pp. 281-306. Mouton & Co. The Hague and Paris.

Swanton, John R. (1952) "The Indian Tribes of North America," Bur. of Amer. Ethnology, Smithsonian Inst., *Bull. 145.* Washington, D.C.

Taylor, Morris F. (1970). "Campaigns Against the Jicarilla Apache, 1855," *New Mexico Historical Review,* April, pp. 119-133. Albuquerque.

Thrapp, Dan L. (1967). "Christian Missions Bested: 45% of Navajos Accept Peyote-Oriented Church," *Los Angeles Times,* 17 August.

Trager, George L. (1969). "Navajo Mountain—Navaho Molehill?" *Newsletter,* Amer. Anthro. Assn., p. 2. Menasha, Wis.

Uintah and Ouray Agency (Ute) (1970). Letter, 3 September. Fort Duchesne, Utah.

Underhill, Ruth M. (1938a). "A Papago Calender Record," *Bull., Anthro. Series,* vol. 2, no. 5, 1 March, 64 pp. Albuquerque.

———(1938b). *Singing for Power.* Univ. of Calif. Press. Berkeley.

———(1940). *The Papago Indians of Arizona,* Sherman Pamphlets, no. 3, 63 pp. Education Division, U. S. Office of Indian Affairs.

Ute Mountain Ute Agency, Towaoc, Colorado (n.d.[a], 1969?). "The American Indians of Colorado," 5 pp. Mimeographed report.

———(n.d.[b], 1969?). "A Brief History of the Colorado Utes," 3 pp. Mimeographed report.

———(1970). Letter, 18 August.

Van Valkenburgh, Richard (1945). "The Government of the Navajos," *Ariz. Quarterly,* vol. 1, pp. 63-73. Univ. of Ariz. Press. Tucson.

Vestal, Paul A. (1952). "Ethnobotany of the Rimrock Navaho," *Papers.* Peabody Mus. of Amer. Arch. and Ethnol., vol. 40, no. 4. Harvard Univ. Cambridge.

Vogt, Evon Z. (1951). "Navaho Veterans—a Study of Changing Values," *Papers*, Peabody Mus. of Amer. Arch. and Ethnol., vol. xli, no. 1. Harvard Univ. Cambridge.

Waliczed, John (1970). "Navajo High School Opens Door at Home," *The New Mexican*, 6 September (from Gallup Independent for AP). Santa Fe.

Walker, George W. (1970). "Celebrating the Arrival of Dr. Charles H. Cook, after Whom Cook Training School is Named, at Sacaton, Arizona," *Indian Highways*, no. 134, December, pp. 4 and 6. Cook Christian Training School. Tempe, Ariz.

White, Leslie A. (1935). "The Pueblo of Santo Domingo, New Mexico," *Memoirs* of the Amer. Anthro. Assn., no. 43, pp. 1-210. Menasha, Wis.

Whitfield, Charles (1971). Personal Information, long distance phone call, 11 May.

Whiting, Alfred F. (1958). "Havasupai Characteristics in the Cohonina," *Plateau*, vol. 30, no. 30, January, pp. 55-60. Museum of No. Ariz. Flagstaff.

Whitman, William III (1947). "The Pueblo Indians of San Ildefonso," *Contribs. to Anthropology, Columbia Univ.* no. 34. New York.

Willey, Gordon R. (1966). *An Introduction to American Archaeology*, vol. I. Prentice-Hall, Inc. Englewood Cliffs, New Jersey.

Yazzie, Ethelou (Ed.) (1971). *Navajo History*, vol. I. Navajo Community College Press. Many Farms, Arizona.

Young, Robert W. (1961). "The Origin and Development of Navajo Tribal Government,". *The Navajo Yearbook*, Report no. viii, 1951-1961 a Decade of Progress, pp. 371-392. Navajo Agency. Window Rock, Ariz.

———(1968). *The Role of the Navajo in the Southwestern Drama.* Robert W. Young and *The Gallup Independent*. Galley, N.M.

Young, Robert W., and William Morgan (1943). *The Navaho Language.* Education Div., U. S. Indian Service Phoenix.

.... INDEX